CW00530302

INTO THE
UNCANNY

INTO THE UNCANNY

A REAL-LIFE INVESTIGATION INTO THE PARANORMAL

DANNY ROBINS

BBC Books, an imprint of Ebury Publishing
20 Vauxhall Bridge Road
London SW1V 2SA

BBC Books is part of the Penguin Random House group of companies whose addresses can be found at global.penguinrandomhouse.com

Penguin
Random House
UK

First published by BBC Books in 2023

Poem extracts from 'East Coker' and 'The Waste Land' from *Collected Poems 1909–1962* by T. S. Eliot, reprinted by kind permission of Faber and Faber Ltd

Picture credits: 12, 143, 282, 294, 324 Danny Robins; 29 Graham Morris; 63 Prime Objective/Stockimo/Alamy Stock Photo; 70 Historica Graphica Collection/Heritage Images/Getty Images; 126 Fortean/Trottmann/TopFoto; 156 Hulton-Deutsch Collection/CORBIS/Corbis via Getty Images; 177 Baltimore Sun; 204 Charles Walker/TopFoto; 238 Mirrorpix/TopFoto/Reach plc; 268 Pacific Press Media Production Corp./Alamy Live News

www.penguin.co.uk

A CIP catalogue record for this book is available from the British Library

ISBN 9781785948091

Printed and bound in Great Britain by Clays Ltd, Elcograf S.p.A.

The authorised representative in the EEA is Penguin Random House Ireland, Morrison Chambers, 32 Nassau Street, Dublin D02 YH68.

Penguin Random House is committed to a sustainable future for our business, our readers and our planet. This book is made from Forest Stewardship Council® certified paper.

For my wife Eva,

and my children Leo and Max,

who are all too scared to read this.

*'I don't believe in ghosts
but I'm afraid of them.'*

EDITH WHARTON

*Who is the third who walks always beside you?
When I count, there are only you and I together
But when I look ahead up the white road
There is always another one walking beside you
Gliding wrapt in a brown mantle, hooded
I do not know whether a man or a woman
– But who is that on the other side of you?*

T.S. ELIOT, *THE WASTE LAND*

'They're here.'

CAROL ANNE FREELING IN *POLTERGEIST*

CONTENTS

CASE FOUR: THE ALIEN IN THE SNOW

CASE ONE PART TWO: THE ENGLISH COLLEGE

EPILOGUE

INTRODUCTION
DO YOU BELIEVE?

I don't believe in ghosts.

That's what I'd have confidently told you any time up until the evening of 22 June 2016. It's the night before the Brexit Referendum, Donald Trump is on his way to being elected, David Bowie and Prince have just died and it feels like the whole world is falling apart or fighting itself, but right now I'm experiencing my very own world-turned-abso-bloody-lutely-upside-down moment, sitting opposite one of my oldest, dearest friends as she tells me she has seen a ghost.

Now obviously I've been in situations before where mates shared tales of things that went bump in hotel bedrooms or felt a cold breath down their necks during stately home guided tours. I'm a bit of a ghost fan if I'm honest; I was that kid who obsessively pored over books like the *Usborne World of the Unknown* in the school library, trying to build the courage to look at photos of alleged spectral monks or that charred leg of a lady who'd spontaneously combusted (I can still see it when I close my eyes). I mainlined *Scooby-Doo*, got thrilled by a teenage theatre trip to see *The Woman in Black*, and hoovered up horror movies like *The Exorcist* and *The Blair Witch Project* but, for all my interest in the supernatural, the older I'd got, the more ghosts had become an abstract concept, something impossibly fictional on a par with Hobbits, Jedi or getting a GP appointment.

Yet, right here right now,* a person I know, like and trust, who, if she'd been telling me anything else in the world, I'd 100 per cent believe, is stating calmly and categorically she has actually seen one, and, well, there's just something different about this, it feels so much more ... *real* than anything I've heard before. Perhaps it's not so much what she's saying, but *how* she's saying it, described as vividly as if she'd had a car accident or witnessed a shocking crime.

What I'm more surprised about, though, is the effect it's having on me. After months of Leave vs Remain campaigning and the culture wars of the US election, I'm fully attuned to the incendiary power of words, but it suddenly strikes me that the deceptively simple sentence 'I saw a ghost' has an almost unique power to silence a room and forever change the way you see someone, or how people see you.

I clumsily mumble, 'You're not the sort of person I'd expect to see a ghost,' and I'm already thinking that, within our tight-knit friend-ship group, people will be forced to take sides after hearing her story. With the clock ticking down to the referendum result, I realise I'm staring at a divide even more seismic than Brexit. There aren't many bigger irreconcilable differences than whether or not you believe the dead can walk again, and if you're sure you have first-hand proof.

This moment gave me the acorn of an idea that would grow years later into my play *2:22 – A Ghost Story*, about a couple where one partner believes there's a ghost in their house and the other

---

* Copyright Fat Boy Slim.

refuses to countenance this is even possible. As part of my early research, I asked on social media to find out how many other people I knew had had experiences like my friend's. I didn't expect a lot of replies and was wary they might come from the more eccentric fringes of my Facebook circle.

The response was astonishing. Stories started to come in, first from friends, then friends of friends, and pretty soon complete strangers, as my request went viral. The accounts were compelling, powerful, often terrifying, and sometimes deeply moving, and they came from rational, sane, credible people. I quickly realised there was no 'sort of person' who sees a ghost; the witnesses spanned all ages, genders, races, personality types and social backgrounds and came from all across the UK and, eventually, all over the world. Their experiences happened at various times of the day in all sorts of weather conditions and all manner of locations. The only real common thread I could spot was the impact these encounters had, changing the lives of the people who wrote to me forever, utterly altering how they saw the world.

I quickly decided the stories couldn't just sit gathering dust on my hard drive, so I decided to do a podcast. I called it *Haunted*, and each episode featured one of the people who'd contacted me describing a ghostly encounter they believed they'd had. There were other shows out there that explored the paranormal, but they tended to sit at one of two extremes – ghost hunters who unquestioningly accepted everything as supernatural, or sceptics who ruthlessly busted any ghost they came across with the proton packs of science and reason. The chills of belief or the cold water of scepticism. I found myself sitting in the middle, though. The more stories I heard, the more

I was genuinely no longer sure what I believed, and so I listened to these people's tales without judgement and then discussed them, exploring the possibilities of what might have happened, including that they might really have seen a ghost. I was surprised and delighted that both sceptics and believers liked the podcast – each side enjoying the stories in their own way.

Haunted was popular enough for the BBC to take an interest and I found myself making *The Battersea Poltergeist* for them – it was a case I'd been sent by a paranormal expert I'd spoken to called Alan Murdie. He told me about a haunting that had taken place in South London in the 1950s, of a family seemingly terrorised by a violent poltergeist that appeared to be obsessed with their teenage daughter. That girl, Shirley Hitchings, had been 15 then, but Alan told me that she was still alive now, in her eighties, and had a box full of case notes from the original paranormal investigator sitting in her attic. Once I'd looked through these notes and spoken with Shirley, I was hooked. The thing that drew me in, to the point where I began to fixate on the case almost obsessively, was simply a quality in Shirley's voice. It reminded me of the way my friend spoke about her experience. I could tell that even 65 years after the events, Shirley was still scared.

We released the series in January 2021, during the Covid-enforced lockdown, a time when we were all prisoners of our own houses, once cosy reassuring habitats that, now we were unable to leave them, took on an oppressive, claustrophobic intensity, the mundane turned menacing, and something about this story of a family trapped in their haunted house resonated. It became a surprise worldwide hit, racking up millions of downloads and I found myself in the surreal position of fielding calls from Hollywood producers keen to buy the film rights. Shirley was on breakfast TV from here to Australia, and suddenly I found that that play I'd been writing, the one that had inspired me to make *Haunted*, hadn't been a total waste of time. There were theatre producers who wanted to put it on. We went to look at a theatre on April Fool's Day 2021, in the midst of the pandemic. It was vacant because one of the big musicals had decided it would close down until Covid was 'over'.* None of it felt real, and it seemed the most insane risk – a new play by a new playwright going on in the West End with a lead actress, the pop star Lily Allen, who had never acted before – but incredibly, *2:22 – A Ghost Story* opened that summer, one of the first shows to be able to play to a full audience after months of weird social distancing, and, again, it seemed to capture a moment. At the time of writing, it is still running in London and has begun to open in countries all around the world.

I'm not saying this to show off,† but because I think it demonstrates something – we are living in an age where we're all collectively fascinated by that question: 'Do ghosts exist?' There are all sorts of reasons you could read into our collective morbid obsession, but clearly it has something to do with the times we're living in. Covid, the existential threat of climate change and the wars we see raging around the world and close to home in Europe have forced us to confront our mortality in a way we haven't had to since the Second World War. Shit, as they say, has got real and we want to

---

* Remember how people thought it would actually go away?

† Okay, I am really.

know, if we are all going to die,* then is death really the end? Or, from another point of view, if the people we love are going to die, will we ever see them again? I think you can draw parallels with the periods immediately after the two world wars when there were huge booms in supernatural interest. Whenever our world seems most unsettled we search for answers by wondering if there is another world beyond it.

The other reason I'm telling you about my sudden ghostly success is because of what it led to. When *The Battersea Poltergeist* and *2:22 – A Ghost Story* became popular, something really remarkable and wonderful happened. That steady trickle of ghost stories I'd been receiving since I launched *Haunted* became a deluge, as more and more people sent me accounts of their own encounters with what they believed was the paranormal.

Alongside the ghost stories, I also started to receive descriptions of UFO sightings and other strange phenomena. Out of these stories would come my *Uncanny* series for the BBC. I boldly described it as 'the biggest investigation into the paranormal ever', which might have come across as hyperbole, but what I hoped for was that somehow, through an act of collective citizen journalism, I and all the people downloading and listening to the show around the world might be able to make sense of these fascinating, baffling and sometimes frankly bloody terrifying mysteries.

Because it turns out that ghosts do exist. We've just been looking in the wrong places. For years, TV ghost-hunting shows taught us we needed to camp out in medieval castles, ruined monasteries and

---

* Spoiler alert, we are, but hopefully not for a while. I reckon you've definitely got time to finish this book.

abandoned prisons – supernatural theme parks, essentially. Ghosts were a historical phenomenon, a rapidly disappearing endangered species that, if you were lucky, you might possibly catch a glimpse of, in the same way you'd find an obsolete VHS player in your parents' attic. These shows, with their exciting blitz of night-vision cameras, screaming presenters and psychics who somehow always managed to channel the spirits just in time for the commercial break, were a lot of fun but, rather than making us believe in the reality of ghosts, I think they did the opposite. Ghosts began to feel like pantomime, enjoyable but ridiculous entertainment, and so, if you were one of that group of people out there who believed they'd actually seen one, perhaps you made a decision.

You kept it to yourself.

Because as frightening as it is to see a ghost, it started to feel more frightening to tell people about it; it brought with it the fear that you'd be mocked, laughed at or, maybe scariest of all, have your sanity questioned, that people might say things like 'you're not the sort of person I'd expect to see a ghost' and view you in a different way. Most of the people who email me have told very few people about their experience, and many have never told anyone, including their partner.

Ghosts didn't disappear, we just forgot how to talk about them. I'm grateful that there was something about my work that made people feel they could trust me with their stories; and, let me tell you, based on what I have heard, ghosts appear to be very much alive and kicking. They live not in castles or stately homes but in ordinary houses and offices. And they definitely exist. By which I mean, people *are* witnessing them. Now we just need to figure out what the hell they are, the dead returning from the 'undiscovered country'* of death, or the product of that equally mysterious and ancient location, the human mind?

But something is going on, because people have been describing these experiences since ancient times in remarkably similar terms. The oldest known ghost story is written on a stone tablet made in 1500BC in ancient Babylon. It is in fact a ghost itself, as the image on it is so ancient it only becomes visible when viewed from above, under a light. It shows a 'ghost' being led back to the afterlife by an exorcist. It seems that what ghosts are and how to deal with them is a problem we humans have been pondering for over three and a half millennia. We may have tried to ignore that problem for a while by pretending it didn't exist, but as the world erupts into another bout of chaos and uncertainty, it is back with a vengeance.

This book is the story of ordinary people who have experienced extraordinary things and want to make sense of them. Each one is a brand new case I have never shared before on my podcasts; modern-day ghost stories that make my blood run cold as effectively as anything that those master storytellers Charles Dickens and M.R. James could rustle up, and they are all entirely true, in the sense that I believe that the events the person is describing really occurred and it is down to us to make sense of whether or not they really were paranormal.

But it's also the story of my own personal journey of discovery, because I've realised something, reading all of these incredible stories sent to me by email or on social media.

I've realised how much I *want* to believe.

---

* Copyright William Shakespeare.

Before that night in June 2016 when my friend came over to tell me her story, I'd spent my life carving out a mish-mash career lurching between writing comedy, travel journalism and documentary-making, with the odd foray into random adventures such as accidentally having a Number 11 hit single (remind me to tell you about that when we meet) and coming second in the UK Air Guitar Championship (I was robbed, we shall not speak of it again, though I did look good in leopard-print leggings). I was, if I'm honest, drifting, trying desperately to be somebody and in the process getting further and further away from myself.

But I've found him again – the me who devoured those ghost books in the school library, who jumped at *The Woman in Black*, gasped at *Scooby-Doo* and doubled my dry-cleaning bill at *The Exorcist*, the me before I listened to all the sensible advice to lump ghosts in with unicorns and fairies, and gave up on magic, wonder and the possibility that there really might be something out there that none of us yet understand.

I still don't believe.

Not fully. Not quite. Not yet. But I'm standing on the brink of the precipice, both feet teetering over the edge. There are some very definite Reasons Why I Want to Believe. They're mostly personal, to do with hopes and fears I have. Some I actually find quite difficult talking about, and you'll have to coax them from me as this book goes on (possibly over a couple of whiskies by a roaring fire in a cosy old pub), and I do know this …

The stories I've heard, the ones we're going to explore together in this book, contain events that I cannot explain, things that, when I'm lying in bed at night, keep me awake, moments that scare the living shizzle out of me, but that I am desperate to understand. So, I have a new job now, a new purpose in life if we want to get all Oprah Winfrey and emotional about it. I'm going to do my darnedest to try and unravel what I believe is the biggest mystery of human existence – are we alone?

I'm not at all sure we'll solve it in this book, or even in my lifetime, but I can promise you the journey will be utterly thrilling. Any ghost story is a detective story. If you're a believer it's a whodunnit, if you're a sceptic it's a howdunnit. Either way, there are mysteries to be investigated and, in reading this book, whatever your own personal beliefs and persuasions might be, you are accepting a challenge: to be the Watson to my Supernatural Sherlock.

Because I can't do this alone. I'm going to need to talk it out, to bounce ideas off you, to explore theories and ask questions. If I was doing all that by myself, I suspect I'd go slightly mad. People are already giving me funny looks in the café where I'm typing this because I read that last paragraph back out loud.

We're going to hear some incredible stories. We'll learn mind-boggling stuff. We may have our very concept of reality challenged. And we're going to be scared. Really bloody should-I-be-reading-this-at-night-oh-sod-it-I'm-going-to-sleep-with-the-light-on scared. So, as you turn the page to begin the adventure, bring with you a sturdy stomach, a brave heart,* spare underwear, and that rarest, most underrated of things in these divided, judgemental, polarised times ...

An open mind.

---

* Copyright Mel Gibson.

SCEPTIC OR BELIEVER?

There's one last thing to do before we start. I want you to write something down. Do it in the Notes section of your phone, or on a scrap of paper, or, if you're feeling really confident, you could even have it tattooed onto your forehead.*

I want you to write down which one of these best describes where you are at, in your head, at this precise moment in time.

TEAM SCEPTIC   TEAM BELIEVER

Don't take all day. Just give me your instinctive inner truth.

Done it? Good. Keep it somewhere safe. Because, by the end of the book, I'm going to ask you if you still feel the same way. And, a word of warning …

You may not.

Enough talking. It's time to start investigating. Let's meet our first witness …

---

* We both know this is a joke, right? But the publisher's lawyers are nervous, so please don't actually do it. Or if you do, make sure it's one of those henna tattoos you get on holiday that eventually (usually) wash off.

CASE ONE

THE ROME
POLTERGEIST

CHAPTER 1

ADVENTURES IN BABYSITTING

'I haven't got long,' says Andrew, stabbing a pork schnitzel with his fork. 'I need to get back on set.'

He's in his mid-fifties, with a beard, collar-length grey hair and the merest trace of an Australian accent diluted by years of living in the UK. A film and theatre producer with a pretty impressive CV, Andrew's taken a couple of hours out from his busy filming schedule, and on any other occasion I'd be giddily tapping him up for celebrity anecdotes, but now is not the time, because we've arranged to meet in this rather swanky restaurant on London's South Bank, a well-aimed sourdough roll's throw from Tate Modern, braving pre-Christmas train strikes and the threat of snow, for one reason only.

Andrew may be about to prove to me that ghosts exist.

I should put on record that I'm not totally sure it's in Andrew's interests to do this. As someone who regularly has to convince people to invest millions of dollars in his movies, the last thing he needs is them whispering, 'That's the bloke who saw objects fly across a room of their own accord'; but we can't choose what happens in life, and the same hand of fate that served him an exciting jet-setting career has also dealt Andrew another role. He's part of that small, select group of people to have encountered a poltergeist.

'Poltergeist' comes from the German for 'noisy ghost'. They're the hauntings you see in horror movies: strange banging sounds on walls, phantom footsteps in the attic, plates flying across rooms, or beds levitating in the air; an unseen force that has a physical impact on the world. They are the most tangible of hauntings and, therefore, the most attention-grabbing – the tabloid headline writer's dream – and yet, in real-life, accounts of full-blown poltergeist activity are rare. What's even rarer is a poltergeist with multiple witnesses, which is why, when I read Andrew's email, I felt a strange tingly feeling in my tummy that's not stopped since and is now preventing me from eating my trendy herb-dusted sweet-potato fries.

'So, Andrew,' I say, 'where do you want to begin?'

He finishes chewing and takes a sip of water. 'My dad was an Australian diplomat,' he says, 'so I grew up wherever he was posted, travelling the world, Paris, Belgrade, and then, for the last four years of high school, Rome.' He sets down his knife and fork with a neat clink and leans across the table, his Australian accent just a little more noticeable for a moment as if he is mentally regressing to being that teenager again ...

'This is the summer of 1983, I was seventeen, and on this particular night, I was babysitting the daughters of a guy called Robert Wilson. He was pretty senior at the Australian Embassy in Rome, a colleague of my dad's, and he and his wife lived in a huge medieval apartment on Via Di Monserrato, this tiny quiet street in the heart of the city. The embassy was renting it from the building next door, the English College – or, to give it its full name, the *Venerable* English College – it's basically where the crème de la crème of English Catholic priests have come to study in Rome ever since the 1500s.

'It wasn't the first time I'd babysat there and I always enjoyed it. The apartment was pretty spectacular, so it felt quite exciting to be left in charge of it. The two girls I had to look after were about seven and nine, we'd play games, like Monopoly and Cluedo. In fact, I remember at one point that night we were playing both simultaneously—'

'Monopuedo?'

Andrew laughs. 'Yeah. They were pretty clever kids, and they were old enough to get themselves to bed, so they'd been asleep for about an hour by this point. I was just sitting on the sofa watching TV, killing the hours until the Wilsons got back. And then …'

Andrew's eyes meet mine and the surrounding noise of the restaurant zones out, because I can feel that familiar shiver down my spine, the tingle of excitement that tells me we are descending inescapably into …

✝

Darkness. The atmospheric, romantic kind that still exists on some back streets in 1980s Rome, where 2,000-year-old blocks of stone litter street corners the way dog-poos do in most other cities. It's a place that resolutely resists evolution, so of course this apartment has no air-conditioning, but the windows are open here in the living room, allowing the warm, soft night to float inside, along with the lilting melodies of people having fun at Caffe Peru, the little coffee shop and bar directly below. The screech of a distant moped is the only real concession to modernity.

Andrew stands by the window for a moment, enjoying listening to the rhythms of Roman life, running his hand over the refreshingly cold stone of the wall. He's been told by the Wilsons that the apartment dates from the fourteenth century, with quite a guest list over the centuries. Say what you like about the Catholic Church, but they're good at keeping a record of who stays on their premises. Henry Bolingbroke, later King Henry IV of England, stopped off here on his way to the Crusades. Andrew wonders if Henry plonked his bottom in this exact same spot as he slides back onto the sofa.

One of the great perks of this babysitting gig is that the Wilsons have MTV, flickering on the screen in front of him now. Andrew is a fan of Duran Duran, Heaven 17 and The Human League. Not quite as sophisticated, perhaps, as the music his older sisters are into – David Bowie, The Cure and The Velvet Underground – but he can still tell the two Wilson girls look up to him a bit. He is the cool babysitter, he thinks, stretching out his legs and congratulating himself on a good night's work – two kids soundly sleeping and the rest of the evening to himself.

The other good thing about the apartment is that the Wilsons have a coffee machine, so, as a cheesy Europop video comes on, Andrew decides to make himself a double espresso. He walks down the corridor into the kitchen, still humming Duran Duran's 'Rio'.

'Her name is—'

What the bloody hell?

He is greeted by a very odd scene.

About twenty postcards of Rome that had been stuck to the fridge with magnets are now lying scattered across the kitchen floor on the complete opposite side of the room. In addition, all of the wooden cupboard doors are open. It's as if a huge wind has swept through the room, creating havoc.

Bit weird, thinks Andrew, there's only one window in here and it's firmly closed, but it must have been some freak gust of wind on this quiet balmy night that somehow snuck in through the living room windows without him noticing and found its way down the corridor, into the kitchen, because what else could it be?

Puzzled, he picks up the postcards. They show churches and pictures of the Vatican, the religious sights of Rome, the sort of things you'd expect to find in an apartment owned by a college that teaches priests. He reattaches them to the fridge with their magnets and closes each of the solid, heavy cupboard doors. He then makes his coffee and strolls back into the living room, consigning the scene to his memory bank of odd moments as he dives back into the joys of Italian MTV.

But then, an hour later … Andrew hears a sound.

Running water. He stifles Bonnie Tyler's 'Total Eclipse of the Heart', playing on the TV, and pads back into the kitchen. There are two sinks (it's a rather grand kitchen) and, in both of them, the taps are on full blast, water splashing down the plughole. But that's not all …

The postcards are scattered across the floor again, in the same place, and the cupboards are open. This really does feel odd now, and it gets stranger still, because some mugs on the washing-up rack that had been standing upside down drying are now all lying on their side, as if each had been lifted and carefully laid to rest horizontally. Andrew's gaze pans down to the floor and this is when he really starts to feel unsettled, because what he sees is truly bizarre.

The plates that were neatly stacked in the cupboards have been arranged across the floor! This is an apartment used to holding official diplomatic functions, so they have a lot of plates. There must be about fifty of them, arranged in five separate piles, like some sort of porcelain obstacle course, neatly stacked, face up, all unbroken.

It's not the wind, then.

Aha! A smile of relief crosses Andrew's lips as he realises what's happened.

He's young enough to remember what it was like to be a kid, the delicious thrill of playing a prank on your babysitter then rushing back to hide under the bedcovers, suppressing the giggles that swirled inside, big bubbles of naughtiness. He can see it clearly now: intoxicated on Monopuedo and the excitement of his sophisticated teenage company, the Wilson girls have found it hard to sleep and decided to creep from their bedrooms to play this trick. God only knows how they managed to make it into the kitchen unheard, but they've clearly arranged this mad scene to mess with him, presumably climbing onto something to reach those high-up cupboards. It must have taken both of them to turn the water on, he thinks, with an amused respect, as he forces the awkward old metal taps grudgingly back into place.

As he heads round the corner to their room, he's already composing his speech, something stern enough to convince them to settle down and go to sleep, but not too authoritarian – he doesn't want to blow his cool babysitter mystique.

He opens their bedroom door. It's dark. He waits there for the laughter to break like waves on the shore.

Nothing.

Silence.

Actually, not silence. Something far more disconcerting. The peaceful, undulating breath of sleeping children, its unguarded rhythms utterly unfakeable. Still, he walks over and leans his head close to their faces, something that would feel deeply weird in any other circumstances, but …

Damn it.

He's no expert on children, yet Andrew is 100 per cent certain these two girls are deeply, utterly asleep. Which sends a very definite shiver down his spine.

Who or what is responsible for the rearrangement of the kitchen? Because last time he counted, there were only three people in this apartment and two of them are currently unconscious. Closing the door, he walks back into the kitchen, all traces of his knowing smile now gone. Unsure what the hell to do, he decides to put back about half of the misplaced objects, but leave the other half as 'evidence' for when the girls' parents get home. He can't imagine how else they'll believe him and, even now, he's assuming he will get the blame for this. Then he goes back and sits on the sofa, MTV forgotten and irrelevant, listening as the sounds of Caffe Peru below gradually diminish, morphing into the noise of waiters putting chairs onto tables and locking up, then the sweltering still of a hot night in the Eternal City.

At 11pm he hears a key in the lock and the reassuring smiling faces of Robert Wilson and his wife Ailsa glide into the room, urbane, lively and excitable after a night of socialising. They are accompanied by his own mother, whilst his father goes to collect the car to take them home. The Australian accents are comforting and familiar after the weirdness of the last few hours, repositioning him back into reality.

'How were the children?' asks Robert Wilson. He's in his forties, solid and manly in an old-fashioned way. Ailsa stands next to him, warm and charismatic, with the physique of a regular tennis player. Both of them have the easy charm of people used to entertaining rooms of diplomats.

'Fine,' replies Andrew, and he's already wondering if perhaps he shouldn't say anything. It all feels so mad now. How could he even begin to describe what he's witnessed to these grown-up, important, busy people? And yet, the evidence is sitting there in the kitchen right now …

But before he can say any more, the decision is taken out of his hands, as Ailsa asks:

'Did the kitchen behave?'

✝

'They KNEW!' says Andrew, leaning back in his restaurant chair, eyes alight, as a waiter collects our plates. I've been so glued to his story I hadn't noticed it has become dark outside. The night is frosty, laced with the threat of snow, a perfect backdrop for the telling of a ghost story. So, is that really what this is?

We order coffees, Andrew clearly still agitated by his memories of the weirdness of that night in 1980s Rome, picturing his teenage self, mouth agape, staring at this apparently sensible middle-aged couple about to crack his sense of reality asunder.

'We wandered into the kitchen to look at the mess,' he says, 'and Ailsa said they hadn't wanted to scare me by telling me, but for about a month, every couple of days, in the mornings when they woke, they'd find the kitchen like this, that same crazy state – cupboards open, plates arranged in piles across the floor, postcards scattered – exactly as I'd found it.'

He shakes his head in disbelief at the memory. 'Anyway, we tidied it up and headed back into the living room to wait for my dad to arrive with the car and then, as we were standing there talking, we heard the sound of running water.'

'Oh my God,' I say loudly, unable to contain myself. The waiter looks at us curiously as he sets our lattes down. Andrew pauses until he has gone, then continues.

'We all walked out of the room, me, the Wilsons and my mother, down the corridor, past the girls' bedroom and into the kitchen … and sure enough, the taps were on full blast again! All the postcards had been distributed across the opposite side of the room, and the plates were lined up in piles across the floor, this time also accompanied by glasses, all arranged on their side.'

'Oh my God,' I utter again. I know I'm being repetitive, but I'm not really sure what else to say. This is, to use a technical term, properly freaking weird.

'Absolutely nothing had been damaged, not a single thing, but the strangest part of all is that the entire contents of the fridge were now also arranged across the kitchen.'

'Oh my – how?'

'I don't know. It wasn't messily, as if they'd fallen out. The fridge and freezer doors were both wide open and each item was placed on the floor, as if someone was doing an inventory. We're talking a half-leg of lamb, eggs – each one sitting neatly by itself on the floor – and the contents of the freezer too. Maybe the weirdest detail was that anything with liquid in it, like the milk and orange juice, was on its side, but un-spilt.'

We each sip our coffees, pondering the brain-bashing bizarreness of this. It's clear that we have a very definite puzzle on our hands. The Mystery of the Misbehaving Kitchen.

'It had happened in the space of five minutes,' says Andrew. 'That's how long it had been since we were in the kitchen tidying it up. Something happened in that five minutes, and I tell you, no one else was in that kitchen or in that corridor. The kids were very much asleep, and it certainly wasn't my mum or Mr and Mrs Wilson.'

'What did you all say?'

'Nothing. None of us really knew what to say to each other, I just went home with my parents, quite shaken.'

For a moment, staring down into the dregs of his latte, Andrew, this winer-and-diner of film stars, the charismatic wheeler-and-dealer at home on Cannes red carpets and at Hollywood premieres, looks like that teenage Australian boy again, genuinely lost for words.

'And that,' he says, 'is when things got *really* fucking scary.'

CHAPTER 2

THE FLYING GIRL

Don't worry, we're going to hear more from Andrew – a LOT more – because he's not wrong, it's about to get really bloody terrifying, but first, I think we need to talk about poltergeists.

Do we actually dare countenance the idea that solid objects can travel across a room of their own accord? That 50 plates can stack themselves and fridges spew forth their contents so delicately that not a single egg is broken or a drop of juice spilt? It's a question I'm asking myself as I walk down a blandly anonymous street on the outskirts of north London. It's a few weeks after I met Andrew, and I've come to the borough of Enfield, like so many before me, to visit a place that should shove a big icy shard of terror through even the stoutest heart.

Enfield Laser Quest. I've just dropped off my ten-year-old son for a party, two hours of intense, sweat-drenched combat played out in stifling windowless darkness between screaming pre-teens and a handful of nerdy loner middle-aged men who always seem to be lurking around to make up the numbers. On the plus side, it's given me a brief window of childcare to make a pilgrimage I've often thought of, but never attempted before, wending my way through rows of monotone suburban houses to ...

284 Green Street.

This ordinary-looking semi-detached house is the scene of what is often described as the world's greatest haunting. Google 'Enfield Poltergeist' and you'll find hundreds of thousands of webpages detailing the strange events that occurred to the Hodgson family who rented the house in the late 1970s, events seemingly witnessed by police officers, journalists and many other serious, credible people. The sort of people who don't believe in ghosts.

Those who make a study of poltergeist hauntings talk about them occurring in stages – the precise order and nature being a source of keen debate.* My friend, the parapsychologist Evelyn Hollow, who takes a particular interest in poltergeists, breaks it down like this:

Stage 1: A sense of presence

Stage 2: Noises

Stage 3: Moving objects

Stage 4: Apports and disapports (that's old-fashioned fancy words for objects appearing and disappearing)

Stage 5: Destruction

Stage 6: Communication

Stage 7: Physical violence or threat to life

Seeing them written down on the email she sent me before I came here, it's a pretty daunting checklist. It shows the general consensus

---

* It's like the paranormal version of 'What is the correct order to watch the *Star Wars* films in?'

between all experts that these cases start small and grow, beginning with unsettling feelings and hearing noises, which could be bangs or scratching or footsteps, before progressing to objects moving, building in intensity to ever more violent and disturbing activity as time goes by.

The Enfield case certainly seems to follow this pattern. Loud persistent bangs were heard, furniture was alleged to have moved, objects were thrown across rooms, then gradually it gets darker and darker, with the youngest of single-mother Peggy Hodgson's daughters, 11-year-old Janet, seemingly becoming possessed, talking in a deep gruff rasping voice that was not her own, a voice that some believed was the spirit of a former resident of the house called 'Bill'. If you search online you can find recordings of it, captured by a BBC journalist. Whether you're a sceptic or a believer, it's properly eerie stuff hearing a little girl's voice sound so otherworldly and sinister. Was this an example of Poltergeist Stage 6: communication – whatever was tormenting the family actually making spoken contact? If you can read that sentence and not feel a little shiver down your spine then you're made of stronger stuff than me.

Over a period of about 18 months, a team of researchers camped out at the house, recording events, led by Maurice Grosse and Guy Lyon Playfair, two heavyweights of the Society for Psychical Research, one of Britain's oldest and most respected institutions for studying the paranormal. The family became a case study. It was that most exciting of things for any student of the supernatural, a live, unfolding poltergeist haunting that seemed to stand alongside, and maybe even outclass, any of the greatest ones in history, and it landed at a time when finally technology had developed to a point where the events could be easily filmed, photographed and taped. TV crews, radio reporters and newspaper journalists descended on Green Street along with many other gawpers, voyeurs and self-styled 'experts', including even, at one point, a well-known ventriloquist determined to see if he could prove that Janet was faking the 'possessed' voice.

The case became national news. Four years after the release of *The Exorcist*, it was like a very British real-life version of it, but the 24-hour attention put an intense scrutiny on the Hodgson family, a spotlight that increasingly focused more and more on Janet. Was she really a vessel for some supernatural force, or was she a precocious hoaxer enjoying deceiving 'the experts'?

The case has spawned endless documentaries and articles since then and been dramatised in a recent Sky TV series *The Enfield Haunting* and, rather more loosely, in the Hollywood movie *The Conjuring 2* (they added in a demonic phantom nun for good measure). For anyone trying to make sense of poltergeists, Enfield becomes an almost inevitable starting point, so huge and all-encompassing is its shadow. It sometimes feels like the supernatural equivalent of the 1966 World Cup – a moment when England had the world's attention, forever to be celebrated and recycled, its unassailable authenticity captured in reams of videos, photos and audio tapes. But, like that World Cup final, it's an event some claim is based on a lie – just as the replays show Geoff Hurst's second goal never crossed the German goal-line, so you will find plenty of sceptics queuing up to tell you Enfield was all a sham, that it is not the most credible of hauntings at all, simply the most photographed, and there is one photograph that has proved more controversial than any other. I'm looking at it right now on my phone, as I stand outside the house, wondering how long I can loiter without looking suspicious to the neighbours.

Even at iPhone-screen size, it's an intensely striking image.

As you can see, it shows Janet's bedroom, which feels like it could have been put together by a TV art director trying to capture the quintessential 1970s teenage girl's room, the décor a jarring colour clash of brown, pink and orange, posters of Starsky and Hutch and bands such as The Bay City Rollers pinned to the walls. You don't really notice any of that on first glance, though, because your eye is drawn to Janet. Thin, small, gangly limbed, in a vivid red nightie and white socks, she's ... well, she's not at all where you'd expect her to be.

She is seemingly hovering two to three feet above the ground, her hair flying behind her, her mouth open and her eyes wide, a look of pure terror.

Janet appears to be levitating.

They say seeing is believing. I think that's why I wanted to come here to Green Street, to make this story that has become almost mythic within paranormal circles feel more real, but I'm not actually sure what I was expecting. I'm a bit like those pilgrims who make their way to Lourdes in France, where the Virgin Mary is said to have appeared to a local woman. Thousands flock there every year hoping for a vicarious touch of the miraculous. What could be more miraculous than a young girl propelled through the air by an unseen force? Looking up at Janet's bedroom, though, just visible through the upstairs window of this demurely everyday house, I don't feel any clearer on what is happening in that picture. It feels like one of those Rorschach test inkblot paintings where how you interpret it will give some insight into your personality. Viewed in one way, the photo shows something phenomenal, impossible. Viewed another way, it is clear evidence of fraud, an attention-seeking child jumping off her bed to trick the gullible investigators, so seduced by this reputation-building case they can't see the tawdry truth staring them in their faces. Because there is another way of looking at that list of stages of a poltergeist haunting, not as the poltergeist growing increasingly disruptive to grab attention, but that a child is doing that, upping the stakes as the shock factor of each previous act wears off, needing to be more and more dramatic to make sure that all of the people who've made her the focus of attention do not decide to go away.

It is as if this single image encapsulates the dilemma at the heart of all investigations into the paranormal. The truth is an uncertain thing, shifting in the eye of the beholder, and the more layers of storytelling that get slathered on top, the more an event becomes a story – as each new documentary or drama gives us their version – the more uncertain it becomes, until perhaps even the person it happened to is no longer completely sure what really occurred.

But there must be a truth, right, buried somewhere deep down inside? Strip everything back, like peeling off coats of paint, and underneath we must be able to find it? And, if that truth is really that yes, there are invisible forces that can move objects and even people across rooms, then wow, I'm not sure if I think that is wonderful and exciting or scary and flipping terrifying, but I can tell you this: if we could prove it, our world would never be the same again. So it seems like there is only one thing I can do right now (after I have picked my son up from Laser Quest, obviously).

I need to talk to the man who took that photograph.

Even in his sixties, Graham Morris has the unflustered, slightly rugged quality of somebody who'd be good in a sticky situation, like, for instance, encountering a malevolent poltergeist. It's a few days later and we're sitting in a greasy spoon café just round the corner from Green Street, surrounded by the lunchtime rush. I first met Graham when I made my series *The Battersea Poltergeist*, for which I looked briefly into the Enfield case. These days, he's retired and lives in Norfolk, but back in the 1970s he was a young jobbing photographer for the *Daily Mirror* newspaper, Britain's left-leaning tabloid. He was working a late shift when a phone call came in from a neighbour of the Hodgson family, a woman called

Peggy* Nottingham.† These were the days when ordinary people still viewed their daily newspaper as some sort of social champion, an ally to be contacted in times of need. Perhaps it helped that the *Mirror* was the newspaper that had broken the story of the haunting of Borley Rectory back in the 1940s, another classic British poltergeist case that went on to grab and enthral the nation. Whatever her reasoning, Peggy had decided the *Mirror* was best placed to help her afflicted neighbours, who were currently hiding in fear at her house whilst, back at Number 284, objects seemingly floated around rooms and furniture moved by itself. Peggy described these events to the journalist who took her call and he, quite frankly, didn't believe her. She was laughingly dismissed as either drunk or crazy, and told to call back 'after the pubs shut', but when she dutifully did so, and told the news desk her story again, unwaveringly, adding in for good measure 'the police officers that are here, they saw it and they can tell you all about it', Graham and a reporter were duly dispatched to investigate whether there really was a story to be had.

When Graham arrived at the Hodgsons' house in Enfield, armed with his trusty camera, Peggy Nottingham's husband, Vic, showed him around.

I tell Graham that, however sceptic-minded I was, I'd still feel scared walking into what I'd been told was a haunted house where objects might hurtle towards me.

---

* Don't worry, you read right, Mrs Hodgson was called Peggy too. It's a little-known fact that it was a bylaw of the Borough of Enfield that all women over the age of 40 had to change their name to Peggy.

† You didn't seriously believe that? It's just a coincidence that there were two Peggys living next door to each other. Or is it? Cue spooky music …

'I was,' he replies. 'I was twenty-something years old and there am I being told to go into a house in the dark with whatever this was, but ... there was nothing happening, nothing at all.'

It must have all seemed like a waste of time to his young mind, a bunch of people who'd got themselves into a right old state over absolutely nothing. But then, around midnight, Peggy Hodgson and her four children returned to the house. Graham, figuring he might as well take some pictures having come all this way, positioned himself in the corner of the living room, camera ready, as the children were carried in, dozing, in the arms of their mother Peggy, Vic and the other Peggy.

'Janet was last,' says Graham, 'and, as she was brought in, suddenly – wow! Here we go!' Graham's eyes light up. 'Things just started flying. There were things whizzing round the room.'

'What kind of things?' I demand, my voice shooting into a slightly overexcited squeal.

'Just tiny things really, the kids' toys, bits and pieces – ashtrays, cups and saucers. I'm concentrating on photographing things, but ... well, I've never seen anything like it.'

And I am struggling to imagine anything like it. Poltergeist phenomena is familiar from a hundred different horror movies, but there we have the comfort blanket of knowing that it is CGI plates flying across a room or that there's an invisible bit of fishing wire yanking the table to send it flying. Trying to process the strangeness of actually being there in person to witness this maelstrom of domestic items swirling like a tornado across the living room of a house a few streets from here is discombobulating. I'm desperate for Graham to suddenly reveal he is joking or mistaken or lying or ...

anything really, other than the matter-of-fact, non-sensational but utterly bloody convincing way he is describing what he saw.

'There were lots of Lego bricks everywhere, as there would be in any kid's house. And these were taking off and flying, and I got hit in the head, just above the eyebrow, by a corner of – well, it was only a little Lego brick, but it must have been going at some speed. It gave me a lump for about four days! It was ...' He pulls up, searching for an adequate word to describe being hit by a paranormally powered flying Lego piece. 'Unbelievable.'

Any of us who have ever stood on a piece of Lego in bare feet will know just how deadly these bits of Danish plastic can be, but, for many sceptics out there, the idea that they can fly will be literally that – unbelievable. Every sinew of my rational being is telling me there must be another explanation here, which I suppose, by default, has to be that the objects were thrown by somebody else in that room, and this is where I run into trouble, because, listening to Graham, I find it hard to countenance that someone so very practical, whose job revolved around observing and capturing moments others might miss, would misinterpret or mistake something so seismically earth-shattteringly unforgettable. Would a news photographer, even one in his early twenties, really be duped into thinking a bunch of people chucking toys at him was objects flying of their own accord? And yet ...

'It's impossible, isn't it, Graham? So how do you, as a rational human being, process that?'

'Well, it's just something that's happening. It's only afterwards when you stop and think, that suddenly, this sort of tsunami hits you and you think, "Wow, what was that all about?" You know,

I haven't ever tried to explain it. I just … press the button. I take the pictures and let other people worry about what it is and what's caused it.'

Other people like me, I suppose he means.

'Could a person have thrown it?'

'No,' says Graham. 'I'm watching the kids, and they're horrified. They're screaming. They're crying. They're not doing it, it's as simple as that. No, this was just happening in the room around them, and they were terrified.'

'When you looked back at the photos,' I ask, 'did they capture what you witnessed – objects flying through the air?'

There is a pause.

'Well … no. Story of my life. You can only take so many pictures at a time. You've got a flash gun that's recharging. It's the days of analogue photography, and you could only take one picture every few seconds.'

I can sense Graham's disappointment, or perhaps it's that he's reacting to mine. It's as if we have discovered the location of the Holy Grail only to turn our backs for a moment and find it's gone. I feel again like one of those Lourdes pilgrims, asked to accept the miracle on trust. One of the most common complaints I hear about hauntings is: 'If the person saw a ghost, why didn't they film it?' Particularly now that we have moved into the smartphone age where our every waking moment can be recorded and played back later, if you're being haunted, why the hell don't you have any photographic proof?

I can understand where the sceptics are coming from, but I will also say this – stop and think for a moment about all those amazing things in life you have missed out on filming or photographing. That hilarious line your kid just said, the perfect smile your partner gave you, the seagull randomly pooing on your mate on holiday or swooping down to steal your gran's chips ... Life surprises us all the time, and sometimes we are too slow or too shocked to react. We capture the aftermath rather than the moment, and so, as much as it is maddeningly frustrating to Graham and to me and you that he didn't become the first person to capture a poltergeist on camera, I'm not entirely surprised that he fumbled to get his shots away in the dark of that room facing the strangest experience of his life surrounded by screaming, crying strangers.

'Never mind,' he says ruefully, 'it didn't take away from what I saw and certainly what I saw over the months to come ...'

And this, you see, is the really interesting thing about Graham's connection with Enfield, because that night wasn't the end of it for him, it was just the beginning. He was so unsettled and fascinated by what happened that he would end up devoting the next year and a half of his life to camping out at the Hodgsons' house photographing and documenting the case.

'I was probably there about four nights a week for eighteen months.'

'Wow.' I tell him I'm amazed the *Daily Mirror* let him do this, and he slightly bashfully lets slip that he was doing it in his spare time, fitted in between his work shifts. The haunting had become a personal obsession, born out of not just a burning desire to make sense of what was going on, but also, I can tell, a deep sympathy for Peggy Hodgson and her kids. Alongside his reportage, Graham found himself helping out with the children's homework and generally becoming part of the family, and one thing he felt very conscious of, he says, is how scared they were.

'The fear was really of the unknown. They had absolutely no idea what was causing it all. Obviously, they wanted it to stop and go away, but they were desperate to know what was causing it.'

Graham got to know 11-year-old Janet well, and liked her. She was the one at the heart of the media storm surrounding the case – a storm that Graham perhaps felt partly responsible for, thanks to his and his colleague's first report in the *Mirror* – and she had become the unwitting public face of the haunting. If I described the photo of Janet 'flying' as being like a Rorschach test, then Janet herself became a walking, talking embodiment of that, with the Great British Public studying and judging her in their newspapers or on radio or television, reaching their own conclusions on whether she was a victim or perpetrator. Quite a burden for an 11-year-old child.

'Did you feel it became a media circus?'

'Oh, yes,' agrees Graham. 'After a while, you had TV and radio, scientists coming from Cambridge University to study it, the Society for Psychical Research, and you ended up with Ray Alan,* the ventriloquist, trying to work out if the voices are coming from Janet or wherever ...'

Graham stops himself, it feels like he's tempted to say a lot more about the ethics of the parade of people who came to poke their noses

---

* Often described as the greatest ever ventriloquist, by the 1970s, Ray Alan was a well-known face on British TV, accompanied by his puppet Lord Charles, a monocled drunken aristocrat, whose catchphrases included 'You silly arse!'

into what was rapidly becoming a freakshow. I wonder if Graham stayed so long at the house because he began to see his role as defending Janet, keeping a photographic record of events in the house that sought to establish the fact that this young girl was not a liar.

'A lot of the time I'd be using the photographs for the equivalent of continuity. I'd be the last one in a room. I'd take a picture of it as it was, and then shut the door. Next thing you hear, CRASH, BANG, WALLOP! I'd go in, take a picture, and then you have two pictures you can compare. You can see exactly what's happened. There was no other access to that room, no one came out, but things had moved in there, so you just knew that people weren't doing this.'

I wonder if Graham is trying to convince me, or himself. It does feel like a form of proof and yet one that would never satisfy the sceptics because, unless we are in that room as the phenomena occurs, how can we truly know what happened? We're all familiar with the idea of a 'locked room mystery' in detective fiction, but the thrill is to witness the seemingly impossible from *inside* that locked room, rather than outside waiting. It makes me think again of Andrew's experiences, how everything happened when he had his back turned. As long as that is the case, there's always the possibility this could be explained by some unseen sceptical reason.

I am reminded of an email I was sent by a woman who told me that she lived in a remote cottage in Wales. Every morning she would come down to find a fire laid in the fireplace in her living room, the sticks positioned in a neat pile in the grate, ready to be lit. How could this be explained in any other way than a ghost, perhaps of some former owner, wanting to keep the new residents warm? The answer to the mystery was one you would never in a million years have seen coming. A family of jackdaws had made a nest in the chimney, and were accidentally dropping sticks down it. Sometimes the rational explanation can be almost as bizarre as a ghost.

But ... Graham really did see those Lego bricks flying, I remind myself, and whilst he may not have captured it on camera, his place in paranormal history is assured for that other picture he did manage to take. It is time to broach the elephant in the 1970s bedroom.

'Graham,' I say, 'let's talk about the levitation photograph.'

Graham nods. 'That was taken one night. This was months into it; by this time, I'd like to think I was just about accepted as a member of the family.'

But Graham had become concerned that his presence had become intrusive. He was keen that the family have as normal a life as possible in their house, and so he put cameras into rooms that he could operate remotely without needing to be in the room himself.

'I had a switch, and we would sit downstairs and listen to live audio through the tape recorder of the Society of Psychical Research guys, and if I heard something, I would just press the switch and the camera would fire. So, on this particular night, we were sat downstairs. The kids had gone to bed, it was quiet, you could hear sort of murmurings and the girls chatting to each other, then they finally got to sleep.'

I am breathless as he tells me this, transported back to the paranormal stakeout on this most legendary of hauntings, imagining Graham sat between the SPR team, led by the charismatic investigators Maurice Grosse and Guy Lyon Playfair. Yes, there's a definite weirdness to a group of adults sitting up all night listening to children sleep and yet ... you know that every single one of them would have been gripped by that sense of possibility, the same thing that makes me write this and you read it … the chance that we might finally be about to lay our hands on it:

Proof that ghosts really do exist.

And so I am totally there for this, Graham poised, alert, finger hovering over the remote button, waiting for the moment, and then …

'Crash! Bang! Scream! So I hit the button and the camera took pictures. Back in those days, you had to get the photos processed in the lab, so I had no idea what had happened until I got them back and then I could see that it was Janet in her red nightdress, and there's a sequence of her coming up from the bed and sort of flying across the room and then crashing onto the floor. Her sister Margaret was in the other bed and she's woken up because of Janet's scream, she's looking horrified and watching her sister fly through the air.'

'What were your initial thoughts when you saw those images?'

'I'm not there to analyse the photographs. I'm there to press the button. They, the Society for Psychical Research and all these other people, whoever they are, who look at the pictures, they decide what they're doing. I provide them with photographic evidence, so all I can say is – there you are, there's a picture of a girl in mid-air somewhere between a bed and the corner of the room where she ended up. That's it.'

Something hovers in the air across the slightly sticky café table between Graham and me. I realise it is anti-climax. I'd hoped that the man who took that photograph might help me find some sort of resolution, some stamp of authenticity, like identifying a disputed Rembrandt as the definitive article, but instead I feel only more uncertainty.

There are some who might say I should ask Janet about the event, but the interviews I've seen with her over the years – she's done very few as an adult – suggest to me that she's been damaged by her childhood experiences. She looks quite literally haunted, and I have no desire to add to her pain by putting her on trial again. Also, I can't help feeling Janet is not the witness, but the event. She, or whatever was happening to her, is the thing that happened in that house to which others reacted, the 'miracle' to be deciphered or debunked.

Oh, to have been in that room, to have cracked the Da Vinci code and actually seen the Holy Grail. I'm feeling slightly despondent as l say goodbye to Graham and jump in a cab to head home. I am thinking of Andrew again and I don't feel any closer to understanding the mysteries of what happened in the Rome apartment. Graham's absolute conviction that he saw things in Enfield that he couldn't explain has had a huge effect on me and, just as with the events on Green Street, the apartment's kitchen misbehaving does seem truly fantastical, but, unless you witness the impossible happening with your own eyes, there will always remain the possibility that some explanation lurks out there … jackdaws, mice, wind, a minor earthquake, a bizarre type of burglar … however far-fetched, they are all possible. Or perhaps the Wilson girls were just incredibly skilled at pretending to be asleep. After all, if we are to countenance the sceptic allegations that 11-year-old Janet was capable of an ingenious fraud that tricked the nation's media, we must be open to the idea that Andrew the babysitter could have been fooled too.

Without another witness, Andrew's testimony is as subjective as the photo of the flying girl. However convincing I may find him personally and however convinced he is himself, we could both be wrong.

I look out of the taxi window, rolling things around my mind, when suddenly I jump at the piercing sound of the ringtone that I keep meaning to change.

The name on my phone screen glows:

Andrew.

I answer ... and his voice reverberates in my ear, the Australian twang just detectable.

'Danny! How do you fancy meeting Ailsa Wilson?'

It takes me a moment to place the name. Ailsa. Mrs Wilson. The woman Andrew babysat for! The mother of the two girls. I do the maths in my head. She must be in her eighties now. Wow. I hardly dare to ask.

'Does she ... remember that night?'

'Oh yes,' Andrew says, 'and she remembers a whole lot more.'

REASONS TO BELIEVE #1

MANCHESTER, OCTOBER 1984, 9PM

Darkness again.

But this time it's that total, heavy, smothering blanket of night that only exists when you're a child. I have to brave it, cutting a path through the heavy layers of blackness as I creep across the room. Everywhere there are eyes, glinting in the gloom, peering out at me – stern, severe, foreboding, disapproving but, in all cases, dead. Looming above them all, he is there, his face so pale it glints like a moon, bearded, doleful, his hands holding out his own heart, dripping blood …

I'm at my grandparents' house, dealing with that childish rite of passage, making it to the toilet by yourself across a corridor that feels familiar and friendly by day but takes on a foreign, nightmarish quality by night. My grandparents are Irish immigrants, deeply devout Catholics from Cork, relocated to Manchester, where my mum grew up, and when we visit their big, dusty old house during the school holidays, I find myself in equal parts fascinated and scared by their bookshelves lined with tomes bearing the reproachful visages of popes, priests, martyrs, monks and nuns, whose eyes now seem to follow me in the dark, and that painting, in prime position on the wall, of Sad Jesus himself, frighteningly realistic, complete with gruesomely torn-out Sacred Heart. Catholicism is, it seems, the only branch of Christianity that takes its aesthetic from horror movies.

By the time my mum had me and my brother, she'd become a devout atheist, put off religion by years of convent school education, nuns who'd beat you for wearing a short skirt, or tell you that you were a whore for having a fringe, and priests who'd sit in the confessional booth listening to your sins, judging you, whilst the potent, sour tang of whisky sat on their breath. Catholicism was in her DNA, she had an uncle who was a monk and an aunt who was a nun,* and, for most of her early life, guilt was her default setting, but as soon as she left home she decided she'd had enough, that she would unpick the faith from her genomes and start afresh.

So, my childhood was a belief-free existence, which made these trips to my grandparents seem all the more alien and intriguing. You are always fascinated by what you are not, and by what your parents have forbidden or removed. I wondered if I was missing out on something, some club that I wasn't a member of. I don't mean Catholicism per se – I think even from a young age I found all the rules and guilt a bit off-putting, the faces of the popes and martyrs in the books just a little too disapproving. No, I mean the very concept of belief. Of course we trust our parents, but sometimes they get it wrong, don't they? What if my mum had

---

* My granny's brother Norman became a monk and took the name Father Celestine. Her sister Gertrude became a nun called Sister Bernard. Yes, you read that right, a nun called Bernard.

been right to ditch the evil nuns* and whisky priests, but wrong in thinking that the world could be explained solely by the actions of humans. I was fascinated by the idea that there might be some other layer of existence, some other realm where magic existed, if only I believed enough.

Some people might have found God, but I found ghosts.

I don't know if I can quite put my finger on exactly where or why that began. Perhaps it was linked to my precocious love of going to the theatre, enjoying the innate spooky drama of ghost stories, but as I got older, the supernatural became the thing that I poured my desire to believe into. The pages of the books about ghosts that I would read in the school library seemed to offer more recent and arguably more believable examples of 'miracles' than the books on my grandparents' shelves.

But, at heart, maybe God and ghosts aren't so far apart,† because whether you believe they are real or imagined, human beings have used both of them throughout history as a way to explain something. Or rather to explain it away.

Death.

It is at the heart of all of this. The hope that death is not the end is the basis of every single religion that has ever been invented, and every ghost story ever told. This is the paradox of ghosts, right? That something so frightening can also bring comfort, because if the dead really can walk again, however terrifying that might be, it also offers the tantalising possibility that we might return ourselves,

---

* No relation to the demonic nun from *The Conjuring 2*, at least I don't think they were …

† Incidentally, I just realised that 'sacred' is an anagram of 'scared'.

45

or that those we have loved and lost could still be out there somewhere, watching and listening.

I don't think I am an atheist like my mum, I'm an agnostic, a coward, if you like, hedging my bets. Not just about God – though I suspect if I was on a plane that was plummeting to earth I might find myself praying – but about the very concept of belief. Because as much as non-believers like to insist that belief is an act of sheer blind faith, it can also be an opinion formed from studying or witnessing evidence: 'After hearing your story, I believe you' or 'After looking out the window, I believe it is raining today'. And over the last few years I have met an enormous amount of people who believe in ghosts because they believe they have seen one.

A lot has changed since I was that little boy in my grandparents' house. I think I'd find that picture of Jesus more kitsch than scary now, and I can definitely go to the toilet by myself,* but one thing remains. As I read these emails about allegedly supernatural experiences, I still feel like there might be a club I'm not a member of, something I am missing out on; the possibility of just the merest glimpse through the curtain of our everyday reality into another world where magic exists.

And I bloody love that idea.

So, Reason to Believe #1 is quite simply this – belief itself. If enough people believe something, is it just possible they could be right, and that we really aren't alone?

And if the answer to that lies in an apartment in Rome, owned by the very Catholic Church my mum escaped from, there's a certain delicious irony to that.

---

* Nine times out of ten, anyway. Nobody's perfect.

CHAPTER 3

THE STRANGE TESTIMONY
OF MRS WILSON

'The smell was the first manifestation. I can only say it was like rotting flesh.'

It's a few days later, I'm sitting in the shed at the bottom of my garden, where I've been working ever since I set up my work desk and recording studio here during lockdown, it having been made very clear by my ghost-averse wife and kids that they didn't want me making my freaky-deaky podcasts inside the house.

Ailsa Wilson is booming out cheerfully from my laptop. She's sitting in what I presume to be the lush greenery of her house in Canberra, Australia's capital.* I can't actually see her, though. This is Ailsa's first time using Zoom, and we have decided getting her sound working is achievement enough; we'll leave the camera for another time. So I'm experiencing her garden vicariously through a backdrop of chirping, provided by the exotic currawongs, cockatoos and galahs who make it home. It's late night here in the shed, the perfect time for a ghost story, but Canberra is 11 hours ahead, and

---

* Yes, I thought it was Sydney too.

I'm wondering what Ailsa makes of reliving her spooky experiences immediately after breakfast in the bright Australian sun.

She's 83, but sounds like she could be 20 years younger, pin-sharp and witty. She still plays tennis every day, and I'll bet you she wins. Andrew joins us on the Zoom, reminiscing with Ailsa about early-eighties Rome. She introduces me to the acronyms 'DBD' (drinks before dinner) and 'DBL' (the pre-lunch variant), which she would apparently partake of with the priests who'd drop by the apartment from the Venerable English College next door. Despite everything she's about to tell us – and trust me, it's going to get pretty strange – I can see she has fond recollections of living there. She tells me the gold-embossed features on the apartment's ceiling looked awfully grand but were actually just jelly moulds an English cardinal had insisted on sticking up there during his residency, a little bit of medieval *Changing Rooms*-style kitsch.

It was Andrew's mum who put him back in touch with Ailsa – after globe-trotting with their respective diplomatic spouses, the two women now live near each other in the Canberra suburbs. Andrew was a teenager when he knew Ailsa, and she had never told him of her own experiences in the apartment, beyond what she'd relayed on that fateful night he babysat, but it seems that the misbehaving kitchen was only one aspect of the strange activity there, activity that began when a mysterious and deeply foul smell appeared in the dining room.

'I've smelt plenty of dead rats and things,' Ailsa says, in her practical, matter-of-fact way, 'but this was nothing like that.'

It was so awful, she reported it to the English College and they sent people to investigate. Oddly, the stench was only present in that one room, so at first it was suggested something might be rotting inside one of the items of furniture. Each piece was dragged out until the room was empty, but the smell was as overpowering as ever.

The ceiling was the next area of suspicion. The college handyman dug it out to see if something had crawled into it to quietly decompose. By now, the smell had been going on for months and Ailsa quipped that it would have to be a cow that had died up there for it to still be smelling so strongly. Nothing was found in the ceiling though, cows or otherwise.

Other theories were pursued, including a fetid water tank. Herbs were burnt in the apartment to try and purge the pong, but all to no avail. 'And then, one day,' says Ailsa, 'the smell just vanished. Nobody knew where it had come from and nobody knew why it had gone.'

But something was left behind ... a strange sense that the family were sharing the apartment with something. I am reminded of Stage 1 on that list of poltergeist activity – a feeling of presence – and this particular presence was about to make itself felt in a way that was utterly bizarre and yet threatened to push the very sensible and down-to-earth Ailsa and her family to the brink of thinking they were going insane.

'Shall we start with the coffee cups?' I say to Ailsa.

'Oh, the cups!' she sighs, as in the background the birds build to a mini crescendo. Though her Zoom screen remains black, in my mind's eye I'm imagining her closing her eyes to block out the Australian sun, allowing herself to return to 1983, and that apartment with the jelly moulds on the ceiling.

✝

'There are six David Jones cups in the dishwasher.'

It's a sentence Ailsa never expected to carry such horror. It seems utterly ludicrous how something so normal, so innocuous, can be so frightening.

She lifts them from the rack, counting each one to be certain, checking for the distinctive David Jones stamp on the base. She asks the girls to count them too and they return the same verdict. Six cups. All solidly three-dimensional, real and bought in a department store that only exists in Australia. It simply cannot be.

There's a back-story, of course. The impossible always requires a context. The custom on diplomatic missions is you bring your own kitchenware for personal use, to save the good ones for official functions, so, before setting off for Italy, she'd popped into David Jones – one of those shops that has all you could ever need, in tasteful patterns – and bought six of everything, including coffee cups.

Then, just a week ago, her husband Robert carried two of these cups, filled with coffee, into the bedroom, as per their morning routine. Though, on this particular day, he really shouldn't have, because they were about to drive off on holiday and had woken too late, so Ailsa was forced to knock her coffee back and then rush in that way that always leads to mistakes. She'd picked up the cups too quickly, and watched one fall to the tiled floor, breaking into pieces, the David Jones stamp on the base fracturing into segments like the pieces of a discarded jigsaw.

Which is how she knows with total certainty that what she is witnessing in the dishwasher drawer is some peculiar form of magic. There categorically cannot be six identical cups in there, because she smashed one. Robert witnessed it. She smashed it to bloody bits, swept the bits up, and threw them into the outside bin. There are no branches of David Jones outside of Australia, nobody has had access to the apartment whilst they were away – this cup simply cannot exist.

It is a ghost cup.

She'd feel so pathetic, trying to explain it to someone. Why can't she shrug it off, be glad to have the cup back? But it's just so damned odd, and oddest of all is that it seems part of a pattern she's been noticing ever since that horrible smell appeared.

The apartment is alive.

It's as if it's involved in some form of conversation with them, responding to things. 'You've lost a coffee cup? Here, have it back.' She shudders at how mad that sounds, but her thoughts are already on the sweater incident.

'Mum!' Emma had called with that shrillness children use to cut through whatever important thoughts you're in the middle of. She can't find her favourite jumper, the one with the bits of leather on it. Ailsa sighs, and prepares to do her parental duty, finding it in the most obvious place possible ... Except she can't today, because the jumper truly is missing. She turns the room upside down, then extends the search to the whole apartment, before tersely saying, 'If you've lost it, I'm not going to buy you another one!'

And then, two months later ... 'Gee, Mum, where'd you find my jumper?' says Emma, and there it is, hanging in the closet in her bedroom. Not hidden, but right at the very front! Almost taunting them. *I'll be damned*, thinks Ailsa. Are they really living with a 'presence' that returns missing items? A helpful poltergeist?

The strawberry bowl was the strangest of all. In the spring, when strawberry season starts, the markets in Rome have piles of delicious, succulent berries, the colour of lipstick. Ailsa purchased a huge scoop to take home and have with cream. She has a special bowl for them, a little antique one covered in roses that she's had for years, except, as she ransacks the kitchen searching for it, she decides she must have left it in Australia.

And then what do you think happens? Of course, the next time she comes home from the market, she walks into the dining room and there is the bowl sitting in the middle of the dining table, as if it has just been positioned to attract her attention. She picks it up, studying the little roses, making sure it really is hers. How is this possible? The apartment has been empty, securely sealed with its multiple locks – almost too many of them really, it requires 11 turns of the key; no one can have got in here, unless they risked their life climbing up the side of the apartment building and through a window, but for what, to go through all the Wilsons' possessions and find a missing bowl?

There are potential other explanations, of course, but she supposes they would involve her loved ones playing deeply cruel tricks on her, hiding and finding things they claim to have had no knowledge of. That feels almost more sinister than a poltergeist and, for Ailsa, harder to believe.

Should she be frightened, she wonders? There's something ostensibly benign about the returning of cherished items and yet ... the idea that there is some invisible presence alongside them in the apartment, that something is watching her, perhaps even right now, is not a comfortable thought.

She shudders. There have only been two moments living here when she's felt real fear. The first, when she woke in the early hours of a hot Roman night, gripped by a coughing fit, a horrible, hacking cough that seemed to come from nowhere. Worrying that she would wake Robert, she'd taken herself into the sitting room, and it was there, lying on the couch, that she'd experienced it. The most total and profound sense of dread. What a funny word 'dread' is. It should always be attached to something – 'I dread flying' or 'I dread Mondays' – but this was simply dread unattached, in its raw state, pure, overwhelming and seemingly motiveless. She simply couldn't bear to lie there any more. She got up and moved into the room they call the study, where Robert's desk is, and the feeling was gone, leaving her confused, as if a stranger had just pushed her in the street for no reason.

It was the second occasion, though, when the fear seemed truly justified. Ailsa was in the kitchen, making breakfast for the children, when—

A SCREAM!

That will always get your attention, and this one came from Ailsa's mother, over visiting from Australia, plus it had been preceded by a very loud bang, which didn't bode well. Ailsa rushes through, fearing the worst, and there on the floor, next to her trembling old mum, is a heavy lead and glass lampshade. It has fallen from the ceiling, clearly missing her by the merest of whiskers, thank God. Any closer and she would have been seriously injured or worse. But the most unsettling thing for Ailsa is the state the lampshade is in.

Utterly intact. Not a single bit of damage. Just like the items lifted from the kitchen cupboards and the fridge, each one positioned scrupulously and unbroken, no matter how high the cupboard they must have fallen from. Later, when Ailsa explains it to Mariolino, the

friendly college handyman, he will look at the lampshade that mirac-
ulously tumbled the length of this high-ceilinged room without a
single scratch, and then at the intact hook it had hung on, a hook the
lampshade would have had to actually lift itself free from in order
to fall, and he will shake his head in horrified superstitious wonder,
saying 'È impossibile!'

She wonders now about the English College's well-meaning
politeness as they sought to reassure her they were doing everything
possible to investigate that smell. Was there perhaps something they
weren't telling her? Ailsa had seen the looks the priests sometimes
exchanged, noticed the hushed conversations that stopped abruptly
as she entered a room.

Gradually, with the easy charm of a diplomat's wife, she
begins to subtly ask around, talking to the student priests, the
young men in their twenties who occasionally swing by for DBDs.
You can tell from their reactions they've been told not to discuss
it with 'civilians', but Ailsa is very good at coaxing details out of
people with that warm smile of hers and just the right amount of
pre-dinner cocktails.

Soon she learns that there have been smells in other parts of
the college. 'The boys', as she affectionately thinks of them, tell her
other things too. Some of them have seen a figure at the end of their
beds, or been woken in the night by the sound of screaming. As she
probes deeper, she hears that a former resident of the apartment had
seen his bedsheets pulled off his body at night by an invisible hand.

It seems the apartment has a reputation. She wonders again
about the smell. It doesn't take a lot of reading around the subject
to learn that, amongst those who believe in such things, the

appearance of a rotten, putrefying stench in a house can be associated with the presence of an evil spirit. Such silly superstition, of course, but it makes one think a little – about that sense of dread, for instance. But would an evil spirit really go to the trouble of finding Emma's jumper or digging out Ailsa's favourite strawberry bowl?

This really is extremely strange, she thinks, holding that sixth David Jones cup in the palm of her hand, perfect and impossible.

✝

'So there were rumours around the college about activity experienced by previous tenants?' I ask Ailsa. It's nearly midnight UK time now, but I don't feel at all ready for bed.

'There were rumours,' agrees Ailsa, darkly.

Rumours, I think, that were perhaps to be expected. After all, if you're going to imagine anywhere is haunted, then high on the list would be somewhere connected to the English College, a medieval building that for centuries has housed priests who were often martyred for their beliefs. During Reformation times, the college was basically a conveyor belt for young men who returned to England to spread the 'one true faith' and ended up getting hung, drawn and quartered for their efforts. Really, you'd almost expect a few phantom priests to be lurking around still in the form of shadowy figures or ghostly footsteps, and yet, Ailsa's experiences don't conform to these traditional tropes of a historic haunting at all; the events she witnessed are so everyday and … ordinary. Mundane household objects shifting their positions. I think again about that strawberry bowl, the thing that, of all of the activity, I think she found the strangest.

'Who could have done that, Ailsa?' I ask, staring into the blackness of her zoom screen.

'Well, nobody. The apartment was locked, we were on the second floor, somebody would have had to climb up to get in, and where on earth would they have found the bowl, that we couldn't find, hunting high and low? I can't explain it, Danny.'

Objects that we lose turn up all the time, I remind myself. Perhaps the bowl was sitting in some unopened box or at the back of a cupboard, but it's *the way* that it and the other items were returned that feels jarring, placed on the table or at the front of the wardrobe, as if to deliberately attract Ailsa's attention – and, in each case, it happened when either the apartment was empty or Ailsa was the only one in it. She must have wondered if she was somehow dissociating – developing a split personality where she was moving things without realising – and yet, Robert saw her break that coffee cup, he knew that there could not be six of them.

'I can't explain these things,' she says, 'but I know they happened. I hesitate to talk very often about them because people think I'm nuts or embellishing or something.'

'This is forty years ago now,' I say, 'and you still remember it so clearly. These events are something that you will never forget?'

'No. I don't forget, I can still feel that feeling as I saw that little antique bowl in the middle of the table, and seeing mother with the lampshade on the floor. All those things made a very deep impression. If anyone asked me, I'd say I don't believe in ghosts, and yet ...'

Another sigh. I imagine Ailsa shaking her head in disbelief, a little shiver running through her octogenarian body in the midst of the Australian heat, pained at the weirdness of it all. Listening to her relive these events of four decades ago over the digital ether from ten thousand miles away, I can't help thinking that the very means by which we are having this conversation would until fairly recently have been deemed 'impossible'. The impossible is not finite, it's a constantly shifting border on a disputed no-man's land between what we know now and what we have yet to learn. Electrical power was once impossible, televisions, telephones, space travel, saving the lives of those who contracted polio or smallpox, being able to tell someone you love them from the other side of the world ... Is what happened to Ailsa and Andrew, and even Janet in Enfield, simply something waiting to be reclassified into the 'possible' category, once our scientific understanding has caught up with it?

Belief is such a personal thing, but I find it easier to get on board with a ghost who rearranges kitchens or finds a missing jumper than the melodrama of headless horsemen and jilted medieval lovers roaming castles and stately homes. Also, those tropey, clichéd things scare me less than the idea that some invisible paranormal force might be operating within a very real and mundane world I recognise, a domesticity just like mine. Because if these things can happen to an Andrew or an Ailsa in their kitchen or dining room ... it could happen to me.

I can tell that the thing that leaves the most lasting, nagging sense of unease for Ailsa is not so much the events themselves but her inability to explain them. Human beings do not deal well with doubt. It scares us, the idea that we're not the masters of our universe, and that the parameters of understanding might exist outside of where we choose to set them.

One of the cases that sticks out most from the many emails I've received is one of the seemingly most innocuous. It involved a pair of jeans. The man who wrote to me had taken them off whilst undressing one evening, placed them on a chair, turned to look at something else and then when he turned back, the jeans were gone. He lived alone. Without pets. No one else had been present in the house. There seemed no obvious explanations for how or why the pair of jeans might have vanished, but they had. He never found them again. Maybe there's a really odd yet rational explanation. It would probably have to feature someone or something crawling through his upstairs window, grabbing the jeans and jumping out just in time before he turned around. That's still theoretically possible though, right? If jackdaws can build a fire each day, then there must be something that can grab a pair of jeans – a rogue monkey? A squirrel on steroids?

Or perhaps there's another explanation, one that might explain all of this, from disgorged fridges and missing jumpers to resurrected coffee cups and fruit bowls.

It really is a poltergeist.

Because remember what Stage 4 of a poltergeist haunting is. Those funny, old-fashioned words: 'apports and disapports'.

'Objects appearing' and 'objects disappearing'.

This is a thing. If we scour the annals of poltergeist reports over the ages, we find many occurrences of witnesses reporting the strange manifestation or disappearance of items. Sometimes it's an object familiar to them, other times it's something completely unknown that seems to have materialised from nowhere, but it has been experienced and reported by people across many centuries, perhaps even millennia. Something is going on here, but what the hell is it?

'Do you feel you saw evidence of a ghost, Ailsa?' I ask.

'Well, I saw evidence of something, Danny. Something I can't explain. I suppose I felt there was something "extra" in the house.'

Something extra. What a wonderful way to describe ghosts. We end the Zoom and Ailsa vanishes back into her bright, sunny Canberra morning.

'What did you think?' asks Andrew, when he calls me the next day.

'I think,' I say, 'that this has got even more interesting.'

If Ailsa's testimony is correct, whatever was going on in that apartment was experienced by multiple people over a considerable period of time, including previous tenants, and was known about by the priests of the English College. It sounds like it was almost an open secret. In short, this is no longer about the events of one evening, or one person, this investigation has just got a whole lot bigger and more mysterious, which means I'm now thinking something else too ...

'Andrew, we need to get into that apartment.'

REASONS TO BELIEVE #2

COUNTY KERRY, IRELAND, MAY 2008

I need you to do something for me again.

Team Sceptic, Team Believer, however you're feeling right now, it doesn't matter, I want you to carefully put down that cup of tea, or mute the music, find somewhere private if you need to, maybe close your eyes, and if you're reading in bed, why not switch off your light …

Because I want you to think about the most frightened you have ever been.

I'm not talking watching-a-horror-movie fear or even looking-at-who-has-just-been-appointed-Home-Secretary fear, I'm talking real body-shaking, pant-changing, never-to-be-forgotten fear; so reach back into that now foreign landscape of childhood, or open the cache of adult memories you keep securely buried, tiptoe into the darkest corner of your mind palace and find me the box that contains …

Your most utterly terrifying memory.

You might not have thought about it for a very long time. Maybe you think about it every day. But you know what it is, and right now, you're going to take it out of the box, hold it, feel it, smell it, touch its contours and remind yourself how intimate your acquaintance is.

If you show me yours, I'll show you mine.

I actually have two moments in my box. One is so scary, I'm going to need those couple of whiskies you promised me* before I tell it, but the other one, ah, what the hell ... deep breath, Danny, here we go ...

I'm visiting Luke Skywalker's house.

It's before he moved in, and this is not Tatooine, but Skellig Michael, an island in the North Atlantic that the *Star Wars* producers chose as the ageing Luke's home in the recent sequel movies. If you've seen *The Last Jedi*, you'll remember its stunning rocky landscape dotted with tiny owl-like creatures called porgs, apparently invented by director Rian Johnson because there were so many real-life puffins, he couldn't get a clear shot, so just painted over them with his own CGI creations.

This kind of sci-fi nerd fame was all a fantastical dream though at the time of my visit. Back in 2008, you only really knew about Skellig Michael if you were a tourist visiting picturesque Kerry on the south-west coast of Ireland. From the charming little town of Dingle there, you can take a boat out over the choppy Atlantic waters to see the island and its smaller sibling, Little Skellig. Other than the outlier that is Iceland, the Skelligs are the most westerly point in Europe. Little Skellig is too small and rocky to land a boat on, but you can disembark on Skellig Michael. It feels like a real-life Craggy Island

---

* In the Introduction – I'm pretty sure you said you were buying? Mine's a Jameson, no ice.

from *Father Ted* and people come here to visit Luke's house, which, in real life, is the ruins of an eighth-century monastery perched at the island's precarious, windy summit. The very name of the island tells you just how difficult it must have been for the monks to build here: 'Skellig' is ancient Gaelic for 'splinter of stone', and the island feels like a collection of them, pointing heavenwards, like a giant pin cushion, savage and inhospitable, building unforgivingly towards two mountainous peaks, the dip between them known as 'Christ's Saddle' (though frankly you wouldn't want to risk your bum sitting on it, and if Jesus really did, no wonder he was looking so troubled in that painting at my grandparents' house).

We have talked about miracles; how the monks managed to construct their monastery must count as one. It sits, in all its unfathomable 1,200-year-old glory, 180 metres above sea level. To see it, you must walk up a steep set of rock steps with no handrails, totally exposed to the North Atlantic elements, so, as our boat docks and I look at the climb ahead of me, it's probably not a great time to realise just how profound my fear of heights has become the older I've got.

It's funny how phobias mature with age, like a good wine or nasal hair. As a kid, I remember jumping off a cliff into the sea, but now, even being on a stepladder gives me the jitters. Still, I don't want to look like a wuss in front of my girlfriend Eva,* so I set off up the steps. The sun is shining, the weather is sweet, and as long as I keep looking straight ahead, focusing on the summit, I should be fine, right?

Yep! Here we are, we're at the top and the views out over the Atlantic are pretty impressive. We take some pictures of the ruined monastery, stare at the puffins pottering about with no awareness of how they will be cruelly photoshopped out of *Star Wars* history, and then …

FUCK.

I've got to get back down.

And, as anyone with a fear of heights knows, that is much, MUCH worse.

DOUBLE FUCK. By now the Atlantic wind has kicked in, sweeping across the island in partnership with a rain that seems to hit us horizontally, like face-kicks from tiny ninjas.

HOLY FUCKING TRIPLE FUCK.

To complete this trilogy of capitalised swearwords – the steps are now slick and slippy from the rain! They're more like bars of

---

* Now my wife, in case you read the dedication at the front of the book and are wondering if I have a wife called Eva and a girlfriend called Eva.

REASONS TO BELIEVE #2

soap than anything I'd want to place my foot onto knowing there's a sheer drop to certain death on either side, but there is no other option – without wanting to sound like a character from *Jurassic World*, we have to get off this goddam island!

And so I tentatively begin my descent, Eva ahead of me, following in the footsteps of an elderly American couple we'd been chatting to at the summit, the man holding a massive tripod he'd been using to take unnecessarily professional pictures of puffins … But –

SHIIIIIT!*

He's just slipped! The tripod was weighing him down, he's lost his footing, and …

OH MY GOD.

He so nearly fell down the sheer slope to the waves churning over the knife-sharp rocks below! His wife is helping him up, presumably telling him he was a bit of a plonker to bring the incredibly heavy camera equipment with him, but he's going to make it home alive.

The question is, am I?

I'm utterly petrified now; the sort of fear that shuts down your critical faculties, until you're functioning on some raw animalistic instinct.

I have become a lizard.

Let me explain – some psychologists talk about the human brain dividing into three parts, summed up by neat animal labels. The 'Monkey Brain' controls reason and language, the ability to communicate that sets us aside from other living organisms. The

* I am working to a 'Three Fucks and You're Out' rule. Other expletives will be applied for the rest of this chapter, and, trust me, we'll need them.

'Mouse Brain' controls our desires – hunger, thirst, love, hate – the things we scuttle after every day. But, under both of these, is the oldest part of the mind, our 'Lizard Brain'. The lizard governs primal instinct, the 'fight or flight' response that's designed to keep you alive. When it kicks in, it pushes the button on that whopping great shot of adrenaline that can hopefully help you outrun whatever predator is trying to eat you.

It may be at the bottom of the brain's pecking order, but the lizard is by far the most powerful of this animal trio. Every other emotion, even love, leaves room in your brain for something else. We can feel happy and hungry or sad and thirsty, we can have a love-hate relationship or be tired yet excited, but when fear takes over, it is necessarily overwhelming, swamping and switching off every other extraneous brain message to focus on the only thing that counts – survival. Because deep down, fear is your body's way of making sure it gets to live another day.

So pick a phobia, any phobia – heights, dogs, crowds, spiders, clowns, dirt, needles, even buttons* – we fear them because somewhere deep down, however irrational it may be, we believe that that thing might kill us. However silly it might seem to others, once that sense of impending threat kicks in, the lizard takes over and it's out of your hands, as your body tries to do everything it can to force you to get the hell away from this situation, effectively shouting, 'RUN! RUN! RUN!' And, even though the monkey part of your brain might be somewhere in the background saying, 'Hey, this may not be quite as serious as you think, buttons are rarely deadly,' the lizard

---

* I once met a man with a button phobia. It was no less profound for him than my fear of heights.

shouts louder, because, as an expert on these things once said to me, 'It's better to be wrong than dead.'

But clearly, prepping you to be able to outrun a sabre-toothed tiger isn't much use if there's nowhere to run to – if you're at school, or on a bus, or giving a presentation to work colleagues – and this is where the usefulness of fear tips over into the absolute uselessness of panic. Which is what's happening to me right now, as I notice that, thanks to the insane amounts of adrenaline flowing through my system, my legs are shaking. Not trembling or vibrating – literally swinging back and forth as the fear courses through me like bad drugs. Walking has become difficult, there's a very real danger that my fear itself is the thing that will pitch me over the side of these slimy stone steps. Oh, the irony.

Eva's looking up, concerned, from below. I feel so stupid. Why is this such a big deal? Even the elderly American has shaken off his brush with death and made it back to the boat with everybody else. Yet here I am, prolonging the agony, my heart beating like a Prodigy bass line. I summon every ounce of courage, and then, finally, slowly … I actually – THANK FUCK* – make it to the bottom!

I consider kissing the last step.

How do I feel? Relieved, sure, but also deeply shaken and somehow changed by the experience. I've seen a different part of me, a weaker version of myself, as if all the fine work of civilisation has been stripped back and for a moment I have become a caveman again, primal fear winning out over reason.

---

* Okay, I lied, but that is the last one, I promise.

So that's my story.

I'm shaking again just typing it out.

If I close my eyes, I can picture every step of that descent, in heightened, hyper-real colours. There's a very small minority of people who listen to my podcasts and then ply the conspiracy theory that the witnesses must be actors and the stories made-up. The line they trot out is, 'There's no way ordinary people could be this eloquent.'

With the greatest of respect, I think that's rubbish. Fear makes you eloquent. For modern humans, true unbridled terror is deeply unusual. Most of us, if we're lucky, will only ever experience it once or twice in our lives. So when you do, my God, you remember it in the minutest detail, every second of what happened carved on to your brain like scars, and you need to find a way to describe it to other people, because it's too much to keep it all to yourself, so you find the words that best help you do that.

Which brings me back to *your* fear. You didn't think I'd forget our deal, did you, and let you get away without telling me about it?

Give the moment a name – 'The time I nearly crashed my car' or 'When I lost my parents in the shops' – however you choose to remember it.

I want you to say it out loud.

Okay. If you're on public transport or sitting in your office surrounded by colleagues, I'll let you say it in your head, but I want you to remember and acknowledge how it made you feel, the degree to which it changed you as a person, and then do this:

Imagine living with that feeling on a daily basis, for weeks, months, years. Try to imagine what it would do to your mind, body and your relationships, because, whatever you believe about the paranormal, the one thing we cannot dispute about the experiences the people who write to me have is the fear they can cause, a fear so real that they cannot countenance the idea the source of it could be anything other than utterly real itself.

And this is what fascinates me. As a student of the human condition, I want to know what could possibly have pushed an ordinary person into this extraordinary state, because fear is not a mood, right? It's a response. Something has to scare you, and so, I ask you, what could possibly make someone who has shown no previous predisposition to fear or anxiety suddenly feel so scared within the security and comfort of their own home that they reach a point where they feel compelled to write to some random bloke* who does a ghost podcast, asking him for help?

What if there really is something to be afraid of?

Yeah, Reason to Believe #2 is fear. It's the hook that lures me in. That little catch in the voice that tells me this person, even decades after their experience, is still afraid. I asked Andrew in an email once how it felt to experience all the things he did, and he wrote back, *'I feel like when we met I played down how scary it was, but it was fucking† terrifying!'*

So, whilst he gets on with emailing the Venerable English College in Rome to see if there is any way he can get us inside that apartment, I think we should look at another case where the fear really is off the scale.

---

* To be fair, I am fairly random.

† Andrew said that one, it doesn't count.

CASE TWO

THE GHOST HORSES OF AVERHAM

CHAPTER 4

A MOST UNUSUAL FRIDAY NIGHT

'I am a Technical Director in the Food Industry with a background in horticulture and farming.'

Okay, so it's not the sort of opening line that normally sets your pulse racing, but once I finished reading the email, I felt convinced I was looking at one of the most unsettling ghost stories I'd ever received.

The sender signed off: *'Best regards from a very sane, rational, non-believing professional woman.'*

But it's the paragraph before that lodged in my head like a splinter of Skellig rock:

'The house was recently on the market and I considered going back to view it, but I am so terrified I never did in the end. Just typing this is making me go cold, I really have been traumatised by the events.'

Which is why I am now feeling more than a little concerned that we are actually standing outside that house's front door, trying to decide whether to knock.

Vee and Maureen look nervous. This is not something they'd planned for. In fact, we specifically decided we *weren't* going to do it. We'll just look around the village, we'd said, we won't go near the house.

Yet here we are, as if it somehow drew us in, magnet-like.

I actually feel like I am crossing a line that I once set myself. You do not turn up on people's doorsteps and tell them their house is haunted. With the apartment in Rome it feels okay, it's a place that people pass through for short periods, but this is someone's home, a financial investment, so what am I going to say: 'Hi, these two women used to live in your house and experienced pure and utter bloody terror?'

I'm sweating slightly as I think it through. Just because the two people behind me had experiences here, it doesn't mean the current owners have or will. Someone once described a haunting to me as a cocktail: you need the right ingredients – the right person or people, in the right stage in their lives, in the right location, at the right time. Or perhaps the wrong time. I've come across stories where multiple people had experiences in a certain place over many years and I've also come across stories where that person was the only one ever to experience anything in their house.

'Something extra', I think, remembering Ailsa's words. We'll tell the new owners that, back in the 1980s and 1990s, Vee and Maureen experienced something extra here. That might be the understatement of the century though, and looking at Vee now, I can see she is virtually shaking at the idea of going inside. Phrases from her email are floating around in my head, lines she wrote about how this seemingly innocuous bungalow so traumatised her. And what about Maureen? For all her neatly coiffured, beige-knitwear-clad orderliness, she is looking similarly rattled. What have I done, dragging a sane and rational technical director in the food industry and her equally sane and rational elderly mother back to the site of events that have haunted them their entire lives?

'That's the living room,' says Vee, pointing to a window, her voice wobbly. 'The area outside there is where they came from.'

They. The phantoms at the centre of one of the strangest ghost stories I have ever received. I take a decisive breath and ring the doorbell, its shriek irreversible, as footsteps come towards us from inside.

'Let's not go into too much detail,' I say. 'We don't want to scare them.'

As we hear the door being unbolted, my eyes lock with Maureen's, as she steadies herself to embrace the horrors of her past, because, whilst it was Vee who wrote to me, in many ways, this starts with her.

Maureen lifts another crisp to her mouth. She is very specific about crisps. Always Walkers, always ready salted. You can't be fiddling around with cheese and onion, prawn cocktail, or worse. Maureen is adventurous in so many ways – she's done sky dives, zip wires and flown in an actual Spitfire – but flavoured crisps are an adventure too far. They'd interfere with this rather agreeable glass of red she's enjoying. Her Friday night tipple. Just the one, you understand, though generously poured, it is nearly the weekend ...

The TV burbles in the background. A BBC sitcom she's been ignoring for the last 20 minutes. She glances at Christopher, not watching either. It occurs to her how little they talk these days. If it wasn't for the girls, would they speak at all? The saltiness of the crisp is tart on her tongue, mingling with the buttery wine as she glances out of the living room window into the ... nothingness.

An unbroken view across dark fields.

Their house faces away from the village, but even if you swung it round, the view wouldn't be much more lively. Nothing really happens in Averham – 'Air-am' as the locals say it – one of those place names the British countryside throws up, designed to confuse anyone who doesn't live within a mile radius. However you want to pronounce it, it is the very definition of 'sleepy', no pub, no shop ...

A ghost town.

Christopher hasn't moved. She can almost see his mind ticking away, full of thoughts she feels increasingly excluded from. Another crisp, and then she really should focus on this sitcom, it seems only polite.

But that's when it happens.

It's the sound of the tack she recognises first. Jingling harnesses, distant, gentle almost. She strains to look out of the window again but sees only her own reflection. There's nothing there, and yet, she can hear them, coming closer ...

A moment later, and any gentleness is gone. The whole room ... well, 'shakes' is the only appropriate word for it. It's like a minor bloody earthquake, the very fabric of the house torn apart by a stampede of pounding, thunderous hooves, as a pack of horses bursts through the window and careers towards her.

There must be a hundred of them, a cacophonic explosion of sound that envelops Maureen and Christopher – the ragged snorts and whinnies of animals spurred to the limits of their endurance, galloping for dear life, directly into the house, cutting a swathe of noisy, steamy, terrifying chaos.

And then they are gone.

Just like that.

The television is still wittering in the background, Maureen's glass of red sits unspilt on the side table, but other than that, this is as unusual a Friday night as it is possible to have.

She looks to Christopher, his usual composure replaced by slack-jawed horror. It would be discombobulating enough to deal with horses charging through their living room, but this is so much stranger and unsettling, because the one thing Maureen couldn't help noticing, and she can tell from Christopher's expression that he noticed it too, is that those horses, all one hundred or so of them, were, well … how can she put this?

Entirely invisible.

For the first time in what feels like months, husband and wife make direct eye contact, sharing wordlessly the single strangest moment in both their lives, and then – isn't the speed of communication between long-married couples remarkable? – in that single glance they make a collective decision on how best to react to this spectacular, violent, inexplicable and totally impossible phantom equine intrusion.

They decide to say absolutely nothing.

Maureen turns her attention to the television. She realises she is still holding that ready salted crisp, in between now shaking fingers.

It's fair to say this has all been rather horrifying.

'Her and Dad didn't speak about it for ten years,' says Vee with an air of exasperation, looking at her mother. It's earlier in the day, before we concocted the madcap idea of jumping into Vee's car and finding ourselves actually back at the house. We're sitting in the living room of Maureen's tidy home on an estate of sheltered accommodation in Newark, a historic market town in Nottinghamshire, a short drive from the confusingly pronounced Averham. There are pictures of Second World War fighter planes on the walls and a spear in pride of place above the main window. Maureen is definitely not your average old lady, as evidenced by her remarkable ability to keep a stiff upper lip even when faced by an onslaught of ghost horses.

'We just carried on being terribly British,' she says with a bashful smile, 'watching television, eating our crisps. I didn't discuss it with the children either, I didn't want to frighten you, Vee.'

Vee tuts. Maureen's 84 now, small, spritely, impeccably dressed, with a big circular pendant round her neck and her hair dyed an ageless gold. I'm pretty sure she'd still jump out of a plane if anyone would insure her, but her mask of bravado is slipping the more we talk about that house.

'I've gone goosey,' she says. 'Feel my hand.'

'You're ice-cold,' I say.

'Ice-cold,' she agrees. 'I'd almost say I've had enough of this conversation.'

'Sorry,' I apologise.

It's at moments like this that I realise, as fascinating as you and I find these stories, we can walk away from them at the end of the day. I can turn off my laptop or you can close the book.* Vee and

---

* Please don't! That was really bad advice, what was I thinking?

Maureen can't switch off their memories, and if you think the ghost horses are scary, trust me, we have only just got started.

One of the oddest aspects of the case is the fact that, for all the extreme experiences they both had at their old home, Maureen and Vee had never actually discussed it together until relatively recently.

'It was Grandpa's hundredth birthday,' Vee says. 'We were at his residential home, having a party, and I remember Mum saying to me, "Did you ever have any strange experiences at Averham?" And I said, "What, Mum? You mean apart from the disembodied voices and the flashing lights, and the horses, and the strange cold and being absolutely terrified and knowing that somebody or something was watching you? Apart from that?"'

She is trembling.

I probably shouldn't be surprised by what it's possible to *not* discuss with your nearest and dearest. Families are the ultimate receptacle for secrets, lies, omissions and festering unsaids, but I'm still utterly amazed it took so long for these two very sensible women to talk to each other about what happened, Maureen burying her terror under her old-school British fortitude and Vee keeping her fear to herself, perhaps worried she would not be believed. But, oh my God, they have so much to share, because that very strange Friday night back in the early 1990s was not an isolated incident, it was the tip of a much stranger, and utterly bloody chilling, great big spooky iceberg that would define both their lives.

Vee's lip is still quivering. I could tell, when she picked me up from Newark train station earlier today, that she was a powder keg of emotion, our conversation scrupulously avoiding the reason I had come here. We talked instead of Vee's career in the food industry with its background in horticulture and farming.

'The biggest part of my job has been inventing new types of tomato,' she confided, sparking a debate about the science of tomato breeding that I never knew I'd find so fascinating. Vee is 50 now, with long blonde hair and sensible specs. Like Maureen, there's a solidity to her, that kind of no-nonsense outdoorsy, don't-be-silly-it's-only-a-little-bit-of-blood robustness you get from people who have grown up in the countryside, and are most at home in wellington boots and stout waterproofs. She's the last person you'd imagine jumping at shadows, just like Maureen, who was happily jumping out of planes into her late seventies.

Vee drove us past the remains of Newark Castle, a Royalist stronghold during the English Civil War, besieged three times by the forces of Oliver Cromwell, finally surrendering only reluctantly on the orders of King Charles himself.

There are many ghost stories associated with it, and there are ghost-hunting companies who organise paranormal investigations there where people pay to spend a night, hoping they might experience some of the spectres said to stalk the ruins, including a hanged man swinging in the king's bedroom (the sounds of his twitching and struggling for breath apparently sometimes audible), chanting, screams, shouting that can be heard at night and a strange feeling of oppression in the dungeon. It's textbook ghostly material in a suitably spooky setting, so very different to the modest 1960s house at the heart of Vee's tale, and yet it is that house that sits like a cold chill between Vee and me right now. Another line from her email floats into my mind: *'it was terrifying for all of its uninteresting appearance*'. A building doesn't have to have ramparts and a draw-bridge, I think, to send a shiver down your spine.

And now here we are, sitting in another seemingly innocuous modern building, Maureen's house, she and Vee on opposite sides of the room. Are they finally ready to tell each other the whole unre-dacted truth?

'I've never …' Vee halts, barely able to get her words out. 'I've never felt terror like it. And I lived with that from being aged seven and a half through to my early twenties.'

I look to Maureen, ruminating on all those years of pluckily eating her crisps in the face of stampeding ghost horses, then back to Vee, her prize-winning tomatoes now the very furthest thing from her mind. I'm not here just to voyeuristically gawp and marvel at their fear and the seismic rift it has caused, but to try and help them get to the bottom of a mystery that has haunted their family for 40 years.

'Tell me about the voices, Vee,' I say.

CHAPTER 5

IT

There are men outside. A group of them. Vee pushes against the wall next to her bed, wanting to make herself as small and insignificant as possible, to become one with the wallpaper, as if by convincing herself she no longer exists, the men won't exist either. On her other side, the side facing the window, she's pulled her teddies into a protective wall, the soft-toy equivalent of a human shield, but it's not really working.

'Dad!'

This is the last resort, because Vee knows what will happen; the same familiar sequence of events that plays out every time the men are outside. The door opens. Her dad is in his pyjamas, but not yet with the patina of sleep on his face. It's early enough that she hasn't woken him.

'They're here again.'

He nods and opens the window, leaning out to look, but it's gone quiet now and she's already regretting calling him.

'I'll go out,' he says, 'check no one's there.'

She hears him open the front door, watches him walk past her window, hears him do a full circuit of the bungalow, and then back round again for good measure, his torch beam sweeping the night, leaving the men with no place to hide.

'No one's there, darling.'

He's back beside her now, tucking her in, pulling the covers up to her chin. She knows that he is right, but she also knows that when he goes, the men will return, their voices lilting in the dark, sounds rather than words, their purpose indecipherable but always with just a hint of menace, right outside her window.

As the door closes behind her father, she presses herself even closer to the wall, so much it almost hurts.

Growing up is imperceptible. You assume there will be a moment when you realise you're an adult, a dramatic, conscious act of casting childishness aside, like throwing away an old hat, but Vee has realised it doesn't work like that, at least not any more. Perhaps it was easier in the olden days, when you had things like initiation ceremonies to welcome you into the tribe, or a young squire being handed his spurs to become a knight. Maybe the besieged defenders of Newark Castle thrust a sword or musket into a child's hand, muttering, 'You're one of us now.' On second thoughts, she's rather glad not to have to go through that. Vee is in her late teens now and supposes she must be grown-up but doesn't remember it happening and, to be completely honest, it doesn't feel like it makes her any more able to cope with what's going on. She's still that little girl, hiding behind a phalanx of soft toys, terrified of the voices, begging her dad to make them go away, knowing with a sinking feeling in her seven-year-old stomach that they'll be back later, and the next night, and the next, their actual words never audible, but the rhythms distinct, like a group of men sitting around a campfire, talking in the dark.

It's not just the voices, of course.

The first thing she remembers is the lights. She'd see them in the hallway. First it was huge great white flashes that would appear and then vanish. At the same time, the doors and windows would shake as if the whole house had been hit by a mini-explosion. Then it evolved into what she'd describe as great balls of light that seemed to float around the house. Sometimes she'd stand in the bathroom, brushing her teeth, and see one reflected in the mirror. She dug out a book about ghosts in the school library and read about 'orbs', strange anomalies of light that show up in photos. Some people think they're the spirits of the dead, others that they are just specks of dust, but these flashes she sees aren't in photos, they're real and in her house, sometimes so bright she'd be convinced a floodlight was shining in from outside. Except, whenever she'd go and check, there was nothing, just the emptiness you'd expect to surround a house that stands in its own land at the end of a long drive, the nearest neighbour a five-minute walk away.

The lights still scare her, even now.

And then, there are the horses. The most dramatic time she heard them came when she was sitting watching television. The curtains were closed and she heard the stampede, heavy-hooved big horses, and, as they approached, the security lights sprung on in the garden, seemingly verifying their realness, and yet, when she threw the curtains back, there was nothing there. She's been getting used to that, looking out into the dark, willing the things she sees or hears to be real, only to be confronted by darkness.

There have been so many nights when she has heard hooves. They run across the front of the house, alongside her bedroom window and then past the dining room and down the side of the sitting room, a circuit of the house, running thunderously at pace, as if their lives, or those of their riders, depended on it.

No, as she has slid unwittingly into being a grown-up, she has not learnt how to deal with any of this. The house terrifies her to the very core of her being, but it is not the lights or the voices or even the horses that scare her most. These, after all, are things you can block out by closing your eyes or holding your hands over your ears. The thing that makes her feel sick to the pit of her panicky stomach is something you cannot shake off so easily.

A feeling – no, sod that, a knowledge – that there is something here.

She knows exactly where it is. In the corner of the living room, by the drinks cabinet. It is dark, oh God, it feels so dark, and hot, like it's a pulsating force of evil.

It watches her constantly, but there are moments when it feels even more intense, like someone stepping out of the background, into focus, and you know when it is coming. That makes it all the worse. You feel a draught around your ankles, like a low breeze that has somehow crept into the house, then the doors and windows start to shake and rattle again. She has felt it in the hallway too, in a corner, by one of the downstairs bedrooms. A cold that comes suddenly and chills you to the bone. Now she feels silly again – how can something feel both hot and cold? It's like having a fever.

Oh no … Oh, Jesus, no …

She can feel it now, that breeze licking her ankles as she stands here in the kitchen making a cup of tea.

It is coming.

'You've referred to "it" a few times, Vee,' I say. 'What was "it"?'

'It …' says Vee with a visible shudder, 'wasn't there all the time, but it was there a lot. It was a … God, I don't know … a being. If I had to describe it, I'd say it was tall. And it had a cloak, and it just used to stand in the corner. It was just there.'

She looks at me, wondering if this sounds silly, cloaked figures lurking in corners, and maybe it does a bit, but it also sounds bloody scary.

And here we have the nub of what so scared Vee about this house, and still scares her to this day; the idea that underneath all those external manifestations of something strange about the place – the noises, the lights, the odd cold, and that strange internal wind – there was a dark spine running through her time there, this sense of presence, the feeling of being watched by something that she can describe in detail and yet only ever felt and never saw.

I think again about Ailsa and her sensation of a presence in her apartment. In so many of the stories I receive, what pushes someone into truly believing that their house is haunted is not a sound or a sight, but that far less tangible of things, a feeling. Sensed presence feels utterly terrifying and completely conclusive to the person at the heart of the haunting, a conviction that there is an intruder or interloper in their house, just one that is invisible. To the rest of us looking in, though, it is the most utterly unprovable piece of the puzzle. We can hear a sound or see a sight, but we will never be able to feel what you feel.

One potential explanation is something called 'Third Man Syndrome', a condition that has been noticed in people in extreme situations, such as mountain climbers, polar explorers and shipwreck survivors, where they become convinced there is an extra person with them. The Antarctic explorer Ernest Shackleton is thought to be the first person to have written about it, describing how a strange companion joined his party at particularly tough stages of the journey, as if helping them on their way. His description of it inspired T.S. Eliot to write the lines of *The Waste Land* that I quoted at the very beginning of this book – '*Who is the third who walks always beside you?*' – coining the name of the syndrome. It's something that can also happen with victims of trauma. I was told a story recently about a woman who survived a serious car crash and afterwards wanted to thank the person who had stayed with her the whole time comforting her and telling her she would be okay until the ambulance came. There had been nobody there.

It's an explanation that sceptic experts have brought up a few times on my podcast. It always feels very neat; and yet, in practice, how many people's houses contain the extreme conditions necessary to generate this type of hallucination? How many of these experiences are sufficiently traumatic? So often the sensed presence is the *first* thing that occurs in the haunting, experienced by a happy person in a balanced and far from extreme state of mind, like Ailsa, for instance.

So where this feeling comes from in hauntings remains mysterious. We can, however, see its effect. I can see it in Vee right now. She is convinced there was something, or 'someone' else in that house. She knew it for years growing up, but it took till that hundredth birthday party for her granddad to have it confirmed, when her mother Maureen finally told her about her own experience of this presence and thereby solved one of the mysteries of Vee's childhood, providing an explanation for why, one day in her teens, she came home to find the front door wide open and Maureen nowhere to be seen, a day that would make that Friday night with the horses seem like a walk in the park in comparison.

'I will never forget it as long as I live,' says Maureen. 'I was in the kitchen, looking out of the window into the sunshine on the trees, and then, all of a sudden, the windows started to rattle* and I thought, *Oh no, here we go again.*'

For so long Maureen had lived in that house without feeling the sense of threat that Vee knew on a daily basis, without even knowing her daughter felt that way, but that was all about to change on this sunny morning in her kitchen.

Vee is tense as hell, wating for her mum to tell this story kept hidden until she was an adult. What a strange sense of relief must have flooded over her when she finally heard it. Confirmation that somebody else had experienced the thing that had haunted her whole childhood.

However, any relief she might have felt would have been short-lived, because what happens next is not very reassuring at all.

---

* This feature of the doors and windows rattling is an interesting one. Both Vee and Maureen have described it. Can we put it on our to-do list to investigate later?

Maureen has the most dreadful feeling. She has never experienced anything like it before.

She is filled with the certain and total conviction that someone is standing behind her.

But the house is empty. Who is this?

She grips the edge of the sink, her knuckles whitening, feeling absolutely frozen in place, as if her blood has turned to cement in her veins.

Wanting it to go away. Whatever 'it' is.

But it doesn't. The feeling intensifies and Maureen knows that she has to do something. Fight or flight. Either one is going to involve something that utterly terrifies her – letting go of that sink and turning around.

One, two, three ... she counts in her head, building up the courage to turn and face whatever it is.

Eight, nine, ten.

She turns, and the cement in her veins cracks and turns to dust, her reality forever fractured by what stands in front of her.

It is a man, tall, dressed in a long black cloak with a hood.

REASONS *NOT* TO BELIEVE #1

LONDON, SEPTEMBER 2019, 9.30PM

The woman frantically slides the old, stiff bolts locking the back door. She nearly slices her finger forcing them into position, top and bottom, but her only thought is to save herself and the children now. She knows that outside, on the overgrown lawn, her husband lies dead, and that soon whoever, or whatever, killed him will attempt to make its way through this door.

She looks out of the window above the sink, her breath coming hard in ragged, panicky sobs. Moonlight glints on the top of the trampoline. She remembers the morning it was delivered, how they built it secretly together, in time for their son's third birthday party, and she is overcome by the realisation that the man she did that with, the person she loves, lies lifeless now, somewhere in the shadows in front of it.

She waits for the sound of footsteps on the path. That horrible crazy paving inherited from the old widow they bought this place from. They have changed so much about the house, ripping out the old 1970s décor and the odd furnishing choices, until they ran out of money and time, here in the kitchen, which is still untouched, the old woman's chintzy cupboards and beige worktops still in place; the splashback row of tiles with twee three-dimensional images of fruit bowls. This back door should have been replaced too. The thin frosted glass could be smashed in an instant, and would the bolts really hold if someone forceful put their weight behind them? Is she about to find out?

The footsteps still haven't come. Has the intruder gone? Are they safe? Or is he … it … waiting out there in the dark for the moment she goes to check on her husband? Waiting to make their children orphans.

Still no sound outside. The garden is as black as soot, a single shard of moonlight the only respite from the soul-crushing darkness.

What the hell does she do now?

My phone rings, loud and shrill.

I'm writing, trying to finish the latest draft of my play. The shed is illuminated by just the glow from my laptop screen and a small Anglepoise lamp, but it's cosy, not spooky. I've got some new stylishly grey blinds that pair rather nicely with the stylishly grey exterior and the stylishly white interior* of my shed, which sits somewhere between garden office and man-cave. I'm enjoying the way the blinds provide a barrier against the cold glass of the windows and that unnerving way your face reflects back at you

---

* What can I say, I'm a stylish man… Okay, I admit it, my wife chose the colours.

against the backdrop of the night, freaking you out as your brain searches unreasonably beyond it for figures in the darkness. Yes, the blinds were a good investment – they keep my lizard brain at bay.

I pause typing and answer the phone.

'Hello,' I say, cheerily.

'YOU'RE ALL RIGHT?!' comes the incredulous, terrified voice.

'Yes,' I say, wondering if I have a reason not to be.

'I THOUGHT YOU WERE DEAD!' says the voice.

'I'm not,' I reply. I look at my watch. It's 9.40pm. This was not the conversation I expected to be having on an otherwise very average Wednesday night. I wonder how best to proceed …

'Thank you for checking, though. Are you okay?'

Footsteps thud across the surface of the shed roof.

I jump, but it's just a squirrel on a nocturnal nut-gathering errand.

I open the door of the shed and step out into the night air, walking, holding my phone to my ear, hearing only frightened, hyperventilating breathing filling my ear.

'I'm coming into the house,' I say.

'YOU CAN'T!' says the voice. 'I LOCKED IT SO THAT THE PERSON WHO MURDERED YOU WOULDN'T KILL ME AND THE KIDS.'

Reader, I married her. The woman, you see, behind that locked door was my wife, Eva,* and what happened was this …

---

* Yes, our relationship survived the Skellig Michael Incident. The next time that my legs would go wobbly in her presence is when I asked her to marry me and she said 'yes'.

She came downstairs from getting the kids to sleep and looked out of the kitchen window to where she'd normally expect to see my shed illuminated at the bottom of our garden. The garden's long, unusually so for a London house, and my shed sits like a lit lantern at the bottom of it. I'd been going through a period of being particularly overworked, burning the midnight oil most nights, but on this particular evening the shed was dark, so she wandered into the living room to look for me, and then up to the bathroom, our bedroom, the guest bedroom, searching every single room of the house … but I simply wasn't there, so she went back downstairs and checked the front door.

It was locked from the inside, with bolts and the chain – there's no way I could have gone out! So, there was only one conclusion Eva could possibly come to …

I had been murdered in the garden and my body was now lying out there on the grass.

'So you decided to lock yourself into the house rather than come and check on me?' I ask, slightly hurt if I'm honest.

'Yes! What good would that have done? You were already dead. If I sacrifice myself too, the children have no parents.'

Eva is Swedish. The Swedes can be very practical people, capable of letting logic triumph over sentimentality.

'What if I'd only been injured? Maybe the …' – I try to decide which weapon my imaginary murderer would have used – 'ice pick had only punctured my lung, and I was still breathing, desperately crawling towards the backdoor, wheezing, "Help me, Eva, help me," and just as I finally get there, I find you've locked it.'

'Well, that just sounds unrealistic,' Eva says. 'And anyway, if I let you in, the guy with the ice pick follows you and kills us both.'

Fair enough. Bloody Swedes.

'I still don't understand though,' she says, 'where you actually were?'

'I was in the shed.'

'But you can't have been! The lights were off!' she says, vexed by the impossibility of this puzzle.

We both look down the long garden to the bottom where not a single chink of light glimmers to alleviate the terrifying, potentially murderer-filled darkness.

'I finally did it,' I say. 'I put those new blinds up.'

I'm not telling this story to embarrass Eva.* Though I would like to put on record (with her permission†) that she is the biggest scaredy-cat I know, to this day she hasn't listened to a single episode of my podcasts and avoids anything on TV with even the mildest peril.‡ I'm telling it to show you something that might be really important for our investigation.

We've said that fear always has a reason, right? And that's true, but it's also possible that, sometimes, the reason we choose is completely wrong. Eva was justified in her terror, knowing her husband had been murdered. She slid effectively into lizard mode,

---

* In case this goes to the divorce court, that's the story you and I need to stick to.

† *Reluctant* permission. NB this footnote was written by Eva.

‡ Let's just say our Netflix profiles are very different.

doing everything necessary to protect herself and our children, her heart beating faster, her brain working more quickly, allowing her to drag those bolts across the back door more speedily than she normally would. If the murderer had actually broken in, that fear might even have given her the extra strength she needed to fight him off. Possessed by a near-superhuman survival instinct, perhaps she would have plunged the ice pick into *his* heart and saved the day.

Except there wasn't a murderer, I'd simply drawn the blinds. In this case, her fear itself was the 'ghost' in this ghost story, a phantom emotion brought to life for a reason that was totally valid but never existed.

Could that be the case with Vee and Maureen? Could they be misinterpreting explainable things happening in their house, putting them together like pieces of a jigsaw puzzle arranged in the wrong order, until they form the shape of a ghost?

In the autumn of 2022, I spent a fortnight in Los Angeles. My play *2:22 – A Ghost Story*, the one I'd been writing in my shed on that unexpectedly dramatic Wednesday night, was being staged at a theatre in Downtown LA.

Whilst I was there, I was invited to the house of Jason Blum, the Hollywood horror producer, whose company Blumhouse have been behind some of the greatest scary movies of the last two decades, films like *Get Out*, *Insidious*, *The Purge* and *Sinister*. The previous year, Blumhouse had bought the rights to my podcast *The Battersea Poltergeist*, and I'd been working with them to develop it for TV, something that, as a horror fan, was mind-blowingly exciting. I'd spoken to Jason a couple of times before on the phone or Zoom, but now, here I was in LA and he had kindly asked me round for lunch, which felt pretty damn cool. There's a point to this, by the way, I'm not just name-dropping, though blimey, he really does have an amazing house, and a private chef, and cutlery and napkins like you get in a posh hotel ...*

Focus, Robins.

Jason made his fortune, and his company's name, by backing a movie called *Paranormal Activity*. It's often cited as the most profitable movie of all time. Filmed on a tiny budget of $15,000, it made over $193 million in cinemas worldwide and spawned a franchise of sequels to boot. The story of how Jason came to release it is the stuff of Hollywood legend. He was a young producer setting up on his own after working for years at Miramax, desperately looking for a script he could turn into a hit, when a tape of a low-budget horror movie landed on his desk courtesy of an agent. The agent said the film had been shopped around everywhere to no avail and he was really only showing it to Jason as a calling card for the director, Oren Peli. The movie was rudimentarily shot to resemble home movie videos spliced together, telling the story of the haunting of a family, but Jason saw something in it and decided he was going to have one final go at trying to get it released.

He didn't have much more luck than the agent. None of the big studios wanted to distribute the film, until he got a call from Dreamworks, Steven Spielberg's company. They didn't want to release the movie either, but they were interested in remaking it

---

* No, I didn't steal them.

on a bigger budget. Jason and Oren Peli thought about this and agreed to the deal on the condition that Dreamworks organised a public screening of the original low-budget film first and invited all of their top executives.

On the night of the screening, they gathered in a cinema in Hollywood. The lights dimmed, the movie played and … about thirty people walked out. It seemed to be confirming everything the Dreamworks executives thought – the movie in this low-budget form wasn't good enough.

But then, the audience research team asked the people who'd walked out why they'd done that, and every single one of them said that it was because they were too scared. They had found the movie so frightening they needed to get out of that cinema.

Everybody involved suddenly knew they had a hit on their hands, because in Hollywood, fear sells. The deal was sealed allegedly when Steven Spielberg himself watched the film in his private screening room at home and, when he went to go out afterwards, the door wouldn't open. Somehow the room had locked him in! The story goes that he was so freaked out he apparently put the DVD into a trashbag and carried it into the office the next day, dumping it on a fellow exec's desk with the words, 'We're releasing this!'

Jason's instincts had been bang-on. When no one else in Hollywood wanted to touch *Paranormal Activity*, he knew it would terrify and all he had to do to prove it was get it in front of some real people. Since then Jason has turned scaring people into an artform and a multi-billion-dollar business. No one knows better than him how to scare people.

Well, almost no one.

Because there's a man even Jason defers to when it comes to the fear factor, and he is sitting across the dinner table from us right now. Couper Samuelson is a hugely tall, athletic beanpole with a collegiate air who you could imagine being a fun youthful academic at Yale or Harvard, the sort of professor all the students try really hard to impress. Over the many years he's worked with Jason, producing hit after horror hit, he has become Blumhouse's resident 'Scare Doctor', the person they bring in to troubleshoot if they feel a film needs to be even more frightening. At the company that has pretty much cornered the market in 'jump-scares' – those sudden shocks that make you jump out of your seat – Couper is the undisputed king of them.

And so we are going to learn from the best here: a nugget of scary wisdom I took home from Couper to pass on to you, the thing he thinks scares us most.

It's not poltergeists, or serial killers or vampires or werewolves, it's something much simpler than that.

A deviation from a pattern.

Or, to put it another way, the breaking of routine.

If we become familiar with a repeated series of three knocks on the wall from the poltergeist in the movie, then it is when we hear the fourth knock that we jump. If the knocks come from in front of us, then it is when they suddenly come from behind that we scream. Establish an open door in the background of a scene, allow it to become familiar, and then the moment you place a figure into it, your audience will jump through the roof.

Routines make us comfortable. They're what we build our lives around, either consciously or unconsciously, and when they shift into something unfamiliar, that uncertainty breeds anxiety or, worse, fear. If you stare down the bottom of your garden at your husband, illuminated, writing in his shed every night, the night it is dark feels odd and frightening.

It's linked to our most primitive evolutionary psychology. Familiarity equals safety, and something unfamiliar presents a potential danger. It is sadly at the root of many prejudices in society; we have an innate tendency to perceive difference as threat and react defensively against it.

Hearing Couper talk about scaring people in his brilliantly wise, geeky, technical way, something leaps out at me about the stories in the emails I've received that hadn't been fully clear until now. There is one other common thread to them. The vast majority occur at a transitional time in someone's life; a period that, to them, feels different.

It could be puberty, or leaving home, going to university, moving house, getting divorced, going on holiday or, in the saddest cases, losing a loved one, but it is a moment when the person leaves behind the comforting security of one established normality to face a new challenge, where the rules, parameters and outcomes are uncertain.

Let's look at Andrew and Ailsa for instance, both in a new city, Andrew shifting from childhood into adulthood, Ailsa kitting out a new apartment. Vee is growing up, and thus perhaps developing an awareness of her parents' marriage breaking down, which in itself inevitably pushes Maureen into uncertainty too.

Shifting states, broken routines.

It's easy to wonder if it's the very uncertainty of these periods that brings to life the paranormal experiences. Left to wallow in our own anxieties, without familiar support structures, we wander into the darker corridors of our mind palace and imagine the worst.

This feels like a revelation of sorts, a moment of clarity in the LA sunshine. Maybe our greatest fear is not of death after all, but of the unknown.

We want our world to make sense and follow predictable patterns, they are the glue that binds our existence together. The fact that our parents kiss us goodnight each bedtime as kids, that our keys hang on a particular hook, that our house makes reassuring creaks as it cools at night and that if we hear a noise downstairs we know it is just our cat. But when our world doesn't obey these patterns, when the noises feel different, when there is a sound downstairs but we can see the cat is in the room with us, or our keys are on a different hook and we are certain we didn't put them there, we don't know what to do.

So here's the big question I feel we need to consider. Could 'ghosts' be simply a product of this confusion, our attempt to impose some sort of explanation on to our uncertainty, to personify it, because maybe a ghost, as frightening as it might seem, is actually less frightening than the idea that we cannot explain some things at all, that life may not actually follow patterns and rules but instead be a chaotic explosion of randomness.

Perhaps this also explains the rise in ghost reports during the pandemic era. It's not that more people are dying, but that we have been faced with a form of life utterly unfamiliar to us, a time when our houses, once we could not leave them, shifted from cosy sanctuaries to oppressive prisons, when routine was broken in a way that it had never been before in human history and every day carried the fear of a future that not even those who ran the country seemed able to predict.

I think it's a question we have to ask.

Maybe I am actually no different to Eva that night, and the ghosts that populate the stories I am told will turn out to be like her murderer in the garden, something we have conjured from our collective nightmares to explain the moments when life just doesn't make sense. Could Reason to Believe #2 end up being Reason *Not* to Believe #1?

Fear. And the fact that we would do anything to avoid it – even invent a ghost.

Maybe. But there is a counter-argument, isn't there?

That being ripped away from our routines, support structures and comfort blankets places us in a state of hyper-awareness, like walking at night, when every sound seems suddenly heightened, or that glorious feeling after vigorous exercise when you feel more alive than you have for a long time.

What if humanity has been so busy looking for patterns that we haven't realised that the gaps in between them are equally important?

The cracks are how the light gets in.

Perhaps in these times when we deviate from the norm, these blips of uncertainty, we may be scared, but we are also more receptive. Yes, we go looking for ghosts, but also, what if it's in these moments that they come looking for us? Because in the horror movies Jason and Couper make, that fourth knock *is* the poltergeist, and the figure in the door often is the deranged homicidal entity. Perhaps ghosts don't fill the gaps in our understanding of the universe, they create them, they are the routine breakers, the bringers of chaos. Not the answer to a problem but the problem itself.

Thanks, it's been good to talk this out. I don't know where your head is at right now but, as ever, I am torn* in two directions on these cases, one foot in Team Sceptic and one in Team Believer. Because there are definitely aspects of these stories that we can attempt to explain away as our brain's reactions to the unpredictable data life and the universe sometimes throw at us, and yet, I see so many other elements that stubbornly refuse to be debunked. Things that stick troublingly in your mind like broken glass trapped on the sole of your foot; moments when the impossible is seemingly experienced by multiple people. Moments like the one we are about to witness. Team Sceptic, you may just have a fight on your hands after all.

---

* Copyright Natalie Imbruglia.

CHAPTER 6

IT STARTED
WHEN THEY DUG

Maureen cannot move. That awful vibration of the windows is like the hum of a rattlesnake's tail in her ears. Everything in the kitchen recedes into the background, utterly irrelevant and trivial in comparison with the threat in front of her. It's like a darkness has spread across the room, cold and horrible, and all she can do is look on helplessly, mesmerised by this figure, its hands raised over its head, and in those hands ...

An axe!

She can't believe how fast her heart is beating. Maureen is a veteran of sky dives and bungee jumps, but never once in the midst of all that adrenaline did she find herself contemplating death in the way she feels she is now, staring at this axe-wielding man in her own kitchen. She thinks of Christopher and the girls, how they would cope without her. Would Christopher even notice if she was gone? She catches herself; this is not a time for uncharitable thoughts. She would be very sorry for the girls if this is the end, all the things left unsaid, the experiences yet to be shared.

She closes her eyes, forcing her lids shut in an act of deep concentration, willing the man not to bring that axe down on her head, yet every sinew bracing for his blow, because she isn't sure how it works with these things. The horses, the voices, this man – can something be simultaneously real and unreal? She doesn't want to be the one to find out. She wills it and wills it, and then gradually …

The window stops rattling. Maureen opens her eyes and sunshine is flooding in. Life is back to normal. Well, no, that's not true, how can anything ever be considered normal again?

She simply cannot be in that kitchen any longer. She runs. How ludicrous is that? She runs out of her own house, down the long drive and onto the main road.

Did she mention that nothing ever happens in Averham? Well it does now. A middle-aged woman in an apron pelting along the road faster than she ever has before, and she becomes aware of a sound accompanying her, something that feels entirely alien and unfamiliar, until she realises it is her own voice.

She is screaming.

Through the mist of her panic she is able to find the home of their neighbours, the Turners; their children are friends with hers. God knows what they will make of seeing her in this state. She thumps on the door.

Does she tell them everything? How do you even begin to describe seeing a ghost – if that's really what it was – threatening you with an axe?

Someone is coming, and now a deep worry sets in at how embarrassing this could be. Perhaps she should just hide, like children do after ringing doorbells, let the Turners find an empty doorstep.

Her brain is still whirring, replaying the last few minutes. Who or what was that in her kitchen? Was he really threatening her? As terrifying as it was, when she thinks about it now, it feels almost as if they occupied two separate realities, him intent on waving his axe, her surprised to find him in her kitchen. Was she the object of his fury, or is it possible that he didn't even see her?

She jumps as the Turners' front door is pulled open. This is certainly going to take some explaining.

John Turner is hiding in his kitchen.

He would dearly like Maureen from Round the Corner to leave right now, but, of course, you can't say that. Being British condemns you to a lifetime of always taking the politest option. There's that film, where Chevy Chase and his family visit London and accidentally run over Eric Idle in their car and he's apologising for being in their way, as blood spurts out of him. That's what being British is all about, staying polite no matter what the personal cost.

So he has offered Maureen a cup of tea, one he is taking his time over making, trying to avoid going back into the living room where his wife Judy is currently trying to calm her down.

The poor woman is obviously in a terrible state and of course he's sympathetic, but you've got to think of your own family first, haven't you, and he knows that this story of Maureen's now threatens to dredge it all back up, everything he's fought so hard to forget, to keep a lid on.

Because the trouble is, what Maureen has just described in the stream of consciousness that poured out of her mouth the minute she lurched into his house, a shaken trembly mess, sounded horribly familiar to John.

It sounded like what Judy and his eldest daughter, Jenny, have been describing to him for years, the things that they experienced in this house. The things he'd told them, in no uncertain terms, couldn't be true.

So, no, Maureen's ghost is not a surprise, it's a bleeding great nuisance, because this all feels very troubling now. Two houses, a few minutes apart, with the same sort of funny things going on inside them is a bit too much of a coincidence. It forces the unwelcome question in John Turner's mind that something very strange really is going on in this sleepy little corner of Averham, and he is not the sort of man who wishes to contemplate something very strange, not that sort of man at all.

The kettle boils, making him jump, because he's thinking of something else now too, how all this began, and the fact that it might actually be his fault.

'Why did he do it?'

'I don't know!' says Judy Turner. 'Men do daft things like that. Burying a toy pushchair!'

Hold that thought. More on the buried pushchair in a moment; this case is going to take an even weirder turn – but the BIG news just in is that Maureen's neighbour, Judy Turner, and her daughter Jenny are sitting opposite me right now, and they have some testimony that is about to blow this case wide open, like a paranormal version of the A-Team escaping from a shed they'd just been locked in.*

---

* How dated is this reference? Seriously, Robins, get a grip, this is not the 1980s any more.

Vee put me in touch with Jenny, but it's been tricky fixing a time to meet. We have finally come together in the kitchen of my colleague Simon's house in Kent, not too far from the village Judy and Jenny have now moved to, far away from Averham. Simon produces the *Uncanny* podcast with me and his house has been chosen as a neutral meeting place. The Turners had made it very clear they didn't want to meet at either of their own houses. I had thought they were just being a bit difficult, or liked to keep themselves private, but now we are together, I realise that it's because they felt even talking about their experiences again might somehow unleash the thing they worried would return when Maureen knocked on their door back in the early 1990s.

'We're both very happy in our houses,' says Jenny, leaving hanging how she feels that might have changed if I'd blundered in there, dredging it all back up.

They seem comfortable, though, unleashing the darkness on Simon's house, reminiscing about their lives in Averham, talking over each other constantly, prompting and correcting details, where they think the other has got confused. Judy is a jolly, short woman in her late seventies – 'Oh God, I'll be eighty next year,' she says, but she looks at least a decade younger. She seems to have an adventurous streak not unlike Maureen's. She worked as a military air-traffic controller in her younger days, which is where she met Jenny's dad John.

Jenny, in contrast, is definitely someone that life has not been kind to. In her mid-fifties, with grey hair, she has a condition called lymphedema, where the body retains fluid, making you swell up so that you look obese, something she is obviously acutely, painfully, aware of. 'It's water she's carrying, not fat,' says Judy sadly, now rendered something of a carer to her daughter. Jenny has to walk with crutches, her mobility restricted. It's a cruel blow and one that she associates with the stress caused by the premature death of her husband when he was only 38. She keeps her spirits up as we talk, but it's clear that it has been a big deal for her to come here today, and I am grateful for it, because the information these two women have could be utterly crucial to our case.

Let's get back to that pushchair. This is in the late 1980s, several years before Maureen's encounter with the man in her kitchen. With his daughters now teenagers, John Turner decided to get rid of some of their playthings, including a toy pram, which for reasons best known to him, and unlikely to be discovered now – 'I've divorced him,' says Judy, 'not because of that …' – he decided to bury in their back garden. By any standards it's an odd way to dispose of an old kids' toy but I guess there weren't any charity shops in Averham and he just wanted rid of it. Anyway, John digs a hole, and in doing this, he makes a discovery.

'He suddenly came across these large old flagstones,' says Judy, 'and because we weren't expecting that, he dug a bit more and found there was a pattern of all these ancient stones on the ground.'

It appeared to be the remains of an older building that had stood where the Turners' house stood now.

'They looked similar to the stones of Newark Castle,' says Jenny.

Intrigued, and a bit unsure what to do about their discovery, they called Newark Museum, who said they'd send out a 'conservator' to assess whether their find was of any historical interest. The next day, a man called Gordon* arrived with a team of student archaeologists in tow to explore the site.

---

* His surname is sadly as lost to the mists of time as John Turner's reason for burying the pushchair.

'And of course, the hole got bigger and wider,' says Judy, her expression evoking the horror any homeowner would feel at the sight of a bunch of students digging up her garden, mingled with, of course, a bit of excitement at the idea that they might have accidentally stumbled across something significant. What might lie down that ever-expanding, deepening hole?

'It went down about five feet, and they were discovering all kinds of bits of pottery, a cup, a candle-holder ...'

The Turners' garden had suddenly become a place of archaeological interest, but perhaps the digging had inadvertently done something else, because in the words of Judy, '... it kind of led from there ...'

It started when they dug. All of the strange things that would happen in their house seemed to emanate from this point, the disruption of the earth in their back garden, and it would come to seem that the strangest of these things focused around Jenny, who was 13 at the time, around the same age Vee would be several years later at the peak of her experiences.

The first event came when Judy arrived home one day expecting to find Jenny doing her homework in the living room; but, as she looked through the window, she saw her lying on the carpeted floor.

'She was crying, so, of course, I got in very quickly and I asked her what was the matter.'

Jenny's story was utterly fantastical. She claimed that whilst she had been doing her homework, she'd had a sensation of sinking through the floor, as if going down in an elevator, and what she believed she was seeing was the area where their house was as it had been in the past. The floor was made of the flagstones the dig had revealed and the layout of the room was entirely different. She was convinced she was in a building from many hundreds of years ago, even the quality of the air felt different.

'I was crying because I thought I was going to get stuck,' says Jenny. 'I mean, how do you come back from the seventeenth century?'

I don't quite know what to say to this. I have had quite a few interesting emails from people who believed they have experienced 'timeslips', moments where they appear to have walked into a different age briefly, experiencing the sights and sounds, and even smells, of hundreds of years ago. Some of them are extremely convincing. There's one particular street in Liverpool, Bold Street, where many people have described this phenomenon, being able to describe the names and positions of old shops that they shouldn't by rights have known.

But ... I also know that teenagers can have vivid imaginations and that maybe this was just a case of Jenny having overdone the homework and having a 'funny turn', coupled with all the excitement of Gordon turning up at their house and discovering artefacts from the 1600s. Judy says she had the same concern. 'I thought, is it puberty? So I kept an open mind about it.'

But then, other odd things began to happen to the family. One day, they came down to breakfast to find the door into their kitchen was locked. Except it couldn't be, the lock had been painted over many years ago and wouldn't budge, but now it was locked and, try as they might, no one could shift it. John Turner was forced to go and get his drill to open it. Oddly, the door was the only thing about the house that had remained constant within the strange vision Jenny had had. It sat in the position that a door had done in that older version of the house she saw. Probably just a coincidence, right? And, again, the Team Sceptic side of me is thinking maybe the house had shifted a bit thanks to all the digging and, as a result, the door was sitting tighter to the frame than previously, meaning it got stuck.

But then, there were the footsteps.

'They went up and down the stairs,' Judy says.

One time, the entire family were sitting in their lounge, including the dog.

'We heard footsteps coming down the stairs,' Jenny says. 'And the lounge door handle moved! There was somebody outside on the other side! I was the only one brave enough to go and look. I opened it and there was just cold air. Nothing else. Yet we'd all heard that.'

I find myself wondering if that cold air was anything like the breeze that Vee felt every time something strange happened in their house.

The clincher for Jenny and Judy that something disturbing was happening came a few days later. This was the moment when the strange sensations in the house would solidify and take shape.

The day Jenny actually saw a ghost. In fact, not one, but two.

Jenny crosses the garden in the dim evening light, being careful to avoid the deep hole left abandoned until Gordon and his team return tomorrow. She opens the hutch door to put in food for Bugs Bunny. Okay, so it's not the most imaginative of names for a rabbit, but she likes it. He scuttles over to grab his feed, and then ...

She hears voices wafting on the air towards her.

She shuts the door and looks up. Walking towards her, across the garden, are two soldiers.

These are not some modern soldiers on manoeuvres who just happen to have got lost. They are dressed in clothes that, to Jenny's eyes, look as if they are from the English Civil War.

They pass so close to her, she can see the patterns of the buttons on their uniforms and hear their conversation. They're using swear-words she shouldn't really know at her age, but does. She makes out the words 'bastard king'.

They seem utterly oblivious to her standing by the rabbit hutch, staring at them. Is this really what ghosts look like? They seem like flesh and blood. She can feel her own blood pumping quicker in her veins, but she thinks it's the surprise of this vision more than fear. There is something wonderfully, weirdly fascinating about it.

She turns and rushes in to tell her mum and dad, so they can share in this sight too. Her dad is sceptical as always, but he agrees to come out and look.

There is no one there.

How could anyone have walked through the garden, he asks her? They'd have had to walk through the hedge on either side, there's no other way in!

She knows this makes sense and yet, she saw those two men, and heard them, as clear as day. She catches herself, because she hadn't meant anything in particular using that phrase, but she realises that was how it felt, as if the men were walking in daytime, illuminated as they would be by the afternoon sun shining, whereas she and the rest of the garden were in the evening gloom. It felt almost like watching a video recording, realistic but unreal.

The next day, she watches Gordon as he and his team dig, looking for more artefacts buried under their lawn. She decides eventually to be brave and tell him about what she saw. He listens unjudgementally and then asks her to draw the soldiers for him. She dutifully goes into the house to try to sketch out the men from memory. She remembers the buttons on their clothing and does her best to outline what the pattern looked like. Then she comes back outside, holding the paper, waits till Gordon has finished talking to one of the student archaeologists, and waves it under his nose.

He looks at it for a long time, and it might be her imagination but it looks like a little shiver goes through him. He looks up at her from his position in the hole and tells her that she's good at drawing.

'I recognise those buttons,' he says.

She sees him later, talking to her parents, concerned looks being exchanged between Judy and him. Judy will tell her later that Gordon believed that the design of the buttons matched the ones worn by the local Parliamentarian army regiment stationed in this area during the English Civil War, drawn with an accuracy he found surprising, but for now Jenny just catches the words:

'We may have disturbed something here.'

She lies awake for a long time that night, thinking about it all, the idea that something came out of that hole at the moment that her father planned to put the pushchair in. That perhaps those soldiers emerged from the building she saw in her vision, a place buried under the existing modern layer of their house. What a strange idea that people or memories could be contained within the soil of the ground. But is history like that, layer after layer that can be peeled away, onion-like?

She's still not really frightened, just intrigued by the idea that they have stumbled across some magical discovery. She feels like the characters in books she's read who find treasure or elves or fairies in their gardens. Of course, swearing soldiers aren't something you'd put in a children's book, which makes it feel all the more exciting.

No, she doesn't feel fear. Not yet. That will come soon, though, and when it does it will be so total that this sense of innocent delight will feel inconceivable.

It's one afternoon, the following week. Gordon is inside the house now, talking with her and her parents. They're sitting at the dining table, he is standing by the door, near to Jenny. He makes it clear to them that he believes she really did see the soldiers. He says he has had experiences of these kinds of things before, where archaeological digs have set off activity in an area, as if the disrupting of the land has somehow woken those who died on it. It turns out that he is much more of a believer than you might expect. He suggests they all say the Lord's Prayer in a homemade attempt to get whatever has been unleashed from the hole to move on.

Our Father, who art in Heaven ...

Her parents pray with him, her mum willingly, her dad through gritted, sceptical teeth, not happy at all this hullaballoo, inwardly cursing the moment he decided to bury that pushchair, resenting Gordon, a man who believes his daughter when he himself does not.

Give us this day our daily bread,
And forgive us our trespasses,
As we forgive those who trespass against us ...

'Are we the trespassers in this story?' Jenny wonders, the house built on the land of others who came before? What is the building that sits under their garden? Gordon has not been able to identify it on old maps, so its use and ownership remains a mystery.

And lead us not into temptation,

But deliver us from evil …

She turns and there, in the dining room, she sees a soldier!

He is a few feet from her, but this is not one of the men she saw in the garden. He looks frightened and she realises that he is not alone. There is another soldier behind him, but they are dressed differently this time, and seem to be enemies not comrades. The face of the man behind curls in contempt. He is holding a pike, and he thrusts the long weapon towards the body of the other man. She sees the metal erupt through the other soldier's flesh, the spike pressing out of his belly like a savage tooth. The injured man's complexion goes a deep purple colour and he falls forwards, crumpling.

She screams!

Her parents look up sharply, stopping their prayer. Jenny's eyes move quickly to Gordon, but he is looking in the same direction she was.

'You saw it too?' she asks quietly, trembly, numbed.

He nods, his face pale.

Later, when they have both recovered, he tries to explain it to her – why they saw this thing and her parents did not.

'Think of it as radio waves,' he says. 'We're on one radio station normally, but you and I just plugged into another one.'

'It all sounds very far-fetched, doesn't it?' Jenny says, looking at me from across Simon's kitchen table.

'It sounds pretty horrific,' I say. 'You actually believed you had seen a man killed in your dining room?'

Jenny nods. 'You don't get counselling for that.'

What are we to make of this vision? And the fact that Gordon saw it too? How much, I wonder, was his presence at the Turners' house a factor in all of this, the arrival of a charismatic history expert who believes in ghosts; there is more than one way in which his archaeological dig could have unleashed things in the house. Could it be the imagination of Jenny that he opened up?

And yet, why would he risk his professional reputation saying that he had witnessed something like that? Surely if John Turner had chosen to report this moment to Newark Museum, with the insinuation that Gordon was making it up, Gordon would have been cautioned for scaring Jenny? Judy's memory is that he was shaken too, both Gordon and Jenny reacting as if they had just witnessed it happen in real life.

Jenny did see things when Gordon was not there, too. She has one particularly vivid memory of waiting for a bus in Southwell, a nearby town where she had a job washing dishes at a hotel called the Saracen's Head, which has its own significant Civil War history – it's where King Charles I handed himself over to the Parliamentarians after the defeat of his army at Newark. She was standing on her own at the bus stop at about ten o'clock at night, desperate to get home after her shift.

'And suddenly I felt these horses going past me, rushing past, and I could hear voices too. I couldn't see anything, but I could hear them. Mum thought I'd finally flipped when I told her that.'

Judy smiles.

'But years later,' says Jenny, 'somebody—'

'I was working at an old people's home then,' explains Judy. 'And one of the care assistants told me she had experienced hearing ghost horses around Southwell too. Apparently, a cavalry regiment had been stationed there during the Civil War.'

I am, of course, deeply struck by this detail, given what I know of Vee and Maureen's story and the horses they heard. Jenny remembers another occasion, when she was around 16, cycling home and she could hear the sound of horses running after her.

'You were chased by ghost horses?' I ask.

'Yes!'

I ask Jenny and Judy what they know of the events at Vee and Maureen's house. Judy says she remembers very clearly the day Maureen turned up at their house, and how upset she was.

'She was a sensible woman,' says Judy, recalling that Maureen had been a Justice of the Peace at one time, and a well-respected figure in the area. 'She was no fool. So she really was worried.'

'When we opened the hole,' says Jenny, 'did we open the problem for Vee and Maureen? I think they had it even worse than us.'

What a strange parallel it is, I think, to have these two sets of mothers and daughters having experiences at neighbouring houses. Can it be explained as contagion? Had Vee and Maureen somehow heard about the Turners' experiences on the village grapevine? The dig in their garden would surely have been local news. Or is there really something more to be investigated here? I've heard a lot of ghost stories in my time, but few with so many, or so compelling, witnesses.

By the end of our time together, Jenny and Judy seem glad that they agreed to meet. I think it's been therapeutic to get it off their chests after all this time, both of them thank me for taking them seriously, aware of how potentially crazy it all sounds. I get the sense that they haven't dared to tell many people over the years.

'When you say it back,' says Judy, 'it feels as though you are just relating a story from a book or something.'

To some extent they are, I guess. All of us compose our memories into narratives, and there is a danger, as we roll them into shape, that they pick up extra details along the way, things that perhaps weren't there at the start. The area around Averham is clearly steeped in Civil War history. Jenny and Judy tell me an evocative local tale about a Royalist blacksmith in the village, murdered by Roundheads because he wouldn't shoe their horses. Can you live somewhere like that and not become a sponge, soaking up all of that bloody, shocking history? Is there a danger that could have coloured Jenny's recollections? Or, as an even simpler explanation, could the two men crossing her garden have been Civil War re-enactors from one of the local Sealed Knot* groups, who act out battles for audiences of locals and tourists?

She laughs at this.

'Oh no, I knew what they looked like. You'd see them all over the place, cycling around in costume or whatever. No, those two soldiers didn't look like them, they were real, and they passed through a solid hedge.'

---

* The Sealed Knot is the oldest historical re-enactment society in the UK, formed in 1968.

Part of me would like to believe that Jenny is imagining things. It would be easier and neater to dismiss this new evidence in our case, but I look at her, having dragged herself here on crutches, and I look at her mum, who clearly utterly believes in her, and who, of course, heard the footsteps in that house too, and I think …

It's quite hard to misinterpret or confuse seeing a man kill another man in your dining room.

If Jenny really did see these things, then we now have two houses, virtually next to each other, with people hearing ghost horses and either seeing or sensing armed men wandering around. And that, I think we can probably all agree, is rather bloody terrifying.

CHAPTER 7

STONE TAPE THEORY

In the early 1970s, a research and development team from pioneering tech firm Ryan Electrics moved into a building known as Taskerlands, a Victorian mansion in the British countryside that had been specially renovated for use as a research facility. Their purpose was to develop a new recording medium that would help the company make a breakthrough in this increasingly competitive market dominated by foreign rivals.

The team was headed by Peter Brock, a respected scientific researcher. On arrival, he and his colleagues discovered that the renovation of the mansion was incomplete. One room had been left in its original state for a reason that seemed frustratingly irrational. The builders believed it was haunted.

There will always be people who hear the word 'haunted' and see it as a challenge, and scientific researchers are probably more curious-minded than most, so the team decided to enter the room to see what all the fuss was about. Inside, they found rough-hewn stone walls, a high ceiling and a set of stone steps that led to a floor no longer in existence. The room, it turned out, was a remnant of a much older building, its foundations laid in Saxon times. Taskerlands had effectively been built around it, assimilating it in the way that trees, by a process called edaphoecotropism, can grow around an object, such as a metal fence, the object itself staying perfectly formed within the tree – not devoured, simply consumed.

As the researchers explored the room, something deeply strange happened. They heard the sounds of a woman running, and then an ear-piercing scream. The sounds came seemingly from nowhere. None of them had been responsible, nobody else was in the room. It was an unsettling experience, but, for one of the team, it had been even more strange and disturbing. Jill Greeley was a young computer programmer and, as her colleagues heard the noises, she simultaneously experienced some form of hallucination, a vision of a woman running up the stone steps and then falling to her death.

The estate manager at Taskerlands, Roy Collinson, decided to look back through old records relating to the house. During his search he discovered that a young woman who had been working at the house as a maid had indeed died in that room in 1890. So had Jill seen a ghost?

Peter Brock did not believe so, but he was excited. He started to form a hypothesis that the stone walls in the room had somehow been able to 'record' the maid's death and play it back. Those stones might in fact be the new recording medium he was searching for! If only he could find out how this process worked. What was it about the bricks and mortar there that allowed them to be able to record and play back the traumas of the past?

All of this actually happened, just not in real life.

It's the plot of a 1972 BBC television play called *The Stone Tape*. Written by Nigel Kneale, who had made his name as the writer of the now iconic science-fiction serial *The Quatermass Experiment* in the 1950s, it was aired as part of a series of Christmas ghost stories the BBC made during the 1970s, in an era when a spine-tingling drama was a popular Christmas TV tradition. But its impact has lasted far, far beyond that Christmas.

Kneale is responsible for a vast body of television drama work. His wife was the equally prolific children's author Judith Kerr, who wrote *The Tiger Who Came to Tea*, a story of an unsettling presence of a different kind. However, unless you are a ghost stories buff or a devotee of 1970s TV, it's possible you may not have heard of *The Stone Tape* until now, but I would make a case that it is one of the most influential horror films ever made when it comes to shaping the way we view and think about the paranormal. However casual your interest in ghosts is, you will almost certainly have heard of the idea that they can be explained by the fact that the very fabric of buildings can somehow record shocking or tragic events and then play them back. Nigel Kneale didn't invent this idea, it had been around in various forms since the 1800s, but he popularised it in the public consciousness and, crucially, gave it a name. In the wake of his TV play, it has come to be known as 'Stone Tape Theory'.

It's a theory that comes up again and again when we are exploring and trying to explain hauntings, because it's such a tantalisingly plausible idea, right? So many of the hauntings we hear about do sound like past events replaying themselves. Perhaps the most famous case to fit this mould took place in York in 1953.

I want you to picture yourself in the dark subterranean cellar of the Treasurer's House, a historic building in the grounds of York Minster, the city's celebrated cathedral. Sections of the house date back as far as the eleventh century, but most of what stands there today is from Tudor times. Working in the cellar on this particular day is a young heating engineer called Harry Martindale. He's only 18 but he has a sensible head on his young shoulders, our Harry, he'll go on to have a 30-year career in the police force, but right now, he's about to witness something that will come to be described as amongst the greatest ghost stories ever and cement York's reputation as one of the most haunted cities in the world.

As Harry looks up from his work, he sees a man in a metal helmet emerge from a wall. That's 'emerge' as in bloody well walk through it, because this guy somehow seemingly magically passes through solid bricks. Harry is utterly flabbergasted. He's no great student of history, but it's clear to him that the man is dressed as a Roman soldier and no sooner has he popped through the wall unannounced than he is joined by a carthorse with at least 20 other Roman solders following it. Harry is so alarmed by this spectral parade that he actually falls off his ladder, stumbling into a corner of the room to hide, just in time, as the men (and horse) proceed to march through the cellar.

From his hiding place, Harry is able to notice something strange. Well, all of it is pretty strange, but he's particularly struck by the fact that he can only see the men from their knees up, it's as if the lower half of their legs, down to their presumably sand-alled feet, is somehow lost beneath the ground. The legionaries pass through the opposite wall, again magically, as if it didn't exist, and are gone, leaving behind nothing of their presence other than the memory etched in Harry's mind.

Harry is profoundly shocked by his experience. Fearing ridicule, he keeps the story to himself for years and years, until the 1970s when he is interviewed about it by a group of academics. With the eloquent clarity of the truly terrified, he is able to outline his experience in great detail, to the extent of describing the legionaries' clothes with a degree of accuracy that, to the academics, seems unusual for someone who is not an expert in the specifics of Yorkshire's local Roman history. One particular detail troubled them: Harry had described the soldiers carrying round shields. This was initially used to debunk his account, as the curved rectangular shape of legionaries' shields is well established, but further research revealed that in the fourth century AD soldiers carrying round shields did indeed replace the Sixth Legion in York. There seemed no way Harry could have possibly known this. However, perhaps the thing that makes his story most compelling is the subsequent revelation through archaeological investigations that a Roman road really had run through the route that the cellar of the Treasurer's House sits on and – wait till you hear this – that road was approximately 15 inches lower than the current cellar floor, or, in other words, about the distance between your knee and your foot. So, if those Roman soldiers were, in fact, walking on the level of the original Roman road, you wouldn't have been able to see below their knees!

It's an intriguingly plausible ghost story, and it is not alone; there are many other similar ones that emerge from the annals of paranormal history, encounters where it feels like someone is having a moment of history replayed in front of their eyes, with the 'ghosts' observing the geography of how the place was and not how it is now. I was contacted on Facebook by a motorcyclist who was out with his group of burly, no-nonsense, leather-clad biker mates for their Sunday afternoon drive, when a woman in Edwardian clothes cycled across the road in front of them, in mid-air – presumably free-wheeling at a level the land would have been at before the new road was dug out.

So, could Stone Tape Theory really be possible? If it makes sense on an emotional level, it feels like it also does on a practical one. We have been surrounded for years by objects that have an ability to record events, from gramophones to smartphones, via CDs and laser discs. VHS tapes, now defunct but once the height of technology, contained plastic strips with iron particles on. When something was recorded on to them, the iron particles were rearranged based on electricity received, to retain the recording. This new arrangement of particles, when placed into a VCR machine, was then interpreted as image and sound, quite literally bringing a memory to life. Try explaining all that to a Roman soldier! If such wizardry can become not only possible but even outmoded, isn't it also possible that the iron deposits in walls could function in some similar way? Why they would choose to only record the more traumatic events in history is perhaps a question to be asked, but the idea that they could record something doesn't seem that big a leap, does it?

And here's the reason I want us to think about this: if Stone Tape Theory is possible, could it explain what happened to Vee, Maureen and Jenny and Judy Turner? Are those sounds of horses running through the house, the voices of men outside the bedroom window, and Jenny's visions of the old house and the soldiers, actually some form of playback from Averham's Civil War past? Could the axeman that Maureen saw be a recording from even further back, a Norman or Anglo-Saxon warrior who fought and died on that site? Basically, can history really repeat itself?

It's a thought that percolates in my head long after talking to the Turners, until, out of the blue, an email pings into my inbox from somebody who thinks he might actually have the answer.

'I spend my time working on cosmology and dark matter, dark energy and particle physics,' says the bald-headed, bearded man opposite.

Professor Malcolm Fairbairn is a professor of theoretical physics at King's College London. I've been entirely honest and up-front that

I don't really have a clue what theoretical physics is and Malcolm has kindly explained it as 'trying to understand funny stuff that's going on in the universe', which sounds oddly similar to my own job.

This isn't the way things usually work. Normally, I email experts and ask if they can explain something, but Malcom actually wrote to me. He'd heard me talking about Stone Tape Theory on a podcast and basically said, 'We need to talk!'

I'll be honest, I'm slightly nervous. No – more than that, I'm feeling defensive, because I imagine it's in Malcolm's job description to tell me that ghosts don't exist and, well, there's something about him – you could imagine Malcolm being cast as the charismatic villain in a superhero movie, arching his quizzical eyebrows and stroking his beard as he fires bolts of 'dark energy' from his fingertips.

'I actually grew up in quite a religious background,' he explains, 'and I was always interested in the truth behind religion. I went through a phase of being quite obsessed by ghosts when I was little,' he adds, and suddenly I feel like he and I are flipsides of the same coin. 'And I think that's because you want to find out how the world works,' he continues, 'and whether there's something going on that you don't understand.'

That's it, I think, in a nutshell, so much of this hunt for answers about the paranormal is a form of FOMO, the paranoia that you're missing out on a really mind-blowing slice of human existence, that you've been looking in the wrong direction all your life. Maybe physicists and ghost hunters aren't the polar opposites I'd imagined, we're both trying to make sense of the universe in our own way.

'The thing I like about your podcasts is that all the people who come on it are rational, believable people,' says Malcolm. 'You haven't found a bunch of crazy people here, these are sensible, upstanding, educated members of the community and they've seen things that they can't understand. If these things are true, then is it possible that there's something that we've missed?'

So does Malcolm have an open mind to the idea of ghosts after all? One of the things that I think often frustrates believers about sceptics is the sense that they've already made their mind up without hearing the story, so sure are they of the correctness of their position.

'Science itself can be quite negative,' says Malcom, 'because essentially you can never really prove a theory is correct, you can only prove it's wrong, so scientists are by definition sceptical because they spend a lot of time trying to kill their own theories in order to find out how strong they are. But yeah, I do keep an open mind, we have things that we don't understand ...'

I'm reminded of that Jim Morrison poster on the walls of thousands of teenage bedrooms at one time, bearing the quote: 'There are things known and there are things unknown and in between are the doors.' Is that what we're all looking for, theoretical physicists and ghost nerds alike, the doors that will take us from one understanding of our existence to another?

Or perhaps we need to look not at the doors, but the walls. Do they really have ears?

'I think Stone Tape Theory is a perfectly rational thing to investigate,' says Malcolm.

This is not what I expected.

'So, could it be one of those things you mentioned that we don't yet understand?' I ask excitedly. 'If people feel like they're seeing a replay of past events, for instance, Henry VIII wandering around the corridors of Hampton Court Palace, it does feel like it makes perfect sense that the walls have recorded it?'

Malcolm nods. 'If you see that, then that's got to be probably the most rational explanation.'

This is definitely not what I was expecting.

'But …' he continues, 'I think there are very good reasons why it won't work.'

Oh dear. Malcolm has lured me into some sort of super-villain trap.

'I said that physicists know there are things we don't understand,' he says, 'but one thing we do understand is walls. In particular, we understand the way that forces between particles make things solid. So the forces which, for instance, are responsible for you not falling through the floor …' – he gestures to my feet with the air of a man who could make me fall through the floor if he really wanted – '… we understand them really well and, in particular, we understand the interactions between the particles within them. The walls and floors are made out of atoms, and atoms are made out of protons and neutrons in the middle and electrons flying around the outside. There's a phenomenon called the Pauli Exclusion Principle …'

To me this sounds like the name of a cult American sitcom from the early noughties. Pauli would probably have been played by Paul Rudd – that's who I'm imagining right now, anyway.

'So Pauli basically states that two particles that are identical cannot be in the same place, at the same time, in the same energy.'

'Does he?'

Malcolm can see a look of panic cross my face. I'm feeling like I used to in science class at school. Once we got past trying to set fire to paper towels with the Bunsen burner, I got a bit lost.

'If I've got two electrons,' he says kindly, holding out his hands in the way you would for a child, 'they are identical to each other. Two protons are the same as each other, two neutrons are the same as each other, and the fact that there is literally no difference between them whatsoever is responsible for the forces which keep them apart from each other.'

I think I'm just about getting my head around this. 'They're like identical twins who hate each other so can't ever be in the same room?'

'Right. They repel each other. So if it wasn't for the fact that they are identical, some of the forces which make the solids in our world solid, would not be there. You could literally fall through that floor.'

Yikes. 'I still don't quite get what this has to do with Stone Tape Theory, though?'

'Well,' says Malcolm, his eyebrows arching, 'for Stone Tape Theory to be true, the information about whatever past event that had happened—'

'Henry VIII at Hampton Court?'

'Yes, that would have to be stored somewhere in the electrons or the protons or the neutrons, right? Because … well, there isn't really anything else in that wall to store it.'

'So?'

'So, then they'd have to be different from each other because one would have one piece of information and the other would have another piece of information …'

'And they'd no longer be identical?'

'Right.'

'So they are no longer repelling and ... the walls would fall down?'

Malcolm nods.

I think about the house-of-cards nature of the scientific laws that govern our existence. Try to explain away one aspect of it and the whole thing threatens to quite literally fall apart.

'One thing that often comes up,' I say, 'is the idea of iron deposits in the walls, and whether it could be like the material in a videotape or a cassette tape. Those are solid objects that record things, aren't they? Couldn't the wall behave like that?'

Malcolm gives this some thought. Have I finally found a chink in his armour?

'In principle,' he says, 'I guess you could have collective arrangements of atoms which could store information, but then you have the idea that any such storage could be heard or seen. If you're seeing things, you have to have some particles of light created – so where would the energy come from for that? If you've got a video-cassette recorder, for example, you use magnetic fields and electric fields to turn that information into an electrical signal, so it's powered, and then you send that to your television, which is also powered. The idea that you could have some arrangement of atoms which would then spontaneously create an image is very problematic.'

I feel like I've been told off. Everything Malcolm says make sense and yet, in my head I am shouting, 'WHAT ABOUT THE ROMANS IN THAT CELLAR IN YORK?' When you think about that, you wonder how it could be anything other than Stone Tape Theory.

'One of the great challenges of sceptical thought,' I say, 'is that the explanations can be very hard to understand. Whereas ghosts are very easy to understand.'

Malcolm smiles.

'You can maybe see,' I continue, 'how people find it difficult to get their heads around the idea of these complex rules that control our universe, but they feel like, "I have actually seen this thing with my own eyes – I have seen Henry VIII walking along," so it must be true.'

As I'm saying this, part of me cringes. I'm all too aware that scientists must hate this argument – 'Yeah, okay, I hear all your boring scientific reasons, Mr Smarty-Sceptic-Pants, but I just want to believe, so there, yah-boo-sucks to you!' You could make a case that the tug-of-war between belief and scepticism is behind some of the greatest schisms we see in society right now, because belief without a desire to corroborate it with evidence can take you to some pretty dark places – the 'Fake News'-spouting populism of the American alt-right, or the fact-denying conspiracy theories of those who say that Covid doesn't exist, Jews run the world, the earth is flat and Hillary Clinton drinks children's blood. It's for people who want all the power of seeing the world in a different way without any of the responsibility of having to prove it is actually true, and Malcolm picks me up on this.

'"We've had enough of experts" is a line that certain politicians threw up recently, and yes, it does take quite a long time to learn how to do quantum mechanics, and it is quite difficult to explain it to people.' He smiles again, those eyebrows arching like the spine of a yawning cat.

'Some people, I think they get a bit depressed about the idea that the universe could have no ghosts, no God, or any of these things. But, actually, I think if you do accept that the universe is like that, it's even more incredible – the way that it created itself to be this beautiful. And, for example, with religion, is it better if somebody is nice and kind to you because they want to be rewarded with eternal life after they die, or because they want to live in a society where you have mutual kindness and respect?'

'As somebody who grew up interested in ghosts,' I ask, 'would you like them to exist?'

Malcolm laughs. 'I would love them to exist. I would love for the universe to be like that, but as I've become more rational and sceptical, I've just accepted that there isn't a magical or mystical element, but I still find it a very beautiful place.'

I hear what Malcolm's saying, but I leave him with a funny, empty feeling inside me, because he's hit the nail on the head there. · Sure, you can look at the tussle between belief and scepticism as raw populism versus expert opinion, but you can see it in another way too, as the search for magic in an increasingly grey and featureless world. The more we have come to understand ourselves as human beings, creating gadgets that can answer our every question, fulfil our every need, and monitor our every thought and heartbeat, a world where machines know what we are thinking before we do … the less room there is for magic and mystery.

I sigh deeply as I walk home through streets of houses full of protons, neutrons and electrons happily repelling their identical selves. A deep ennui* sets in. Has Malcolm just explained away the

---

* Posh word I looked up meaning 'listlessness and dissatisfaction', pronounced as in the name of the famous former Arsenal striker Thierry Ennui.

entire point of my existence for the last few years, not only hitting the nail on the head but also hammering it into the coffin lid of the idea that ghosts exist? I've been so desperate to prove their existence, but have I been chasing shadows, albeit quite cool ones that look like Henry VIII?

The walls do not have ears or eyes. They cannot. Because in the words of Malcolm, and also Paul Weller's The Style Council, they would come tumbling down. As I muse on the twisted wreckage of my attempt to prove the existence of Stone Tape Theory, I'm reminded of that scene in *Jurassic Park* where the visitors watch an instructional video explaining how the park's scientists created dinosaurs by harvesting their DNA from blood-sucking mosquitoes trapped in prehistoric amber. It's such a brilliantly ingenious yet simple idea, but ... it's impossible.

So, if Stone Tape Theory is not the answer, how do we explain what happened in Averham? Because I am not at all convinced that Vee, Maureen, Jenny and Judy were all imagining things, are you? I think it's time to get into Vee's car and go on a little drive, because if the past can't come back to us, then we must go back and confront it.

CHAPTER 8

NOT A HAPPY PLACE

'I feel sick. I'm cold and clammy. I literally want to run.'

As I mentioned, this is not how it was supposed to turn out.

We were just going to go for a little drive in the countryside, take a tour through quaint, sleepy Averham in Vee's Porsche SUV* to help me get a sense of the area. It really is the quintessential English country village, it turns out, and dead as a doornail on a weekday afternoon. There is no one to be seen; it feels like an out-take from *28 Days Later.*

We decided we'd drive past the Turners' house too, to give me a sense of the geography of the story, just how far Maureen had to run when she was terrified out of her mind. It turns out it's further than I thought, she really did leg it quite a distance, fuelled by the lizard power of the axe-related terror in her kitchen.

The drive-through felt like a good way of bringing the story to life, for me, but also for Maureen and Vee. Being in the place where something happened to you always helps unlock your memories, whether that's for good or bad …

---

* The tomatoes have been good to her.

But it was meant to be a drive-*through*, we weren't going to stop. Except we did, and we are now taking 'bringing the story to life' to another level, a Victor-Frankenstein-flicking-the-switch-to-send-electricity-through-the-monster kind of level.

Because we are actually inside Vee and Maureen's old house, face to face with …

The current owners.

Dave and Lesley* bought the house just two years ago. They're in their early sixties, I'd guess, and are absolutely bloody lovely. Some people, faced with a strange bloke knocking on their door accompanied by two women who claim to have lived in their house, might have turned us away, but they've been nothing but friendly and welcoming, even though, it's fair to say, we are behaving in a slightly weird, edgy way.

I was really careful not to talk Vee and Maureen into this, knowing from Vee's email just what a big deal going back to the house would be, but I think there was part of her that needed to finally face her fear, confront the bogeyman that has lived in her head all these years. Maureen, too, was nervous, but both of them were intrigued to see what the house was like now and how it would feel to them to be back inside.

We made a pact that we'd say as little as possible about our reasons for being here, have a quick look around and then politely leave.

It hasn't worked out like that.

Being back is having a BIG effect on both of them, but particularly on Vee. As we leave Maureen talking to Dave and Lesley in

---

* Not their real names. I want to respect their privacy.

the kitchen and walk towards the living room, the place where Vee always felt that cloaked figure standing in the corner, she is literally shaking. She surveys the room, remembering how it was laid out when they lived here.

'Over there is where the TV was, the lamp would have been in that corner, Mum's chair was in that corner, Dad's chair here and, that … that's the corner where I kept telling you, "it's there, it's there".'

Her body quivers in one big involuntary sob.

'I'm fucking having the most horrendous reaction to being here.'

Summoning her bravery, she leads me towards the dreaded corner.

'Jesus Christ, how cold is that?'

'Icy,' I say.

It is. But then it is near the window, and an exterior wall, and Dave and Lesley have just told us they've had a new heating system put in and perhaps it's not working properly yet?

'I cannot believe that I'm in here. I used to sit there in Dad's chair, and these doors and windows would rattle. I told you about the wind – it would start up when "it" was here.'

In this corner. Even I am shivering now.

'And the horses.' She touches the nearby French doors. 'This was a window then, and you can imagine, I've opened the curtains, the lights are on. There's nothing there.'

Her lips thin into a grimace.

'I hate being in here.'

She says it with a force that takes me by surprise. It's like she's almost become a different person since we entered the house, going from the calm, composed 'sane, rational, non-believing professional woman', to somebody swearing like a trooper and on the verge of nervous collapse.

After this, she goes into her old bedroom by herself and I see her actually weeping, remembering all the nights she spent in there, hugging her soft toys, feeling scared, and I wonder if she wishes we hadn't come here after all. I think maybe I do, and I'm glad Dave and Lesley aren't witnessing any of this. The one thing I'd said to Vee before we came into the house was that we shouldn't say too much to them about what she experienced here. It wouldn't be fair to scare them in their own, only recently bought, home. They seem happy, and I'm reminded of what Jenny said Gordon told her, that people are like radios and only some of us will ever tune in to what is going on in a house. I guess Vee and Maureen found themselves tuned to a certain frequency that Dave and Lesley don't pick up on.

At least, that's what I thought, but then I overhear a conversation between Lesley and Vee as we all walk out into the hall. Vee's remembering how there used to be a rickety staircase here built by her dad that turned the attic of the bungalow into an extra bedroom. She asks Dave and Lesley if they would consider putting a new staircase back in.

'No,' says Lesley, 'because I don't know if we're stopping.'

'Oh,' I say. It seems odd to be thinking of moving only two years after buying a house. In your sixties, surely you're looking for the place you can comfortably spend your retirement years.

'Are you thinking you'll only stay here for a short time then?'

'Um, I don't know,' says Lesley, looking to Dave, as if she instantly regrets saying anything.

'It's okay here,' she says, not sounding like she means it.

'It's all right,' says Vee, not meaning it either.

'It's just not a place that … It wouldn't be my forever home,' Lesley says.

Dave looks keen to move the conversation on, and we leave it at that. It's the first sign I've seen since arriving that they are not completely happy here.

We go out into the garden. One thing you can't help but be struck by when arriving in Averham is something that looms large on its outskirts, a boil on the face of this pretty English village – Staythorpe Power Station. It's a gas-fired power station that provides energy for up to two million British homes, and it has stood on this site since 1950, though the actual building itself has changed over the years, being demolished and reconstructed so that the current power station is known as Staythorpe C.

Earlier in the day, we'd pulled up in Vee's car to get a good look. It's like a cathedral of fossil-fuel-guzzling power with two chimneys shooting skywards like towers. Now, we learn that Dave actually used to work there, servicing the boilers. Maureen reminisces about

how they watched the old power station being pulled down before this new one was built. It's clearly such a huge part of village life, and not necessarily a positive one, a giant ugly modern interloper amongst Averham's historic rural beauty. Look one way and you could almost imagine you are in the Britain of Civil War times, look the other and you are somewhere that feels more dystopian, dominated by this symbol of our unsustainable need for energy, pumping its smoke out, polluting the landscape. Before I came here, I googled the power station and found an article from the *Newark Advertiser* newspaper about a protest from local people at plans to build a new energy-storage facility there, and there have been other protests over the years from people who would rather it wasn't here at all.

But could Staythorpe have been doing something to the people of Averham that goes beyond just spoiling their views?

'There's a lot less pylons, now,' says Vee to Dave.

That is the other thing you notice at Staythorpe, the huge long row of pylons that stretch out, carrying its power across the country. I'd been struck by how many there are, but it turns out that this is a big reduction on what there used to be when Vee lived here. They've been pulled down as we have found other ways to transport electricity, and this has got me thinking …

Pylons emit EMFs – electromagnetic field radiation – and that can be harmful to humans. It's been known to cause headaches, depression, lack of concentration, changes in memory, irritability and fatigue, and it's been suggested that it could affect children in particular, with some studies showing raised levels of hyperactivity disorder, anxiety and social problems in children living near to power plants. These days, there are guidelines about testing homes in the vicinity of power stations to make sure they are safely below EMF guidelines, but these guidelines were only introduced in 1998, so it's impossible to know how much EMF radiation Vee and her family were exposed to when the old power station was here back in the early 1990s.

Could EMF have been a factor in that strange feeling of presence Vee had, the sense that the house was not a comfortable place to live? I'm not suggesting that living near to pylons can make you hallucinate a man with an axe or hear phantom horses, but it's an interesting thing to chuck into the mix as a possible contributing factor. It's also one other thing that both the Turners and Vee's family had in common, of course, their proximity to Staythorpe, though if this really was the breakthrough theory, I suppose you'd need everyone in the village to have been reporting their homes were haunted.

The other thing Vee notices is how much noisier the road next to the house is. It's a main road that didn't exist when Maureen and Christopher bought the house – it was built two years before they moved. Could that increased volume of cars, and now even big lorries, passing their home explain any of the bright white lights or the shaking doors and windows? It's the sort of detail I can imagine the more sceptically minded of you leaping on, and it would be great if we could neatly tie the start of the haunting to the building of the road, but the lights and rattling windows started many years before its construction. It makes me wonder though, if it's wrong to look for just one reason why hauntings like this occur. Is it possible that there are both environmental and paranormal factors at play here, one feeding the other?

Out here in the sunshine, Dave questions us in more detail about our reasons for turning up on his doorstep. He clearly suspects there is more to it than simple curiosity and it feels wrong to lie. Vee tells him about the horses she used to hear. She says she's always wondered if it was something linked to the Civil War.

'It's got that much history, this place, it wouldn't surprise me, to be honest,' says Dave. 'Spooky innit? I'll keep an eye out in future.' Then he adds: 'I won't be sleeping tonight!'

We go back in to say our goodbyes. Maureen and Vee linger in the kitchen, remembering more mundane domestic times here.

'I remember there were cork tiles on the walls,' says Vee, 'and a table here. You used to sit and have your toast there in the mornings, didn't you?'

Maureen nods.

'She eats burnt cold toast,' says Vee. 'What's that all about?'

For a moment, we are back to how any mother and daughter would be, squabbling, wandering around the place that holds so many memories of formative experiences for both of them, good and bad. Perhaps we have exorcised something by coming back.

We say goodbye to Lesley and Dave on the doorstep, apologising for this odd interruption to their lives, and then, just as we are about to walk away ...

'She said she was never happy here,' says Lesley, nodding towards Vee.

'Yes,' I say. Lesley clearly has something else to say before we leave.

'I never sleep properly since I've moved in here. It's ...' She looks to Dave again. 'I don't know what it is.'

'A funny feeling?' says Vee.

'Yeah,' says Lesley, 'because I don't think it's a happy place. Do you?'

This stops us in our tracks.

'It isn't,' says Vee, feeling vindicated.

'I'm happy,' says Dave, trying to break the mood, and I think he genuinely is, his radio resolutely tuned to a different station to everyone else.

Back in Vee's car, I think we're all a little shaken by the idea that Lesley may have had some of the same feelings about the house Vee and Maureen did, all these years later. I ask them how they feel in the wake of a momentous, unexpected visit to their old home.

'I feel like I'm in some parallel universe,' says Vee. 'I got really quite emotional.'

'Yes,' I say, 'I saw you go into your old bedroom and actually have a cry.'

'I was so unhappy there,' she says. 'It was horrible, horrible! And, you know, I'll tell you what was going through my head. Jesus Christ, if I stay here, this thing will come back. I'll feel it again. It will come back because I'm here.'

Maureen has been oddly quiet the whole time we have been at the house, though she was so talkative back in her own home.

'Maureen?'

She considers for a moment.

'I made a point of reining in my emotions and choosing to reduce my thoughts as much as I could, because I didn't want to be there.'

That stiff upper lip again, battening down the emotional hatches so nobody knows how you really feel on the inside. Despite her cool reserve, I like Maureen hugely. She's a remarkable, bold woman. Vee told me she did her most recent zip wire just two years ago, sliding at high speed across a Welsh valley in her early eighties – in Vee's words, 'She's got her own broomstick, hasn't she? So she's not too much at risk.' Maureen has lived her life without fear or inhibition, so seeing her in this subdued state is chastening and it occurs to me again just how scared she must have been the day she ran screaming to the Turners' house, to have let go of her steely self-control in such a dramatic, public way.

I ask them both what they made of Lesley's own reaction to the house.

'She wanted to get out,' says Vee. 'She said that, completely unprompted, unsolicited.'

'She said to me earlier, "I don't like it here",' says Maureen, 'and I didn't comment in any way, because I thought, "I don't want to say something that might plant an idea in your head".'

'And,' says Vee, 'she said, "I hear all sorts of funny noises. I won't be here on my own. I hear all these noises." And her husband said, "Oh, I put it down to the sheep and the pigs next door." And you kind of think, "Do you? Do you, indeed?"'

Vee turns the key and we set off, deciding we need to find a pub, to download our experiences over a drink, but before we do that, there's one more bit of this strange story I want to share with you, because I came into this thinking I was exploring just the experiences of Vee and Maureen, and then I discovered Jenny and Judy, and now we have Lesley too and I'm wondering how many other people living in this area have been affected by 'it', whatever it is, and, well, it turns out, we know there is at least one more.

Somebody Vee and Maureen knew incredibly well, but did not suspect shared their feelings in the slightest bit.

What a day, thinks Maureen, staring into the bathroom mirror, wondering how the Turners are feeling back at their house. A flush of embarrassment colours her cheeks as she remembers herself jabbering almost incoherently as they let her in. She doesn't know whether she feels reassured by her discovery of the full extent of their shared problems or utterly horrified by what it means.

That this is real.

There's a noise behind her.

Her gaze shoots to the mirror. A man stands watching her.

Christopher.

For once, she doesn't feel like arguing. She decides to tell him everything that has happened, not just today, but all the other things she has felt in the house, and he does what he always does, nods and digests the information with absolutely no outward display of emotion. Now, more than ever, she is fuming, she needs something back, something that tells her she isn't going mad …

And then …

'Do you mean,' he says, 'when you're in the sitting room and it all goes cold?'

She looks at him in deep shock.

'Yes!'

This is news to her. Has he really experienced other things, beyond just the horses on that strange Friday night? Her heart is racing.

'Have you seen the white flashes?'

'Oh yes,' he says, seemingly unfazed. 'I've seen those.'

And then he utters the words she will never forget.

'And have you seen the figure?'

'Well that just finished me off,' says Maureen.

We're in the pub now, the closest nice one we could find to pub-less Averham.

Vee and Maureen are across the table from me, Vee sipping a Diet Coke as she's about to drive me back to the station, and Maureen relishing a voluminous Pinot Grigio, having rolled her eyes at me when I asked the question, 'Small or large?' And we're all tucking into a well-earned scampi and chips.

'What kind of figure?' I ask. Had Maureen's husband Christopher seen the cloaked figure she and Vee had seen too?

'He said, "You know, the one that goes round the house. She's kind of bent over a bit. I think it could be an old woman, and she's got something on her back, like a sack or something."'

This really is news! A *female* figure? This is unlike anything any of our other witnesses have described.

'So he had been regularly seeing a ... ghost?'

'Yes.'

I'm knocked for six, aren't you? This family, living together, each experiencing extraordinary things and each keeping it entirely to themselves, year after year after year, and now we discover that Maureen's husband Christopher, the quiet, thoughtful, emotionally distant university lecturer, who I'd had pegged as a background character in all of this, the sceptic in the mix, has one of the biggest revelations of all. Alongside the horses, the axe man and everything else we have learnt about this little rural corner of England, we have an apparition of an old woman too.

Suddenly it seems ghosts in Averham are like London buses, you wait to be able to prove the existence of one and you're deluged as several more pop up to haunt you. Christopher had been experiencing all of these things for years, it turns out, and yet it had never crossed his mind to share it with anyone.

'Dad was very laid-back,' sighs Vee. 'He was almost horizontal.'

She tells me that after Maureen and Christopher separated, her dad never discussed the events that occurred in the house again until just a few months before he died in 2020. Vee finally sat down with him and asked him what he remembered. He told her that when he used to sit smoking in the living room (something expressly forbidden by Maureen and therefore done in private) he would sit with his back to the door and, one time, he heard the door open and something that he described as 'a shadow' walked through the smoke.

'It gave him quite a fright by all accounts.'

How Vee's heart must have leapt at that revelation. Was this the dark, cloaked figure she felt to be resident in that room, the man Maureen saw in the kitchen? But there was one memory she wanted to ask him about in particular.

'I said, "Do you remember how I used to tell you that I could hear people talking in the garden?"'

I think this is the most important detail of all to Vee, perhaps because it's the one she's most unsure of. Those later events – the horses and the strange feeling of being watched – come from a time when, as a teenager, she felt fairly confident in her judgement, but delving back to being that tiny kid sandwiched between a wall you wished would swallow you up and an army of soft toys arranged to protect you, it is totally possible she was imagining things, that the voices were a dream or fictitious fear conjured from her childish mind.

'What did he say?'

'He said, "Darling, I used to hear them all the time."'

I feel a shiver down my spine.

It's time for me to head back to London. Vee drives me to the station, Maureen in the back seat, a little giddy on Pinot Grigio and the thrill of being out of her retirement village. Today has felt like an adventure, but it has taken us to some dark places on our hunt for old ghosts and we are all glad to fall into a conversation about that most reassuring of subjects – tomatoes.

'I call her the Tomato Queen!' proclaims Maureen proudly.

Spending time with them both, I've seen how they can rub each other up the wrong way, but I wonder if today has brought them closer through this therapeutic purging of long-held secrets and fears.

Maureen has one final revelation for me as we approach the station and the tomato conversation finally dries up. After Christopher told her about the ghostly woman he saw, she felt she had to share what was going on in the house with someone outside the family, as if to tell somebody else about it might help her make sense of whether or not their entire family was going mad.

Vee's sister had married the son of a local farmer named Ian, a level-headed, down-to-earth man. He lived in Staythorpe, the next village along, but only a few minutes' walk from their house, the two villages being almost one and the same.

'So, I thought, I'm going to go and see him, and when I got there, I said, "Ian, you've farmed here for a long time, do you ever have anything strange happening?"'

Ian looked at her through his shrewd, countryman's eyes.

'What do you mean exactly, Maureen?'

She told him about what had been happening and finished with Christopher's account of the figure he sometimes saw walking around their house, the woman bent over, with the bag upon her back.

There was a pause as Ian rubbed his chin.

'Oh, yes,' he said. 'I know who you mean. That's Old Meg. We often see her in the fields around here. We're used to it.'

A silence fills the car. We are close to Newark station now, and the moment our adventure will end.

'Wow,' I say. 'Old Meg? Who do they think it was?'

She shrugs.

'It was Old Meg.'

I open the car door and step out into the station car park, the night air prickling my skin. Is Old Meg* yet another layer? Another fragment of history somehow stamped on the fabric of that house through some process as yet unknown to science? Or another thing imagined by a group of people – if it is possible for

---

* There is a poem by Keats called 'Meg Merriles' that talks of a wandering gypsy called 'Old Meg'. The final lines are 'God rest her aged bones somewhere / She died full long agone!' I wonder if the name given to the apparition seen by the locals in Staythorpe and Averham was inspired by that.

them to all imagine the very same things without ever actually discussing them?

As I say goodbye to Vee and Maureen, I'm thinking of Vee's intensely visceral reaction to being in her old childhood bedroom. We can argue over whether buildings have the capability to record events, but indisputably *we* do: we record them in our brains and then reluctantly play them back for a lifetime. Haunted houses are lived in by haunted people and, as I meet Vee's eyes one last time, I can see that loop playing, clear, precise, undulled by time.

On the train back to London, I open the inbox on my phone and an email from Andrew appears. He's forwarding me the response from the Venerable English College to our request to gain access to the apartment.

A cursory glance tells me it's a flat no.

Damn! It seems they don't wish to connect the college to paranormal activity.

I sigh disappointedly. Andrew is clearly frustrated.

'It's ridiculous! What's their problem? Someone once said to me, the Catholic Church invented ghosts!'

He has one other idea, to try and contact someone in the Australian Embassy in Rome, through his old diplomatic connections. It seems a long shot but I wish him good luck.

Oh well, I think, one step further away from getting answers on that case, but maybe I'm chasing a red herring anyway, wanting so desperately to get inside a building, if I have decided the stone in its walls cannot hold the answers?

I find myself looking around the carriage at the rows of faces surrounding me, a motley collection of commuters, families, tourists and pensioners – a slice of everyday life – and I have an epiphany.*

There's a reason why I became obsessed with trying to understand if ghosts are real, and it was never about places.

It was about people.

All those people who write to me, who've seen truly strange and compelling things, people who have experienced what they believe is the presence of other people, dead ones.

What if the thing that is communicating across time and place is not bricks and mortar, but us? Maybe Gordon from the Newark Museum is right with that 'people are like radios' theory of his. Somewhere out there, somebody from the past is broadcasting in some way and, sometimes, a few of us have the ability to tune in. The ghost is not actual light or sound, but that most human of things, the quality that sets us apart from the animals we have evolved from.

Emotions. What if a ghost is an emotion brought to life?

I scroll through my remaining emails, mostly spam, and then, just as the lights of London are appearing through the window of the train, I see it, another of those messages that stop you in your tracks ... One that might put this new theory to the test.

Because if ghosts are like radios, then what I am now reading about might just be the clearest reception I have ever come across.

Am I really looking at an indisputable message from the dead?

---

* Posh word I looked up meaning 'moment of sudden realisation', often preceded by a gasp – NB do not precede it with a gasp whilst on a packed train. You will get several funny looks and quite possibly be reported.

CASE THREE

THE PREDICTABLE DEATH OF SHEILA MASON

CHAPTER 9

A MESSAGE FROM AUNT CONNIE

Never mess with Ouija boards.

It's a thing ingrained in all of us from an early age, like 'don't talk to strangers' and 'eat your broccoli'. There is something about these devices, once staggeringly sold as fun toys to children, that, in a world with increasingly few taboos left, still feels like a wanton transgressive act. I've met many resolute sceptics who dismiss Ouija communication as impossible yet still go pale at the idea of sitting around one by flickering candlelight trying to summon a spirit. Whether we think the dead can return to talk to us or not, it seems a risky idea to put it to the test.

So it's with a degree of trepidation that I set out on the short journey from my home in Walthamstow to neighbouring Leyton where our next case takes place, because it involves a Ouija board, and it involves death and … well that's quite enough to make me feel unsettled. As much as I desperately want to believe in ghosts, the idea that it's possible to actually have a conversation with one can't help but scare me. What secrets might they be privy to now that they have moved beyond this mortal coil? What terrible visions would they pass on? Or, you might just meet a really annoying ghost, perhaps that cousin you always found quite irritating at family events, and they'd choose to pester you until the end of time.

For me, communication is the greatest enigma of paranormal belief. As human beings, we've evolved communication to a highly sophisticated level way beyond the capabilities of any other living organism on this planet. We are the GOAT* of communicating and, like anything you're good at, you want to show it off. So, we spend our entire lives filling our world with a mass of messages, texts, DMs, emails, phone calls and scribbled post-it notes. We write essays, letters, books, poems, newspaper articles, plays and films and make YouTube videos, TikToks, Facebook Lives, Instagram Lives, blogs, vlogs, Spotify playlists, stand-up comedy routines, one-person theatre shows, mime acts and experimental dance performances, all so that we can communicate to other people and have them communicate back to us.

Because we have become so bloody good at it, we tend to be a bit obsessed with communication, looking to analyse every single tiny potential message in our surroundings, however minute or fleeting. Like body language, for instance. What is the position of that person we fancy's eyebrows or the tilt of their head conveying? Does our business rival's handshake suggest weakness or superiority? It's a pursuit of meaning that runs the risk of pushing us into seeing messages where perhaps there are none.

There's a popular trend within ghost hunting for people to take an audio recorder to a 'haunted' location and leave it running. When they play the recordings back they can hear voices that

---

* 'Greatest Of All Time' for anyone who's not down with the slang and thought I was just shouting at them about bearded horned animals.

nobody heard at the time. This 'Electronic Voice Phenomena', or EVP as it has become known, throws up some creepy and compelling examples, and many ghost hunters swear by it as a form of spirit communication, but it's always so hard to know if we are simply hearing sounds that we then unconsciously reform into words, in the same way that we spot shapes in the clouds, or the face of Jesus on a slice of burnt toast.

But let's just say we can receive messages from the dead – because that's an incredibly exciting, slightly scary, change-the-whole-flipping-nature-of-the-universe idea – the thing that has always troubled me about it is why the dead are so patently bloody terrible at communicating.

Let me explain.

If you've ever sat watching a medium do their thang, you'd be forgiven for thinking that the spirits are utterly obtuse and useless. There's the poor psychic, onstage, doing their very best …

'I'm getting a name – it begins with B, or it could be C, or D … He died in an accident, or it might have been an illness, or it could have been old age …'

It's all just so utterly vague.

If you were a spirit and you'd made all that effort to return and communicate, knowing your wife was in that audience, wouldn't you be more specific? It feels like the equivalent of making an emergency phone call from an old payphone with your last 10p and then spending the tiny time you have making the person on the other end guess what colour your socks are.

Or, psychics aside, what about the theory that poltergeists are the spirits of the dead and the knocks on walls or objects falling off shelves are their attempt to make contact? Would we, nature's greatest communicators, really be reduced to such banal methods, rearranging the contents of someone's kitchen, as in Andrew's case, or throwing stuff across rooms, like some petulant psychic toddler?

Where are the ghosts who communicate like actual human beings? Where are the phantom emails, tweets, DMs? The spirits who appear in your room to discuss how Aston Villa need to reinforce their midfield in the next transfer window, or what they thought of the latest series of *Love Island*?

But maybe I'm being unfair here, imposing our living, breathing standards on those who are neither. Maybe when you die your personality changes, or fragments. We could draw an analogy with dementia, that there are still aspects of the old you, but coherent communication becomes a lot harder, and so you do end up chucking objects about in a desperate, frustrated bid to get heard.

Who knows. But I do know one thing, we are never going to solve this mystery of whether ghosts are real unless we can find some way to successfully communicate with them. Which is why I find the Ouija board so intriguing, I guess. As much as it scares me, if you listen to those who claim it works then it does seem to offer the best hope of a coherent and clear channel to the other side, where words and sentences can be spelt out, questions answered and messages exchanged, like a ghostly SMS service.

But it's silly, right? There's no way that pushing a glass or wheeled planchette around a bit of cardboard with the alphabet printed on it could really be a way to contact the dead. It would require so many breakages of the laws of physics that I can feel Malcolm Fairbairn somewhere getting a migraine coming on. Of all the things we have discussed, it is surely one of the most impossible.

That's what I'm telling myself, repeating it inwardly again and again, hoping it is true, because I know that we are about to hear a story that might just make us believe the complete opposite.

As the cab pulls up, and I get out into the area of east London where this next truly extraordinary case takes place, I take a deep breath, wondering if I'm about to meet somebody who really did have a conversation with the dead one Sunday night in February 1988.

David flexes his fingers. There's nothing particularly 'scary' about these sessions. They agreed they won't go for the theatricality of a séance, dimmed lights, candles and all that hoo-hah. It feels so unscientific, to plunge yourself into darkness. Basic evolutionary psychology tells us we have feared the dark since the Stone Age because when it falls our senses fail, leaving us vulnerable to those who hunt and kill nocturnally. Switching the lights off seems likely to achieve nothing other than make you imagine ghosts.

So the room stays lit, the family budgie still wittering away in the background and the dog snoring under the table, domesticity uninterrupted by an attempt to contact the dead.

The Ouija board sits on the table and there's a story to it, bought in Saudi Arabia* where David met his wife just a few years before.

---

* As odd as it seems that Ouija boards would be sold in an Islamic theocracy, David tells me they were stocked in toy shops there under the misapprehension that it was a kids' board game!

The boards are still classed as toys there, he'd bought it and given it as a Christmas gift to his sister a couple of years ago, when he and his wife moved back to the UK.

There's always been an interest in ghost stories in their family. None of them are what you might call sceptics, though David likes to think he approaches paranormal matters with a rational mind. It feels arrogant to dismiss what we can't explain as bogus, though, like those who queue up to dismiss Chinese medicine as fraud, simply because they don't understand how it could work, despite the fact that many people seem to be cured by it when all Western medical techniques have failed. It reminds him of when you were at school and you wouldn't get full marks for a sum unless you could prove your working. Who cares how you get to the answer if the answer is right?

His sister is the most deeply interested of the family. Her tastes run to tarot cards, palm reading and clairvoyance. He sees a hunger in her for a knowledge that he thinks perhaps we humans should not be in possession of. What does it profit us to know the future if we cannot influence it?

It is she who always insists on bringing the Ouija board out on these Sunday evenings when they have dinner at their parents' house here in Leyton. She's 33, four years older than him, but still living at home, and he sometimes gets the impression these sessions are a weekly highlight, a deviation from the humdrum. His mother joins in, a willing participant, enjoying the melodrama, but his father laughs and makes fun of it, a mockery that perhaps hides a sense of unease that there may really be something to this. Likewise, David's wife, he has noticed, recedes into the background as the board comes out, careful not to get involved.

So it's just the three of them with their fingers on the plan-chette, the little wheeled device that came with the board, an object which, if you believe in these things, will be physically possessed by the spirits to spell their messages out.

David has never known it not to move. It's remarkable really, that familiar tug of excitement as it begins to slide around the board, spelling out words that he and the others will then attempt to infer some meaning from, usually unsuccessfully. The process feels a bit like putting up an aerial from an untuned radio, you get snippets of something, but more often it's unconnected gibberish, the spectral equivalent of white noise. Either the dead need more practice at using this technology, or they just don't feel in the mood for passing on a coherent message.

But the planchette does move. Always. And it's the hope that keeps you going, right?

David has an ulterior motive for his own desire to take part in these Sunday night sessions, a deeply tragic one. Six years ago, when he was 23, his best friend's girlfriend, Jacqui, was a bridesmaid at a wedding. She looked lovely in her dress, everyone said she'd have been the one to catch the bouquet at the end of the night, a future full of happiness ahead of her, except she dropped dead at the evening reception in full view of everyone. Heart failure, at the tender age of 21, shocking and truly awful. It's Jacqui who David always hopes to contact through the board. Sometimes there have been messages purporting to be from her, but never anything he could substantiate.

They have had one somewhat frequent visitor who they've christened 'the Onion Man' as his contact always seems to come with a strong smell of onions appearing in the room. David's father even walked into the room and commented on it a couple of times, so it was undeniably real, not – what's that word? – 'phantosmia', the condition where you smell things that aren't really there. Whatever the source of the phenomena, there was never any clear detail from the board who the Onion Man was. At times, jokingly, they would blame the dog, not that he ever ate onions, but only because the alternative felt scarier. Mostly, though, the board has felt like a murky pond, hinting at greater depths but throwing up nothing but the weeds of confusion.

This evening, his dad is already cracking his familiar jokes, David's wife making herself scarce. He sits with his mother and sister, watching the planchette move beneath their fingers, struck as ever by its strange fluent certainty as it lurches from letter to letter. All is as usual, but then, when they ask who they are speaking to, the typically random gobbledygook is replaced by a very clear sentence, spelled out with precision.

'A-U-N-T C-O-N-N-I-E.'

At last, this is a name they are all familiar with. Constance, to give her her full name, had been married to David's grandmother's brother, Fred, and had lived just around the corner with her two daughters – another Constance, named after her mum, and Sheila, both contemporaries of David's mother. Constance junior married into money, whilst Sheila has stayed single, just turned 55 now, and had been living with her mum until Connie passed away this Christmas. David has had no contact with that side of the family for years, not since he went out to Saudi, but his mother attended the funeral, just a few weeks ago, so, if this really is Connie, she is a very recent arrival in the spirit world, fresh off the boat, so to speak.

Always the keenest at the table, his sister asks: 'How are you, Aunt Connie?'

They watch as the planchette shifts across the board spelling out: 'F-I-N-E N-O-W.'

More questions follow. The board's answers are short and unremarkable, like those annual phone calls you have with distant relatives, going through a polite checklist of questions until you run out of things to say.

But then, things take a turn for the surreal. The board spells out the sentence ...

'I-M W-A-I-T-I-N-G F-O-R M-Y D-A-U-G-H-T-E-R.'

'Which one?' they ask, surprised.

'S-H-E-I-L-A,' it says.

David's mother and sister exchange a sharp look. They tell David that they know that Sheila has just been referred to Whipps Cross Hospital. There has apparently been a mumble on the family grapevine about 'women's problems', but certainly no suggestion it is anything too serious.

Intrigued, they ask the board, 'What is wrong with her?' A moment's pause and a word is spelt out:

'C-A-N-C-E-R.'

They all react with shock. Sheila has always been a fine specimen of good health, a non-smoker who drinks only in moderation.

The board continues:

'L-I-V-E-R.'

How dearly now they hope that this is not true, that it is not really Aunt Connie but just another example of the odd randomness the board can throw up, and yet they have a horrible sinking feeling, as if a heavy stone has been placed in their hearts. The atmosphere in the room is one of sombre profundity; it is quite something to be granted contact with the other side, but it comes always with the caveat that you may not like what you hear.

They ask one final question:

'When will she join you?'

The board responds:

'O-C-T-O-B-E-R.'

The specificity of it seems astounding. David sits there long after they have pulled their fingers away from the planchette, wondering if the board can be trusted. Could this novelty item, bought from a toyshop in Saudi Arabia, really have found a way for his Aunt Connie to make contact over the dining room table, months after her demise, to predict the premature and entirely unexpected death of her youngest daughter?

'That was a prediction for eight months in the future,' says David, ruminating over it to me 35 years later. 'A prediction for the death of someone who, as far as we all knew, was going into hospital for a routine investigation and showed no outward signs of illness. None of us knew any more. In fact, no one knew any more, not her doctor, nor the hospital. Later in March, about six weeks after that night with the Ouija board, the hospital diagnosed that Sheila did, in fact, have cancer of the liver.'

My jaw is dropping.

'She declined rapidly over that summer,' David continues, 'finally succumbing to the disease in the autumn and dying in ...'

I can hardly bear for him to say this.

'... October.'

The message from the board – the message they believed had come from Aunt Connie – had proven correct in every detail.

'And,' says David, 'the message had been given at a time when no one alive had that information.'

I am getting the feeling I really hoped I wouldn't get. The feeling that my fear of Ouija boards may not be so irrational after all.

'I could never explain it,' says David, 'but it called many things into question. Does life persist after death? Is the future pre-ordained? These premises strike at the very heart of our idea of free will, but how else do you explain what happened?'

CHAPTER 10

THE MYSTERIOUS TALKING BOARD

My head is hurting.

I'm trying to find an explanation for what David experienced that doesn't involve the G-word* and it is proving tricky.

I receive quite a few emails from people telling me a Ouija board has somehow changed or defined their lives, people who used it for a joke, dare or ghostly thrill when younger and then felt it unleashed something frightening and uncontrollable. People who regret asking it a question about themselves or about their husband or wife. Some of the stories are extremely unsettling, with loud noises, sinister dark figures or disembodied voices appearing in the person's house in the wake of a message they believe they received.

These stories feel complicated. To get to the tantalising prospect that a Ouija board really is able to open up a communication path with the dead, we first need to wade through the murky world of the power of suggestion, because if you tell someone, especially

---

* 'Ghost' not 'goat', in case you are still getting over the whole GOAT debacle.

someone young and impressionable, that an object has the awesome power of necromancy, then it's got to have some kind of effect, right?

So, could all the strange bangs and sinister apparitions really be just the placebo effect, like those experiments where people get drunk on non-alcoholic beer they've been told is full-strength? We can't underestimate the impact of planting the idea that you're breaking rules by using this thing, whether they be the imagined natural laws of the universe or the doctrine of religious groups who tell you that it's sinful to mess with the dead.

Everywhere you look, the horror genre is full of stories where a protagonist brings their fate upon themselves by doing something they were told not to. Take the utterly terrifying *The Ring*.* If you've seen it, you'll have that female figure in the white dress, with the long black hair obscuring her face, forever glued into your night-mares, and why did she appear? Because a bunch of kids were dumb enough to press play on a videotape they'd been specifically told would lead to their deaths if they ever dared watch it. WHAT WERE THEY THINKING OF? *It Follows* is another brilliant, slightly less well known, take on this. In that movie, the horrendous stalking spirit who tracks your movements until it eventually kills you, is spread by unprotected sex, brilliantly tapping into one of the biggest real-life transgressions of its target audience. It's basically a demonic STD, like *Hellraiser* with chlamydia.

You can probably think of a host of other examples that play to this deep-rooted anxiety that it is ALL OUR FAULT. We can cope with the idea that bad stuff is someone else's doing, we'll happily

---

* The American remake's not bad, but go to the Japanese original if you really want to guarantee you'll never sleep again.

grumble away about that till the cows come home (or are killed by a Satanic cow murderer) but when we have brought the horror upon ourselves, it feels overwhelming.

Is there any more corrosive human emotion than regret? Fear may be capable of scaring us to death, but regret's slow drip is a far crueller and more painful demise. We can probably trace the roots of this kind of thinking back to the myth of Pandora's Box, where Pandora's curiosity to open the mysterious jar* her husband had been given by the gods lead to her unleashing all the evils of the world. If only she hadn't done it, we think, but curiosity will always get the better of us.

Curiosity, the only emotion with any hope of trumping fear. It's what guided David to buy that Ouija board for his sister back in the 1980s and what kept them glued to it every Sunday night, and it's why you and I are currently working our way through this investigation together. We're curious about the idea that the paranormal might be real, flirting with it under the comfort blanket of knowing we'll probably never get an answer, until some of us, like David, feel like we do, and then have to accept that that answer might be a bloody terrifying one.

But curiosity is no bad thing in itself, of course. It's led to all of the greatest inventions humankind has come up with, including, of course, the Ouija board.

When it was first invented, the Ouija board was not viewed as a first-class ticket to Satan's boudoir, but as a positive thing that allowed the Victorian-era public, who were fascinated by spirit

---

* The jar has become referred to as a box over the years, just in case you found that reference 'jarring'. Alright, sorry, I'll get my coat.

communication, to do it for the very first time within the privacy of their own homes. The idea of the board first emerged in America, in the wake of the Civil War of the 1860s, when American society was reeling from mass loss on an unprecedented scale. War is undoubtedly the greatest spur to invention and the most effective advancer of technology. Just look at the way aircraft changed during the Second World War, from the biplanes that began the conflict to the jet planes that emerged at the end of it.

In the Ouija board's case, it was the aftermath of war that provided the conditions for its genesis, the thousands of parents and spouses mourning their loved ones whilst in some cases never knowing how they died or even where their bodies were. It was a climate of emotional devastation that provided a fertile breeding ground for the burgeoning industry of people claiming to be psychic mediums and the fledgling religion of Spiritualism, a form of Christianity based around spirit communication, which had started life in the 1840s and seemed to offer a have-your-cake-and-eat-it option for deeply religious American society whereby you could make contact with the dead without it feeling sinful.

By 1897, Spiritualism had more than 8 million followers in the US and Europe. Meanwhile, mediums filled theatres and concert halls as if they were rock stars, proof of a society that, more than anything else in that moment, craved to be in touch with those it had lost. Then, of course, less than 20 years later, the First World War arrived, bringing a brutal mechanisation and globalisation to the slaughter of young men that, alongside the ensuing Spanish Flu epidemic, created mass grief on a scale never seen before. As organised religion crumpled in the face of this onslaught, unable to provide the answers or relief the grieving millions needed, the demand for answers of another kind grew stronger.

There's one other truism about technological advancement. It starts off in the hands of the few, but will inevitably at some point pass into the hands of the many. Think back, if you're old enough, to when only rich businesspeople had mobile phones. Any new invention is eventually democratised; we can now all edit our own films or record our own music, one day we will probably fly our own spaceships, and the same was true of the nineteenth-century innovation of contacting the dead.

What does a society that's grieving and desperate demand? The ability to do it on their terms, of course, whenever they want, and at a price they can afford. Out with the expensive tickets to see mediums or the inconvenience of having to find a spiritualist church near you, in with a device that will allow you to channel your lost loved ones around your own kitchen table after dinner. There was a definite gap in the market for the right inventor, and when they stepped forward, it was to unleash a 'mysterious talking board', as the newspaper adverts referred to it, that would come to define spirit communication for the next century and more, and, ultimately, provide rocket fuel for all our nightmares.

It is February 24th, 1927, and William Fuld is on top of the world, or at least that's how it feels to him. On a literal level, he is on top of a factory, *his* factory, sweeping his proud eyes proprietorially over all he owns. He's up here nominally to supervise the installing of a new flagpole on the roof, but the real reason is to take a chance to survey his dominions, as proud lord and master of a burgeoning empire, built on his shrewd business skills and one other extremely important factor …

The spirits.

The spirits have been very kind to him, because the most popular item that the William Fuld Manufacturing Company produces, fast becoming a staple in American households, is the Ouija board. Fuld is sometimes wrongly credited as the inventor of it, a notion he does nothing to dispel – after all, that is good for business – but instead, he sees himself as a conduit. Just as the planchette is seized upon by the spirits to spell out their messages, he has been the vessel through which this miraculous device has found fame across the nation.

Or perhaps he's just very good at selling stuff to schmucks, he's never quite sure.

He's sure as hell worked for this, though, doing things the hard way. He started on the shop floor, so to speak, as an employee of the Kennard Novelty Company, set up in Baltimore in 1890 by Charles Kennard and a group of other wily businessmen, to market their creation, the Ouija board. People often think the name comes from some amalgamation of the French and German words for 'yes', but Fuld was told by his mentor Elijah Bond, one of Kennard's fellow investors, how it was actually christened by Bond's sister-in-law. Helen Peters was a medium and engaged in a séance to ask the spirits what they should call this new invention. 'Ouija' was the answer that came back. When quizzed on what it meant, the spirits replied, 'Good luck.' Fuld has always enjoyed this detail – the Ouija board, the only invention that ever named itself.

The idea of a 'talking board' was not a new concept in itself; they'd been used in Spiritualist camps for a few years by that point, an innovation to make the contacting of the dead more efficient. Prior to that, mediums had to read out the alphabet, waiting until they heard a thump from the spirits to signify the letter they wanted to use. Spelling out sentences could be truly laborious. Kennard and his colleagues had no affiliation to Spiritualism, but they could see that in the right hands – namely, theirs – these boards could be mass-produced and mass-marketed in an extremely lucrative way.

To protect their investment, they needed to get their Ouija board patented, and this is a story that still makes Fuld smile – again, told to him by Elijah Bond, who had taken Helen Peters with him to the Patent Office in Washington. They knew that it would be hard to get the patent approved, as they could not easily prove that the board really allowed you to contact the dead. The Chief Patent Officer looked disapprovingly down his nose at them and issued a challenge. If the board could spell out his name – which was unknown to Bond and Peters, and therefore, he considered, impossible – he'd give them their patent. It was intended to be an obstacle that would send them off empty-handed, but as the three of them placed their fingers on the planchette, sure enough, the board did indeed correctly spell his name. Fuld has always cited this as proof of the board's accuracy, though a little bit of him wonders if perhaps Bond or Peters had actually known the man's name. Whatever the truth of it, a short while later, ashen-faced, the man granted their patent and, by extension, a licence to print money. The popularity of the board exceeded even its creators' expectations. By 1892, the Kennard Novelty Company had six factories in America and one in London. It was one of those rare products that you simply couldn't make enough of.

Kennard and Bond were wily, but not as wily as Fuld, and when internal strife led to them both being ousted in a coup, he took over, having slowly built his standing within the company, plotting a route from the factory floor to the boardroom. He's never been afraid to make tough decisions, like cutting his own brother out of the business. They've never spoken since. The feuds and recriminations that have followed his dealings have played out across the pages of the *Baltimore Sun* newspaper, the betrayals and attempts at revenge almost Shakespearean. Kennard, Bond and others have done their best to market their own 'talking boards', but it is the Ouija board, controlled and expertly marketed by Fuld, that has vanquished all before it, the spirits having a say on their preferred means of communication. Everyone has their own brand preferences, even the dead.

The Great War has helped business, that's for sure, creating millions more dead to contact. Fuld tries hard not to think of it in those cynical terms; he is providing a service, he likes to think, allowing people a degree of power that was previously in the hands of a tiny few. The mediums do not like him for it. Ouija has eaten away at their business – after all, why would people shell out good money to go to a séance when they could give Fuld far fewer dollars and walk home with one of his boards? The psychics complain that it's risky, giving amateurs the keys to the spirit world, but screw them. Fuld has made his fortune and, as he approaches the end of the 1920s, he feels hugely optimistic for the future. There are very few certainties in life but death is one of them, and as long as it exists, it will drive demand for a device that claims to be able to unlock the mysteries of what lies beyond. Wasn't it the *New York Times* who described the board as being as popular as bubble gum?

He uses it himself, of course. You have to have confidence in your own products, right? He will consult the board over big decisions in business, to see whether the insights of the spirits will give him an edge on his competitors. It was the board that advised him to build this, the latest of his factories, the impressive three-storey building in Baltimore that he stands atop right now.

The workmen have nearly finished with the flagpole. Fuld puts his hand on to one of the metal supports for the pole. He's standing by the edge of the roof; he doesn't want to slip as he leans back to study their handiwork. He grips the pole tightly, positioning himself carefully, and then –

CRACK!

The support has given way. He topples back over the edge of the building. *His* building. He feels himself falling, terrifyingly, towards those dominions that just a moment ago he was proudly surveying.

But he is William Fuld, he will not be defeated by something as inconsequential as gravity. He reaches out a hand, grabbing on to the sill of an open window, hanging suspended above the ground, his heart racing, but safe, until –

SLAM!

The window crashes shut, sending him falling again, and this time he crashes painfully to earth with a –

THUD!

He groans in pain. He has definitely hurt himself, possibly badly, but he is alive.

He can see the workmen looking down, concerned, from the roof above, the new flag fluttering behind them. A crowd is gathering around him now. Winded and unable to get up yet, he feels his chest. He's broken a few ribs, he'd say. It hurts like hell, but he'll survive.

As he is helped into a car to transport him to the hospital, he feels an intense gratitude. The spirits have always taken care of him. That has been their bargain: as long as he continues to manufacture the means by which they can communicate, they will continue to watch over him. Any lesser mortal, without this form of celestial protection, would surely not still be breathing and – however painful that breathing might now be as he watches the road go by outside from the speeding car – he is relishing this second chance at life he has been given.

Will he do things any differently now that he has been saved? He doubts it, he's done things pretty well his way so far, he's not about to become a monk or donate all his earnings to charity. He'll keep serving the spirits and they'll keep serving him.

The bump in the road catches both the driver and him unaware. It has never been the smoothest of routes, this stretch, but on any other day such a bump would have given him nothing more than a shock. Today, however, he feels the most terrible searing pain, a sharp agony that sweeps through him like the opening of a sluice-gate, sending a numbing, tingling coldness throughout his body, followed by a darkness as he feels his senses ebbing away.

He cannot know it then, but the jolt has pushed the splintered end of one of his shattered ribs upwards, puncturing his heart. Although he will make it to the hospital, he will die there from this freak injury, a cruel pulling away of the rug at the very moment he was celebrating his survival.

As the life seeps from him, Fuld's final conscious thought is that the board really should have warned him about this. It seems the spirits are fickle after all. Despite all he has done for them, in building their empire here on earth, enlisting millions to their thrall, it is they who have decided to call time on the bargain. Or perhaps it really was all just so much horseshit and the board is just a useless inanimate object that becomes a mirror for our own desires.

Oh well, he thinks bitterly, the darkness now overwhelming him, this will be his chance to find out, because if he's about to join the spirits, he's damn sure he's going to come back and tell people here on earth about it. That thought is of little solace, but it's preferable to the alternative, that he's spent his whole life marketing a cheap scam and is about to be reduced to silent nothingness, a mush of decomposing organic waste to be filtered back into the fabric of a universe where the dead stay dead and silent.

The strange circumstances of the death of William Fuld, chief architect of the Ouija board's success, have helped to feed its infamy, in the same way that Lord Carnarvon snuffing it from an infected mosquito bite sealed the deal for the Curse of Tutankhamun. The fact that Fuld is often miscredited as its inventor probably helps, the idea of the person who came up with this thing being inadvertently killed by it, falling from the roof of the factory it told him to build, is certainly a neat full stop on the story.

Interestingly, the woman who actually did give the Ouija board its name, the original investor Elijah Bond's sister-in-law, Helen Peters, apparently really did believe the board had ruined her life. When some old heirlooms went missing at her house, she asked the board who had taken them and the name of a family member was spelt out. Half the family believed this and half, including Helen, didn't, and the schism proceeded to tear their family apart. Afterwards, Helen spent the rest of her days telling people never to go near the board because of its lies.

These events have helped lay the ground for a continuously evolving narrative that links tampering with the board to disaster – strange deaths, suicides, murders and, of course, the ever-present possibility of unleashing the fury of hell. It feels odd that the board has such a bad reputation now, because for nearly a century it was looked upon as a benign, helpful, comforting and even fun tool, a parlour game that could be harnessed to enlighten and enthral. The newspaper adverts for it promised the board was *'Amusing! Scientific! Instructive!'* and *'Lots of fun and just the thing for parties!'*

If the original demand for the Ouija board was born out of the horrors of the American Civil War, the shift in public perception of it came in the 1970s, thanks to another seismic moment of American horror, the release of *The Exorcist*, a film which had a cultural and social impact beyond any horror movie before or since. It planted an enduring image of demonic possession in the minds of all who saw it but also showed the means by which it had occurred. Regan, the little girl who becomes possessed, has been using a Ouija board to befriend a spirit known as 'Captain Howdy', who actually turns out to be a terrifying hellish entity. The film is so effective at scaring the living shizzle out of anyone who watches it that the device that was once happily pulled out by bored housewives at suburban dinner parties now took on a deeply sinister edge. Despite its origins in the Christian Spiritualist movement, in the wake of *The Exorcist*'s release, Christian groups would label the Ouija board as evil and encourage boycotts of shops that sold it.

Which all seems rather dramatic, you might think, getting so upset about a fictional depiction of an object that was only ever promoted as a game, not to be taken that seriously. But was *The Exorcist* homing in on a truth, shining a beacon in that way that art sometimes can, that the boards could indeed be dangerous? There are many things that were previously thought to be 'lots of fun' that have since been proven to be risky as hell. Cigarettes, for instance. Heroin. Or asbestos. Okay, you'd have to be pretty weird to think asbestos was fun, but you get my point.

What if there really is something about this object that – in some way we haven't quite figured out yet – opens up a way of contacting those who have passed away? Given what we've seen of the life-changing nature of the seemingly paranormal moments in our other cases, handing that ability out willy-nilly feels a major risk. Not everyone can cope with the enormity of the idea that the paranormal could be real and there may be times in our lives when we are particularly ill-equipped to deal with it, for instance when we are teenagers, or if we are processing grief. With that in mind, the dangers of the board don't even have to be real – as long as you are imagining you are contacting the dead, the impact would be the same.

I can feel myself coming back to a familiar place, trying to separate the 'ghost' from the 'story'. Which is real? What are the chances that an object invented in Baltimore, bought in Saudi Arabia, and used in East London, could accurately predict the death of a woman who, to all intents and purposes, had been entirely healthy up until that point? It seems staggering, but could it really have been Aunt Connie moving the planchette that night?

CHAPTER 11

THE HARDCORE SCEPTIC

'There's a short answer to that and a long answer. The short answer is "no", and the long answer is "noooooooooooooooo."'

I'm sitting with my old friend Ciaran O'Keeffe, self-proclaimed 'hardcore sceptic', and he is doing what he normally does, pissing all over my dreams that I've inched closer to proving that ghosts exist.

We're in his lab at Buckinghamshire New University in High Wycombe, a commuter town an hour so from London, where Ciaran is a psychology professor, specialising in parapsychology.

Parapsychology, for anyone who doesn't know, is the study of alleged paranormal phenomena, and Ciaran does this through a very specific lens, channelling a childhood obsession with ghosts that mirrors mine – he's wearing a faded vintage *Ghostbusters* T-shirt now for good measure – with, unlike me, a near certainty that they don't exist. We've been friends ever since we worked together on a TV series called *The Bullshit Detective*, which set out to debunk pseudoscience, collaborating on an exposé of fake mediums.

Ciaran had form at that kind of thing; he was the person who exposed the trickery of the well-known TV psychic Derek Acorah, who was once the star turn on *Most Haunted*, the paranormal show that has pretty much defined the British view of ghost hunting for the last 20 years. Derek, a twinkly-eyed, slightly rough-around-the-edges Scouser, had briefly been a professional footballer before he became a medium. He'd actually been signed by Liverpool's legendary manager Bill Shankly and apparently gave one of their star players, Emlyn Hughes, a scare by predicting a car accident that Hughes did then go on to have. By the time *Most Haunted* turned him into a household name, Derek came with a spectral wingman, his 'spirit guide' Sam, who he claimed he'd met in a previous lifetime, '*when I was an Ethiopian boy and Sam was a friend of the family. This is about 2,038 years ago.*'

Ciaran, who'd been installed as *Most Haunted*'s resident parapsychologist,* had his doubts about Derek. He wasn't totally convinced he was always telling the truth, and he was suspicious of Derek's uncanny knack of always, without fail, channelling the spirits at every haunted location they went to, discovering lots of accurate historical details from these spectral conversations. Derek claimed never to have researched a location in advance, so was he really communing with the dead, or was he lying, reading up about the ghosts rumoured to haunt somewhere and then just pretending to speak to them?

Ciaran thought he'd put this to the test, and, at two reputedly haunted locations, decided to plant the names of potential spirits somewhere that he thought Derek would find them. The premise was that these were people who had died there, their names were Rik Eedles and Kreed Kafer, and Derek did indeed channel them,

---

* Watch some clips on YouTube, he's great – and see how young he looks!

even in fact becoming 'possessed' at Bodmin Jail by Kreed Kafer, a murderous South African jailer.

The only problem was that both of these men were entirely fictitious, created by Ciaran, their names actually anagrams of, respectively, 'Derek Lies' and 'Derek Faker'.

The point of all of this is that Ciaran doesn't suffer fools and he is quick to sniff out anyone he feels is acting fraudulently. I'm presuming he doesn't think David is on a par with Derek, though?

'No, not at all. I think he has had a genuinely strange experience.'

'But do you think he has been genuinely contacted by Aunt Connie?'

'No, unfortunately not.'

'So, I say,' sipping my takeaway coffee, 'how the hell do you explain it?'

'The most viable explanation here is something we know about called the Ideomotor Effect, which is basically unconscious movement based on prior expectation or suggestion. Effectively, your brain is sending signals to your finger, but you're not aware that that is happening. The classic way of illustrating this is that if you ask the name of the spirit, and you've all got your finger on the glass, and you go to J, then O, then H, you will then automatically go to N, because your brain will be telling you to spell out "John" and will be sending that signal to your finger before you're consciously aware of it. But you are not *trying* to push it to N, which is why David is right in thinking nobody was *consciously* moving the glass, because that's not what you're doing, it's your brain instructing your muscles to do it without you realising.'

'Like your brain's little secret?'

'Yes! So even if we hooked you up to a lie detector afterwards and said, "Did you push that glass to 'N'?" you will say no, and you will pass the polygraph without an issue. We've been aware of this effect for decades, even centuries. Michael Faraday, one of our most famous British scientists, well known for his work on electro-magnetism, wrote about the Ideomotor Effect back in 1853. There's an article that was published in *The Times* where he cited it as an explanation for the Victorian passion for "table turning", which is where a group of people would sit around a table and, in theory, the spirits would show they were present by moving the table. It was happening in séance rooms up and down the country and being held up as an example of spirit contact, and Faraday said no, that's the Ideomotor Effect.'

Ciaran digs out a bit of string with a small weight on the end of it from his pocket.

'May I directly address your readers, Danny?'

'You may.'*

'You can do this yourself if you've got a necklace or any kind of pendant. Take it off and hold it between your first finger and your thumb, let it hang down, so it's dangling like a pendulum, like this ...'

Ciaran hangs the string and its weight from his fingers to show me.

'Consciously do not let it move. Then say, "Show me what 'yes' is. Show me what 'yes' is," and I guarantee you that it will start moving ...'

---

* It's fine, listen to him, just don't look into his eyes.

Ciaran's pendulum is indeed moving!

'It will either rock from side to side or twirl in a circle, but are you moving it with your fingers? No. You will tell me, "Absolutely not, Ciaran, I'm doing nothing," but your brain is telling your muscles, "You've got to move it now because you're asking me what 'yes' is."'

'Okay. Can you stop staring at my readers like that?'

'Sorry.'

I am worried that Ciaran is enlisting you all to the dark side of hardcore scepticism. He's very convincing, isn't he? But don't worry, the small rebel fleet that represents my quest to prove ghosts exist is about to make a run down his Death Star trench. And no, that's not a euphemism.

'I get that,' I say. 'I totally get it. It makes a huge amount of sense that, if we are presented with a name that begins J-O-H, we decide it must be John. We know we're always looking for patterns, we hate incompleteness, so we summon up an N without even realising we're doing that. I think you can explain the N that way. I think you could probably explain the H that way. What the hell, I'll even throw in the O. What I don't get, though, is where the J comes from. As much as our brains might be trying to finish the message, I want to know why the message *starts*.'

I feel like I'm the opposing barrister making my case against Ciaran, with you, the jury, watching on. My next point needs to be something really sensational – the knock-out punch.

'It's like yoghurt, isn't it?'

'I'm sorry?' says Ciaran, confused.

'Well, you need to use yoghurt to make yoghurt, so how did the first yoghurt start?'

'Well, yoghurt historians believe that it was probably spontaneously fermented by wild bacteria in the bags made from goats'* stomachs that people used to carry milk back in Mesopotamia around 7,000 years ago.'

I love Ciaran, but sometimes I hate him. He really is the Emperor Palpatine of sceptical thought, always returning for one last battle just when you think he's been slain.

'Really? Is that true?'

'Yes. It wasn't invented by ghosts, if that's what you were thinking.'

'I didn't think yoghurt was invented by ghosts. Obviously. I just thought it ... appeared.'

'In a ghostly way?'

'No! Let's just forget about yoghurt,' I say. 'How the hell could the Ideomotor Effect lead people to spelling out something that none of them knew, yet is entirely accurate – that Sheila had liver cancer? She didn't even know that herself at that point! And even if it was just a complete guess, isn't it the most spectacular coincidence ever that she then dies at exactly the same time the board says she will?'

I look Ciaran in the eye, and he meets my stare unblinkingly.

'You have always told me that the dead cannot communicate with us,' I say to him, 'and I've always figured you might possibly be right because most times I saw somebody claiming they'd had spirit contact, it felt frustratingly vague, but this, Ciaran, this is the polar opposite of vague, it could not be more specific. So, do you, hardcore

---

* I've had it with these goat references. They are really getting my goat.

sceptic and destroyer of false mediums that you are, not think it is at least possible that David really was talking to Aunt Connie?'

'It's possible,' says Ciaran. 'I can't prove to you that it is not, but if it came down to a choice between Aunt Connie and Michael Faraday, I'm with the Victorian dude.'

'So how do you explain it?'

'Like you say, it is the most spectacular coincidence. But coincidences do happen.'

'Has anybody ever used a Ouija board?'

A few hands go up. I'm at one of the live recordings we sometimes do for the *Uncanny* podcast. We've just been talking about Ouija boards on stage and now I'm opening things up for discussion.

We start with a couple of stories from people about how they scared the bejesus out of themselves messing with them as kids, the sort of stories you'd expect really, and then I come to two women in their twenties in the middle of the auditorium, both with their hands stretching expectantly into the air and an excited look on their faces that tells me they have good stories to share.

And this, I think, is a coincidence. Two women of about the same age sitting next to each other, both with Ouija board stories to tell, what are the chances of that?

I hold the mic out to the girl on the right. It's hard to know what makes me choose her first, perhaps it's just that she is marginally closer, or maybe she's waving her arm slightly more energetically.

'Hello, my name's Kate,' she says, 'and I would like to take this opportunity to confess to all of my friends that as a teenager, it was me. I was pushing the glass.'

There is a little gasp from the audience at the boldness of her admission.

'We did try other times, and I thought, I'm not going to intervene here, but after ten minutes it gets boring, so I just got it started, and then other people filled in the blanks.'

Blimey, I think, Kate was the J in J-O-H-N.

And then she turns to the woman next to her.

'I'm sorry, Michelle.'

Oh God, I suddenly realise, this is not coincidence; they're not sitting together randomly, the two women are friends. Michelle's face has fallen in utter shock; her hand slowly retracts itself. Poor Michelle, I think, they were going to tell stories about the same event, but different stories. Michelle thought the messages from the Ouija board were real.

That old line flashes into my head: 'It's not ghosts you have to worry about, it's the living.'

How can we ever ascertain if Ouija boards really work, when humans are so bloody unreliable themselves, either through the unconscious impact of the Ideomotor Effect or the mischievousness of someone like Kate messing with Michelle. Maybe we will never know if, under all that noise, there is a voice trying to get through. We humans are like a drunk at a party, monopolising the conversation with our own irrelevance whilst the spirits, if they exist, recede into the shadows.

David remains confident that there was something guiding the hands of him and his mother and sister that day. He tells me that they used the Ouija board only a few times after that fateful night. Perhaps they all felt shaken by what they'd heard, or that they'd peaked and anything after Aunt Connie's revelation would be anticlimactic. Or, perhaps there was another, slightly more unsettling reason …

Before the Sunday night meetings completely fizzled out, in those last few sessions, David found himself studying the movement of the planchette around the board.

'The scientist and engineer in me kicked in, and I decided to conduct an experiment without telling my sister or my mother. I thought that for the planchette to move, someone or something was viewing the table from above and guiding our hands, or that that same someone or something was using our eyes to observe the scene and then guide the movement.

'So on one evening, whilst the planchette was moving and spelling out words, I kept my finger on it, but deliberately closed my eyes.'

What happened intrigued David.

'The planchette continued to move, but in a small circle and dithering. When I opened my eyes, it started to spell out words again. The inescapable conclusion was that something was using my eyes to observe the board. I really didn't like the idea of being used as a puppet by some external force.'

It's an eerie idea. Is that what we are when we use 'the mysterious talking board', marionettes conducted by some offstage spectral puppet master? I think about that tableau of a family sat around their kitchen table in 1980s East London, frozen in time thanks to David's testimony. Just like the photo of Janet above her bed in Enfield, it feels like the meaning of the scene lies in the eye of the beholder. Do we believe that the glass's loss of purpose when David closed his eyes was because something that was controlling him could no longer see, or because, without vision, the Ideomotor Effect would not work?

David says he avoided Ouija boards after that.

'But my sister got dragged more and more into these grey areas between life and death. My wife and I found contact with her became increasingly difficult. My sister always seemed to take an unhealthy interest in our business, and seemed to know things about our life almost in real-time. At first, I thought this was my mother gossiping, but I found out later that my sister's use of tarot cards and the Ouija board was becoming compulsive, and it seemed like she was getting an inside track on our lives.

'From my point of view, I had no desire to believe the future was pre-ordained, and if something bad was going to happen I had no wish to know in advance.'

The awesome and destructive power of this simple object, I think, from its roots as a soother of Civil War widows and plaything to excitable Victorians, to its present-day status as a Christian-upsetting rouser of demons; the Ouija board has had a quite striking ability to destroy friendships and family relationships and introduce fear and unease into previously happy lives. Whether it allows us to communicate with ghosts remains frustratingly hard to pin down, but, as I think about Aunt Connie and her impact on David, I am pretty sure that the board does have the ability to haunt you if you dare to put your fingers onto that planchette but are unprepared for the consequences. Somewhere out there, perhaps William Fuld is watching on, and I wonder if he feels pride, or regret and a desire to close his very own Pandora's Box.

REASONS *NOT*
TO BELIEVE #2

LONDON, NEW YEAR'S EVE, 2022

We're having a party. There's a gang of feral children running around the house waving toy weapons and the adults are just getting started on some fizzy wine whilst my wife oversees a Beef Wellington she's got in the oven.

And then all hell breaks loose.

The air is filled with a horribly high-pitched screeching, even more horribly high-pitched than the children. In fact, it's bad enough that they run downstairs, hopping up and down, shouting, 'The smoke alarm is going off!'

I sigh. We've got super-sensitive smoke alarms. They have a habit of going off at moments of intense cooking action. I grab a stepladder, head upstairs and climb so I can reach the reset button.

I press it. One long loud screech.

Then it starts beeping again.

This has never happened before. The alarm won't stop going off. The children are running around with their hands over their ears and it's definitely not the chilled-out party vibe we were aiming

for. Our smoke alarms are hardwired into the house's mains electrics, but each one has a back-up battery, so I figure the battery in
this one must have gone and it's beeping to tell me.

But damn it! We're out of nine-volt batteries! Thinking wist-
fully of my glass of fizzy wine downstairs, slowly losing its bubbles,
I grab my coat and dash to the corner shop, the alarm screaming
like a banshee behind me. Moments later, mission successful, I'm
back, climbing the ladder, to change the battery and save the day …

Phew.

Oh no.

IT IS STILL BEEPING. Like it's utterly furious with us for
having a party and wants to COMPLETELY RUIN IT.

At this point, my friend Simon* comes upstairs to help. Let's just
say that everyone downstairs is now pretty desperate for this noise to
end and he's been sent to help bring an end to their aural suffering.

We confer and decide that, if it's not the back-up battery, it must
be to do with the wiring in the smoke alarm itself. There's nothing
for it then, we're going to have to turn off the mains electricity to
see if we can somehow reboot it. My wife is not delighted by this
idea. Her Beef Wellington is at a crucial stage, and turning off the
power to the oven is not going to help.

But desperate times call for desperate measures. I head down to
the cupboard under the stairs and flip the main fuseboard switch.

Darkness descends. It's like the moment at a murder mystery
party when the killer has to strike.

---

* Not Simon my *Uncanny* co-producer, whose house I met Judy and Jenny
in. This is another Simon, though funnily enough he too is an audio
producer. Coincidence, or something more sinister?

I can feel the collected bated breath of everyone, adult and child alike.

BEEP!

The bastard alarm is still going off!

How is this even possible? Confused and uncertain, we switch the mains power back on. We are finally going to have to do the thing no man ever wants to resort to.

Reading the instructions.

I google 'what to do if your smoke alarm won't stop going off' and find a YouTube tutorial that tells me alarms like mine have a 'residual power', so that even if the mains electricity is turned off, they can still work. Aha! Residual power sounds like something ghost hunters would cite to explain how Anne Boleyn still stalks the corridors of Hampton Court, and, to be fair, I do now feel like I am being haunted by this alarm, still drilling its evil beeping into my ears long after it should be dead. The way to circumvent this function, the video tells me, is to turn the mains power off and hold the reset button down for 20 seconds to drain the alarm of its power. I guess it's the smoke alarm equivalent of holding an exorcism, or driving a stake through a vampire's heart, but, bloody hell, it means we're going to have to turn the mains power off again.

My wife is apoplectic now, as the house is plunged into darkness a second time and her Beef Wellington is plunged into critical condition. We offer hopes and prayers for its chances of recovery as I hold the reset button one more time, desperate to end this.

It emits the now-familiar horrible long constant wail.

A beat of glorious silence. This must have stopped it. We have won.

BEEP. BEEP. BEEP.

NO. You cannot be serious.

Simon and I agree this makes no sense. We have literally turned off all the power in the house and this thing is still going.

We switch the electricity back on and, as the lights reappear upstairs, I spot something. On the side of the smoke alarm it says, 'Replace by Jan 2023'. Has it really chosen tonight of all nights – though, to be fair, only one day early – to loudly and publicly sign off from active service? I don't know how it's doing it without any electricity, but it seems this now malfunctioning device is telling me I need to get rid of it.

Well, if that's what you want, my friend, then let's do it.

I grab the toolbox from downstairs and root out a crosshead screwdriver. Simon holds the ladder as I head up it again, feeling like a superhero preparing for a final showdown with my nemesis.

I unscrew the smoke alarm from the ceiling. Behind it are big, important-looking electrical wires. No neat unpluggable connection. Fuckity fuck fuck.* I'm about as practical as Mr Bean at the best of times and after a few sips of fizzy wine I do not trust myself to be slicing through live wires. As much as I love the idea of proving ghosts exist I don't want to do it by actually becoming one.

'We need to call an electrician,' says my wife. She's watching from the stairs, a desperate urgency in her eyes. This is a noise designed to make sure you cannot bear to be in the house, to force you to run away and escape. It is not the noise you want your party

---

* Sorry, I know I promised to behave after the Skellig Michael incident.

guests to have been subjected to for – checks watch – oh my God – an entire hour now.

But an electrician on New Year's Eve? How mind-numbingly expensive will that be?

'I'm going next door,' I state decisively. Our neighbour, an Italian man in his early seventies, is very practical, great at DIY, and we often call on him to help us with problems in the house, like some kind of surrogate dad. His name is Leo, the same as my older son, so we refer to him as 'Big Leo', and I know that Big Leo knows a thing or two about electrics.

I knock on his door, apologising for interrupting his New Year's Eve, begging for his help. He can spot a man at breaking point and so, moments later, Simon and I are holding the ladder whilst Big Leo stands at the top. We go through every step we've already been through, just to double-check. I can hear my wife's moans of despair as we turn the mains power off again, her Beef Wellington now well and truly screwed.

But nothing can stop the screeching.

It's crunch time, we need to take the only option left. 'I can cut through them,' Big Leo says, looking at the wires. 'If that's what you definitely want?'

'We have to,' I reply.

Whatever this ultimately ends up costing me in getting an electrician out to fix the damage later, I can't take this any more.

And then, Big Leo looks at me and says something that will – to paraphrase myself – completely change the course of this investigation.

'Are you totally sure the noise is coming from here?'

What?

'I mean, is the noise definitely coming from this smoke alarm?'

What kind of dumb-ass question is that? Simon and I haven't been standing here staring at this bloody smoke alarm for an hour and a half for no reason! It seems blatantly, painfully obvious where the noise is coming from. I've stood next to that thing holding the reset button, it's scream slicing through my eardrums. But, to humour Big Leo, I go into our bedroom next door – no smoke alarm in there. I pull the loft ladder down and go into the attic – nothing doing up there either.

And then, as I am coming back down from the loft, my eyes pan down, and I see a bag on the floor of the landing. A bag full of old junk we collected to get rid of. And I remember something.

I reach into the bag, and there, at the very bottom, is an old carbon monoxide alarm that my wife once bought after reading a scare campaign about the danger of CO poisoning. An alarm we never really used. An alarm that is now running out of batteries.

BEEP. BEEP. BEEP.

I open the back of it, take out the battery, and the noise stops.

I look across at Simon, then up to Big Leo, perched on the step-ladder, then at my wife standing on the stairs, her Beef Wellington a distant memory, and at our party guests nursing their injured ears behind her.

I feel a total and utter fool.

I replay the last 90 minutes in my head, how it all began when I ran up and the children shouted, 'The smoke alarm is going off!' How, from that point, I was glued to looking at the alarm, and trying to solve the problem it presented. How Simon became equally sucked in to helping me, so that we never once considered the noise could be coming from elsewhere.

And we had evidence, because the smoke alarm *did* emit screeches, extremely loud ones, but only when I pressed the reset button. The rest of the time, all those other beeps were coming from somewhere else entirely.

Humans, we love to join the dots, but sometimes we come up with the wrong picture.

I think about Staythorpe Power Station, the new road through Averham and the Civil War history of the area, of David and his sister's thirst for paranormal knowledge, Aunt Connie's recent death and the fact that Sheila had gone for her hospital check-up, and I wonder if these were all dots that somehow got joined into ghosts. There are details in all our cases that could possibly be explained away.

But then there are a whole lot more details that can't. Like how do you explain a man with an axe in your house? Or an inanimate object that can predict the exact time and means of someone's death? And how about the kitchen in Rome that repeatedly rearranged itself? This is what I love about this adventure we're on, it's like a game of Whack-a-Mole – for every Reason Not to Believe, another Reason to Believe pops up.

With that Roman kitchen in mind, I call Andrew a few days later. He tells me it's still a no from the Venerable English College. I tell him how much I have built this up now. His story is a huge part of my book, if we don't actually get into that apartment before the final chapter, it is going to be a massive anticlimax. I will have egg on my face, and not in an exciting 'egg thrown by a poltergeist' way.

Andrew promises not to give up and fires off another email to his influential sources in Rome.

As I hang up, my inbox pings with that familiar sound.

Another case has landed, and this one, on a cursory read, seems like it has watched all of the weirdness and scares of the last few chapters and then said, 'Hold my beer.'

Be warned this next stage of our investigation is steeped in the stuff of our deepest nightmares. It's a story of utter unparalleled bizarreness, but it doesn't feature a ghost.

It's a UFO.

CASE FOUR

THE ALIEN IN THE IN THE SNOW

CHAPTER 12

THE ODD BALL

The taxi driver's being careful, to Peter's relief. You can hardly see out of the windscreen, the road's a blur, like the telly when all the programmes end for the day. It's the sort of snow you don't see much these days, the stuff of Victorian Christmas cards, a thick, all-encompassing layer that shuts things down and cancels plans. Normally, Peter would be travelling back with the barmaids who live near him, but their husbands came to collect them tonight, keen to personally ensure they got home safely in these treacherous conditions, so he's alone, staring out the window of the cab as the streets of Middlesbrough disappear from view under a blanket of white.

It's mid-January, far enough away from Christmas for the New Year blues to have set in, in this first year of a new decade. 1980. Wow. It has a futuristic ring to it. Only four more years till we get to see if George Orwell is proved right and the world does end up an authoritarian shithole. Not that anything looks to be changing much in Middlesbrough. It's still its down-at-heel, depressed self, the North-East town everyone forgets about, fixating on its noisier neighbours Newcastle and Sunderland. But Peter knows from the 16 years he's spent growing up here that there's always something going on. His brain's replaying the events of the evening, doing his rounds collecting glasses from the tables of the working men's club. The conversations overheard, the jokes cracked, the drunken attempts at romance he politely averted his gaze from. It's not a bad job, glass collecting. You get none of the grief the bar staff do, shouted at by drinkers impatient to get served. Everyone's happy to hand over their empty pint glass, to make room for a full one.

'You're going have to jump out, mate,' says the taxi driver.

'What?' Peter's attention snaps back to the here and now as the cab pulls onto his street.

'I can't stop in this snow. I'll get stuck. I'll go as slow as I can, you open the door, and jump out.'

'Oh … all right …'

Peter's not the sort of teenager to argue with a grown-up, however bonkers the plan may sound. So he pays the driver, and, as the car slows, he reaches for the door handle.

'Now!' shouts the driver, and Peter opens the door, looking down as the snowy road moves beneath him, then springs and leaps, feeling like a paratrooper in a war movie, jumping into the drop zone.

He runs after the cab to slam the door closed and the man honks his thanks and trundles off, turning into Cargo Fleet Lane, already obscured by a white haze. Peter turns his collar up and walks across the narrow street, towards home. The street lights glare off the snow, making it surprisingly bright. He passes his neighbours' houses, the curtains all drawn tight. The snow's pristine, the only footsteps his. He enjoys this time, being the only one out. And then, about 20 yards away from his house, he notices something. It sits on the pavement, in front of the low privet hedge his dad keeps so neat.

It looks like a ball. A dark, leathery sphere. It reminds him of those heavy 'medicine balls' the teachers used to make you lift in school PE lessons. It's slap-bang right in front of the gate, and even from this distance, he can tell there's something ... odd.

There's no snow on it.

In this blizzard, where every other object – hedges, cars, roofs, walls, lampposts, postboxes, and certainly Peter himself – is wearing a hat of white, the ball sits entirely undusted, dark and stark against the snow, like a pupil in the white of an eye. It's as if it has just been placed there. How else can you explain the absence of snow? And yet, as he moves closer, Peter notices something else.

There are no footprints leading to or from it, no evidence of the person who must surely have dropped it. It's like the ball fell from above and just landed there, he thinks, looking up into the freezing night sky. He remembers an old story he was taught at school, about how some ancient Greek playwright was killed when an eagle dropped a tortoise on him. Apparently the bird thought the bloke's bald bonce was a rock and so dropped the tortoise to try and crack the shell, poor bastard. Did some big bird just drop this? Has Peter narrowly escaped being twatted on the head too? But what the hell's big enough to fit something like that in its claws or beak?

He moves closer towards it, but then something makes him stop, a feeling that creeps over him, almost a muscle spasm, but a certainty that something is wrong, without any direct knowledge of what that something is. He just knows that there is no way in hell he should approach that ball.

Bugger. The sogginess of the snow is saturating him now, finding its way into every nook and cranny, down the neck of his coat, up his sleeves and into his eyes and ears. He wishes he was inside, in the warmth, greeting his parents who always wait up for him, but this is a stand-off now, him standing out here like a flipping idiot, staring at the odd ball. He should go in, but –

Oh fuck!

Suddenly, horribly, grotesquely, the ball starts to move.

No way. No fucking way, mate.

It's as if something is silently hatching out of it.

Peter is frozen in horror as he sees a large, hairless head emerge from the ball's leathery casing, a face that he knows he will never be able to adequately describe, so unique is its horror, its total weirdness, but one that he will never ever forget.

It appears to have no mouth, no nose, no ears and no eyes, and yet it is still recognisably the head of some living creature, growing out of this ball.

This cannot be happening.

Whatever it is emerges rapidly, unfolding itself as if it were a puppet being pulled to attention. The head is followed by a neck and chest, then arms, a waist and legs. It's not so much that the figure is coming out of the ball any more, but that the ball has become the figure, all of it happening without a single noise, like a magic trick performed in a silent movie. The only thing audible to Peter is the sound of his own heart pumping like a sodding express train.

The 'hatching', or whatever the hell it was, seems to be over, and the figure, fully unfurled, stands, stick thin and uncommonly tall.

Peter guesses it must be seven feet, towering over his dad's hedge, but its spindly legs are only about the width of the cardboard tube in a toilet roll. They look almost too thin to hold its weight. Everything about it feels anthropomorphically impossible, its body too slender, its arms too long. It has a spider-like quality, fragile and delicate. Over the surface of its body, it wears what looks like a leathery, skin-tight black suit that reflects the moonlight, the collar covering its neck, so only the face protrudes, pale, bald and featureless.

Peter's wondering how the hell he is going to explain this to his parents, or anyone else for that matter. What the hell even is it?

'It' is facing the front door of his house now. Peter cannot move. He feels utterly immobilised as if he'd been glued in place. All he can do is pray that it doesn't turn to face him, because he doesn't think he could bear to look at that freaky eyeless face full-on. He thinks of another Greek legend he learnt at school, Medusa, who could turn blokes to stone just by looking at them.

This is utterly mad, cast-iron frigging bonkers, but it's happening right in front of him. He pinches himself for good measure and, unfortunately, he is all too wide a-bloody-wake. There's no 'I was only daydreaming' get-out-of-jail card here, he's standing on his own street, with a ... a what?

And then it moves! Lurching forwards, its motion shaky, awkward, like old film footage being rewound. It feels like something learning to use its body, unsure of its footing, but with a mechanical, almost robotic quality. Maybe it is a robot, Peter thinks, and yet, everything about the way it appeared felt so organic, like a creature growing out of a cocoon.

For all the thing's uncertainness, its movements are quick, and it doesn't make a single sound.

Oh no … You can't be serious! It suddenly makes its way down the path of Peter's house, up to his front door! Bloody hell! What if it went in? His parents are in there! But then it takes a sharp turn right, then left, and vanishes into the shadows down the side of the house.

He breathes out for the first time in the last couple of minutes. At least it didn't look at him. What would have happened if it had? Would he have been viewed as a threat? As prey? For all its willowy fragility, there was something of the hunter about the way it moved.

Peter has a problem now. He has to get inside his house, but he knows the door will be locked and feels too scared to even knock on it to summon his parents, in case the sound alerts the creature and draws it back. So, with the hazy logic of the panicked mind, he decides to roll snowballs to throw at the window. One, two, three, four, they pound gently off the glass until, at last, the porch light clicks on and his dad opens the door, wondering what the hell Peter's up to, playing silly buggers, but then concerned as Peter runs into the house, closing the door as quickly as he can, his mum wanting to know why he's got such a funny face on him.

Peter is still fresh with fear and it pours out, a description of the strange figure and its eerie 'birth'. His parents are clearly sceptical, but they have never seen their son like this, shaking, scared, hyper-ventilating, so they agree to go out into the snow to investigate. They wander around the house, looking for traces of an intruder, but there is only snow, thick, pristine, untouched by human feet, or any other kind of marks.

As Peter stands by the gate, flakes falling softly, layer piling upon layer of whiteness, there is no evidence that the odd ball was ever even there.

'They thought it must have been my imagination,' says Peter. He's in his fifties now, grey-haired, still with a strong North-East accent despite long stints living elsewhere in the UK. He works in the TV industry now and our conversation has been preceded by several assurances from me that I won't say anything about him that would reveal his identity.

'I wouldn't want to be putting my name out there,' he says quietly, 'just because, you know, it would cost you work – people would think you're a lunatic or something, but it was real.'

He meets my gaze earnestly, challenging me perhaps to dispute this assessment.

What he has just described is one of the most fantastical encounters I have ever heard, and yet, Peter is so very ... normal. That can sound like an insult, but there's just something kind of ... reassuring about his softly spoken North-East burr and open face.

It's entirely possible that he is a pathological liar, a cunning prankster, or that he has some condition that makes him fantasise or hallucinate, but, at this moment, sitting here on the sofa of his house in Middlesbrough, the hometown he moved back to a few years ago, none of that feels very likely.

The standard view of people who reveal experiences like this publicly is that they are attention seekers, wanting publicity or payment, desperate to make tabloid headlines or appear on some Discovery Channel series about alien encounters. Peter is literally the polar opposite of that. He shudders at the idea that anyone might link his story to him, to the point where I wonder why he is telling me it at all.

'I feel disturbed by it, still,' he says. 'There's unanswered questions, and I'd like to know the answer to them.'

'Unanswered questions', now there's an understatement. This story troubles the hell out of me. If we accept that Peter is describing something that he actually saw that night, what the blazing hell was it? It's so much easier to dismiss things seen out of the corner of an eye or in a darkened room at night. How do we make sense of something like this, viewed in plain sight over several minutes? If he'd spotted it 30 years later, he could have whipped out his phone and filmed it, but we have only Peter's memory to rely on, and memories are inevitably unreliable. Was it some waking nightmare? There was certainly no evidence of the figure ever having been there, no one else saw it ...

Or did they?

'Two days later,' Peter tells me, 'a milkman knocked on our front door very early one morning. He said he'd seen a very tall, odd-looking bloke walking down our path and that he'd vanished down the side of the house. My mother went out to look and, this time, she found prints in the snow. They led to the garden gate, down the side of the house, which was always locked. It's a huge great eight-foot gate, and the prints just stopped there. There were no marks or prints leading off across the garden. They just ... stopped. Whoever it was had got to the gate and then vanished.'

'So they would have had to somehow get through that locked gate?'

'Yes, which they couldn't have. It was still locked. But the footsteps only went in one direction – down the path – they didn't come back.'

Hmm. A head-scratcher worthy of an Edgar Allan Poe or Arthur Conan Doyle story. A locked-gate mystery.

'So, do you think the milkman had seen the same figure you did?'

'We still have no idea, but, I have to stress, what I saw ...'

Peter hesitates, making sure he finds the right words for this.

'It was no hallucination. The figure was there, and I can still see it in my mind's eye, it's not something you can easily forget.'

I wonder if he wishes he could.

Looking into Peter's eyes, I feel like I can see the memory of that night replaying in all its twisted peculiarity, the everyday landscape of his home street transformed into something alien and frightening, like a scene from *Doctor Who*. But this story is about to get even stranger, because if Peter has a whole load of unanswered questions, then number one on today's agenda is ...

Why him?

Why on earth would this thing, whatever it is, choose to reveal itself to a 16-year-old boy on the way back from his part-time glass collecting job?

Peter wonders if the answer to that lies in something that happened to him two years earlier, something else deeply strange and discombobulating, but this time experienced by nearly his whole family.

The day they saw an unidentified flying object.

CHAPTER 13

CLOSE ENCOUNTERS IN MIDDLESBROUGH

I grew up in the North-East, in Newcastle, but I think I've only been to Middlesbrough once before. It gets a bad press, even locally, often dismissed as boring, or showing up high in rankings of 'the worst places to live in the UK'. It was not always so. Back in the nineteenth century, William Gladstone, the future prime minister, visited the town and was so impressed he called it 'an infant Hercules ... the youngest child of England's enterprise'. Forged in the country's Industrial Revolution, Middlesbrough was seen as a fast-developing symbol of Britain's manufacturing might. Back then, the blast furnaces of the steelworks roared and the mills hummed.

Those days are long gone, sadly. Peter tells me the town experienced massive unemployment when he was a kid. Middlesbrough had gone from infant Hercules to knackered old codger, but, despite that, his memories of growing up there are happy.

'Blissfully happy,' he says. 'I loved my mates and I loved the area. It was a good place.'

For all the unemployment, he remembers the town's spirit. 'People always found humour. They had a heart and got through and coped.'

His mum was one of those people, someone who seemed like a tower of strength in Peter's life. She had a habit of taking the kids shopping every Thursday, timed perfectly to fit in with another communal family activity.

'We'd always go so that we'd get back in time for *Top of the Pops*.'

Top of the Pops, the weekly chart-music programme on the BBC, was such a big deal in Peter's house that he is able to tie down the precise specifics of exactly when this incident took place by remembering who was on the programme that day.

'It was the time that Terry Wogan had a chart hit with "The Floral Dance".'

Terry Wogan, for anyone unfamiliar, was a venerable bastion of British broadcasting, famous for his chat show and for doing a sarcastic but affectionate commentary on the Eurovision Song Contest each year. I hadn't been aware of his one-hit-wonder pop career, but a quick glance on YouTube will tell you the song is a twee, old-fashioned number performed by a twinkly-eyed but slightly tuneless Terry to bemused teenagers who look like they'd much rather be listening to David Bowie.

Anyway, this is the thing that Peter remembers. It's odd how these little details lodge in your mind, anchoring your memories into chronologically verifiable reality. Terry had made it into the Top 40 and appeared on the programme on 5 January 1978. Peter would have been 14, walking to the shops as normal, on a stormy North-Eastern night, with his mum and younger brother and sister.

'What's that?' says Peter.

His mum stops pushing the pushchair containing his little brother and looks up, following the line of where Peter's pointing, whilst keeping her other eye on his younger sister. Above them, in the sky, is a red light, directly above their heads.

'Is it a helicopter?' she wonders.

'It's not making any noise,' Peter says.

It's bright, really bright. A plane would be higher in the sky, and would be moving faster. This just feels like it is hovering, its movements slight and slow, unaffected by the force of the wind as the storm buffets all around it.

'That's odd,' his mum says, already transferring her attention back to his siblings, then – 'Come on, we'd better get a move on if we want to be back for *Top of the Pops*.'

They continue on their way, but Peter hasn't taken his eyes off the red light and, if it was odd before, it's odder now because it appears to be following them, tracking their movements as they walk up the road.

He tugs his mum's coat sleeve, pointing again, and now, as she looks up, he sees a flash of something in her eyes that looks like concern. She quickens her step, forcing the pushchair on, but the light isn't going anywhere, it matches their pace. Peter keeps his focus on it. They have been walking for ten minutes and the light has followed them the whole way, hovering above their heads. Peter's mum is walking unusually fast, almost dragging his sister along, her head resolutely set forwards. Peter thinks she might be frightened.

They can see the supermarket now, over the road, Frankie Dee's, one of a local chain of North-East stores. As usual, there's a row of prams out the front, babies left there sleeping whilst their mums are inside shopping.

'Let's see if it follows us over the road,' Peter's mum says, shooting a quick glance skywards. They cross over by the traffic lights, quickly, too quickly really, and the light does follow them, quickening its own pace. Peter's mum almost charges into the shop and Peter sees the light pass over them, as if it is now hovering above Frankie Dee's, before it disappears from view as they find the sanctuary of the shelves and aisles full of groceries.

They are in the shop for about 45 minutes, long enough to almost forget about the light, but as they emerge again, loaded up with bags of groceries for the journey home, his mum says, 'I wonder if it's gone?'

And it has.

They scan the sky above them but there is no sign of the red light. Maybe it was a helicopter. Some new kind that travels silently? They wait at the traffic lights to cross the road again. Peter has an instinct to look behind him and …

It's there again!

It blinks at him, and then it moves, as if it is coming straight towards them. He prods his mum and she sees it too as the light moves undeviatingly back into its favoured position, directly above their heads.

'Run!' shouts his mum, and she doesn't even wait for the traffic lights to go red, she just charges the whole family across the road, and then they are all running down the street, Peter's heart going like the clappers. There's something deeply unsettling about seeing your parent scared, the person you have always relied on to soothe your own worries and anxieties now reflecting and amplifying them back at you. There doesn't feel any question about it any more, the thing above them is a threat, something that means harm.

They run and they run and they run, the light following them step for step, with the eerie certainty of one of those zombies in a horror movie, constant and ominous, unshakeable.

'Into the park!' shouts his mum, and she veers the pushchair and his now crying siblings in through the park gates.

'Under the trees!'

They run for the cover of a group of trees and Peter realises they are hiding, literally cowering from whatever this thing above them is. Is this what it was like in the Blitz, he wonders, taking cover, knowing the sky was full of menace? He dares himself to look up. The red light is visible through the leaves, as if it is searching, probing for them, or perhaps just biding its time until they are forced to break cover.

They stand there, clutching the shopping bags, his brother and sister sobbing, his mum pale and silent, waiting for what feels like a really, really long time, until finally, when they look up, it is gone.

It's funny, but *Top of the Pops* no longer feels like that big a deal.

'Could it have been a helicopter?' I ask.

'I don't think so. It was a really stormy night and it seemed crazy that a helicopter would be out in that weather. And you'd hear a helicopter, right?'

I think about the intense noise I hear every time a police chopper or the Air Ambulance passes over my house.

'We couldn't hear any noise from it at all,' Peter says.

The incident clearly made a big impression on him. Even now, several decades later, he remembers it in crystal-clear detail, but I can't help wondering if the thing that scared him most was not the odd red light, but his mother's reaction to it. Fear is contagious and never more so than when it comes from someone we have previously felt is immune to it. But what was it about that light that scared her so much? She was a down-to-earth, no-nonsense woman, there was clearly something about this flying object and the way it seemed to track her family up and down the road that felt like a genuine threat. Peter tells me she went as far as calling the local Teesside Airport to ask them what it might have been. They told her there were no scheduled planes or helicopters flying over that area at that time.

There is a further odd instalment to this, which might make us wonder if that red light was indeed something deeply unusual.

'About two weeks later, I was at home,' says Peter, 'pottering about, and I just had this feeling that something was outside. I had an urge to go to the window.'

So Peter looked out.

'And I saw that same light.'

It was back!

Peter's heart must have skipped a beat. If the light had felt like a horror-movie zombie tracking his family, then this is the point in the film when you realise you haven't actually killed the zombie after all and it's come back to have another crack. Weirdest of all, though, is that odd instinct he'd had that made him cross to the window.

'It was like I'd *felt* it was coming.'

Suddenly, this all seems very personal to Peter. As if there is some connection going on between the red light and him.

'It was just hovering there over the street, so I ran and got my telescope and set it up so I could view whatever was making this light.'

Now, my heart is beating faster, is this the chance to finally see what it was that stalked them to the supermarket and back, lurking suspiciously over the park, intimidating a mother and her kids?

'What did you see?' I ask.

'It was a big orange object that looked like a tube with long elongated windows and a row of lights underneath. Inside it, I could see people moving, silhouettes in the window.'

Okay, I'm not quite sure what I was expecting, but this is a lot, lot weirder. Peter looks to me, gauging my reaction. It's the gaze of someone caught between his certainty of what he saw and the awareness of how it sounds to say it out loud.

I need to have a response here, but to be honest I feel totally unsure what it is, because just as with Andrew, Vee or David, I don't feel I'm talking to someone who's contacted me for the attention or has been spending too long in their own heads and started jumping at shadows. Peter is a sensible, sane person in a responsible job who just has one big and very unusual problem.

He can't get over the fact that he saw something all those years ago that, on paper, is utterly absolutely impossible – potential proof of alien technology hovering over Middlesbrough.

Blimey. Peter is still looking at me, searching my face for some sort of sign of how I feel about hearing his strange experiences. The truth is, I feel like I'm a long way outside my comfort zone.

Ghosts are something I've been obsessed by since I was a kid. UFOs are a much more recent interest, or at least the idea of making a serious investigation of them.

Don't get me wrong, I've always found reports of 'flying saucers' fascinating. Like loads of kids, I grew up on a diet of science fiction, I can quote *Star Wars* lines with the best of them, hell, as you know, I've even been to Luke Skywalker's house, but I'd never moved beyond the fantasy to explore reports of actual alleged sightings. Even after I embarked on my serious quest to investigate ghosts, if I heard people talk about 'Roswell' or 'Area 51', I tended to cloud over, assuming it was just conspiracy-theory-mongering. If sceptics like Malcolm Fairbairn complain that ghosts are the easy answer to a lot of complicated questions, then UFOs felt like the opposite. Isn't the most likely answer for secrecy around a US Air Force base in the desert because they don't want any old Russian or Chinese spy wandering in, rather than because they're hiding a bunch of aliens there?

The other thing that bothered me was a big fat WHY. Why would an alien race travel all the way to Earth and then choose to reveal themselves to just one bloke in a trailer park in Arkansas, or a boy and his mum in a Middlesbrough park? Surely, if they were sending their emissaries, they'd do it in a slightly more thought-out way? Basically, why land by Peter's local supermarket when you could land on the White House lawn?

But then, amongst all the ghost stories being emailed to me, I noticed a definite sub-genre. Stories that talked about a different kind of encounter. There were people writing to tell me they had witnessed flying objects or strange figures that they couldn't explain, things they felt could only be described by words like 'UFO' or 'alien' and, by the way they described them, I could see that these experiences had left the same kind of impact as if they had seen a 'ghost'. In fact, you could describe them as 'UFO Hauntings'. The witnesses certainly felt haunted and, sometimes decades later, were desperate for answers. It suddenly felt utterly wrong to be open-minded to the idea that some people might have really seen a ghost and yet dismiss these UFO accounts as imagination, or suggest the witnesses were so obtuse or credulous they'd mistake everyday objects for the fantastical.

So I started to explore the stories in more detail, wondering 'what if'. Was it possible these people did witness something that sat outside the normal parameters of human experience? If it truly is evidence of something 'unearthly', that feels as exciting, ground-breaking and mind-blowing as discovering whether ghosts exist; and, if they can be explained sceptically, then is there anything we can learn from these experiences that might help us to understand other types of hauntings?

Because it feels like UFO experiences and ghost experiences are similar yet different. They both involve a moment where a witness is confronted by something which changes their view of reality, which can be frightening and something they'll find hard to explain to others due to the worry that they will be judged, mocked or considered 'mad'. Where the experiences differ is that ghost sightings often come with a 'build', there are stages to the experience – quite specific stages if we're talking about poltergeists, but even in regular hauntings, there is normally some form of progression. You move in, you have strange feelings, you notice odd things, and then the ghost appears, to be seen or heard or felt, but it is the climax of a process, whereas most UFO sightings are normally 'one-hit wonders'; you're driving along a road or walking down a street and suddenly see something above you or in the distance that you cannot explain. You can take people into your haunted house and ask them to wait for an appearance from the ghost, but you'll never be able to show anyone the thing you saw briefly zip across the sky at an unexplainable speed.

There are UFO cases, of course, that do involve some kind of progression, perhaps multiple sightings as in Peter's case, or a sense that the first sighting has had some sort of impact on you as a person. There are people who believe they have actually had contact with whatever was on board that flying object, and feel changed as a result. These more involved UFO encounters throw up another key difference I've noticed: that witnesses in ghost cases often feel it is simply bad luck they became haunted – they bought the wrong house or booked the wrong hotel room – whereas witnesses in UFO cases sometimes feel a sense of having been targeted, or 'chosen' to witness this sight – the UFO came and found them. We see this definitely in Peter's case. He is a rational person, the idea that extra-terrestrials would travel from outer space to find him and his family above a Middlesbrough supermarket and then return to scare him by lurking around his gate to hatch out of a ball should seem so implausible he dare not say it out loud, and yet, he knows what he saw, and it feels hard to explain it any other way.

The more I explore the reports I receive, the more I feel like the greatest similarity is that UFOs throw up the very same question for us that ghosts do. If we accept that the person telling the story is neither lying nor insane, then we have to accept that they did see something. That there are dots to be joined.

If we, on this journey we are on together, taking in poltergeists, ghost horses and Ouija boards, allow ourselves even a flicker of a possibility that the dead can come back to life, are we also open to the possibility that there could be people amongst us who have had encounters with alien spacecraft or even alien beings that strayed into our world accidentally or intentionally, perhaps to investigate us, or maybe just to gawp in the way we do at exotic animals in foreign countries?

I can imagine what your head is telling you right now, maybe you're thinking we've strayed too far into the stuff of movies and cheap novels, but it might not be as big a leap of belief as we think. After all, believing in ghosts involves us doing battle with the accepted laws of physics, believing in aliens just involves us not having explored beyond the tiniest fraction of the universe yet. To deny the possibility that we are not alone is like saying there's definitely no one in this house when you've only looked in one room.

But ... and it's a big but.*

If these aliens were coming to earth, even if it was just to briefly joyride over Middlesbrough for shits and giggles, wouldn't we know about it? When you look at the amount of gaffes and leaks that befall governments here and in the US on a daily basis, the idea they could successfully conceal the arrival of aliens feels unlikely to say the least. Some cabinet minister would surely have accidentally announced it by now:

'I just want to say that this year's alien landing figures are extremely healthy – damn it! I meant employment figures! Not

---

* I like big buts and I cannot lie.

227

aliens! Forget the aliens! Hardly any of them have landed – I mean … Oh God, I'm resigning and going on *I'm a Celebrity*!'

Basically if you can't keep the expenses you've fiddled secret, how do you conceal a Martian invasion?

That's what I'd always thought, but what if I told you there were a spate of strange sightings in that same period Peter had his, and that two of the most key sightings came the very same year that he saw the figure emerge from the ball, 1980. How about if I threw in that the sightings have similarities with his in more ways than one? And what if I told you that there was potential evidence of a conspiracy to silence the witnesses to these sightings? That would really seem just a bit too much like a science-fiction movie come to life, wouldn't it?

And yet, there is a very definite real-life mystery to be explored here, as deep, dark and unsettling as anything else we have come across, so I'm already on another train, my walking boots packed, heading north, because the next stage of this investigation will take us to the wild, rugged moors of West Yorkshire, and a town where seeing strange flying objects is not considered unusual at all, but almost the norm.

All aboard … we're going to Britain's busiest UFO hotspot.

CHAPTER 14

WELCOME TO TODMORDEN

As I walk down the street from the train station, a man hurries past me in a T-shirt with an alien's face on it and the words 'I Believe', so I figure I'm going in the right direction.

Todmorden, or 'Tod', as the locals affectionately call it, sits where three steep valleys meet amongst the rolling hills of the vast Pennine moorlands, about 17 miles from Manchester. Go in one direction and you'll find the moors of Emily Brontë's *Wuthering Heights*, go in the other and you'll find the moors of the 1960s Moors Murders. It's a landscape that contains romance and darkness, and Todmorden sits in what feels like a crater carved out of it. You have a very definite sense of being surrounded; everywhere you look as you walk through town, the imposing, steep hills gaze balefully down, their colour scheme a sombre dark green.

Historians think the name 'Todmorden' comes from Old English words meaning 'Totta's border valley', though who Totta was is lost to the mists of time. There's an alternative etymology though, sometimes bandied around, that it derives from two words for 'death' – the German 'Tod' and the French 'Mort' – which sends a pleasing shiver down the spine for one such as me, who spends their days chasing ghosts.

Though for once, of course, I am hunting different game, something that, if you believe the locals, has been spotted in abundance, hovering over the town for the last few decades.

Not wanting the man in the alien T-shirt to feel I'm some shadowy government agent following him, I slow my pace and allow myself a moment to take in the street I'm walking down. The buildings in Todmorden have that solid unfussy grandeur of a northern mill town. Like Middlesbrough, it received the Industrial Revolution as a thirsty plant takes on water, growing and blossoming from village into thriving manufacturing hub where several large cotton mills generated thousands of jobs that drew people here from far and wide. In the late twentieth century, as the mill industry declined, the population receded to its present-day 15,000 inhabitants and Todmorden has developed a different kind of reputation, as somewhere that attracts people who favour an arty, alternative lifestyle. I walk past a yoga studio, a 'Wellness Centre', art galleries, trendy cafés and a place called Spiritual Connections, which sells all your pagan and witchcraft needs and also does dreadlocks. It's definitely a new-agey place to live. Like Glastonbury's Arthurian legends and converging ley-lines, the idea that Tod might be on an extra-terrestrial flightpath gives an air of romance that's a beacon for anyone who walks the road less travelled, which has led to another nickname for the town – 'Odd-morden'.

So why are there so many UFO sightings in Totta's Death Death Border Valley, and can it throw some light on the mystery of Peter's case? In the hope of finding an answer, I follow in I-Believe-Man's wake into the Golden Lion pub, buy a pint for a jaw-droppingly low £2.50* and head upstairs to a room normally used for music gigs that has probably the stickiest floor I've ever walked across. In front of the small stage is a circle of chairs fast filling up with an eclectic mix of old men in woolly hats, middle-aged women, punks, young hipsters with beards and tattoos, and a few smartly dressed people who look like they've come from work and are slightly out of place. There's even a man with a strong American drawl from West Virginia. They all have one thing in common though, which sparks a sudden wave of panic in me – will I be the only person here who hasn't witnessed a UFO? It feels ironic, worrying about being stigmatised for *not* having had a paranormal experience, but it's too late to back out, the curtains are being drawn, and a small silver statue of an alien has been placed in the middle of the circle as an expectancy fills the air. It's time for tonight's session of Tod UFO Meet.

I've never been to a meeting of Alcoholics Anonymous, but I imagine it probably feels a bit like this. The thirty or so people in the room sit politely, nodding and listening supportively as, one by one, people in the circle share their experiences. A softly spoken guy in his thirties describes seeing a giant silver metallic sphere floating in the sky above the hills outside town; a spiky-haired, well-built man in his fifties talks about seeing a UFO with his mum as a kid, an experience that reminds me of Peter's. There are a few eccentrics

---

* Possibly the most unbelievable but true detail in this whole book. I love you, Yorkshire.

here, for sure, but in the main it's ordinary people talking about extraordinary things, so you can imagine I feel right at home.

The group has been meeting every month since 2017 in a bid to try and make sense of what is happening in Todmorden and give people a chance to talk about what they have seen. It's presided over by its founder, Colin Lyall, sitting at what feels like the head of the circle, if such a thing can exist, his long denim-clad legs stretched out in front of him. Colin is in his mid-sixties and has the air of a trendy wizard, in a little beanie hat and white beard, which he strokes as he listens. I first met him a couple of years ago when he appeared on my podcast, and I liked him hugely for his calm, measured take on a subject that can attract its fair share of crazies. It struck me that he and I were alike. We'd both found a way to provide a safe space for people to discuss experiences that they'd previously bottled up for fear of sounding mad. With his background as a teacher and training as a psychotherapist, Colin has created an environment at these monthly meetings that feels therapeutic and non-judgemental despite the sometimes extreme experiences people share out loud. I find myself wishing I could bring Peter here, to show him he really is not alone.

That kind, respectful atmosphere is vital, because a few stories into the evening, it's clear to me that, even in a room of fellow believers, there is a real wariness from the people sharing their stories. I can understand it, because as a society, we've turned people who think they've seen UFOs into a comic trope, conspiracy theorists who wear tin-foil hats so the aliens can't read their minds, or American hillbillies who claim they were abducted by little green men. Some of the people here describe the bullying and mockery they've received when they've talked to people they know about what they saw. One man is visibly trembling as he describes his experience, another is offered the chance to tell his story by Colin, but decides he is too nervous. All he'll say is that he's seen something he can't explain, 'and where do you go with that?'

It's a phrase I hear a few times across the evening, the idea that these experiences leave you feeling trapped, unable to discuss them with friends or family. The mystery of what you saw becomes a private one that sits locked, stubbornly unsolvable, in your psyche. One of the regulars, in a moment of casual profundity, says, 'It makes you the alien,' no longer sure how you fit in to normal life and everyday conversations.

There's another reason for the wariness too. When one or two people ask the spiky-haired man where his sighting happened, he clams up. 'I'd better not say too much more,' he mumbles quietly. Another woman says something similar when describing seeing a UFO as a teenager with her boyfriend. I learn that they are worried their stories could have real consequences, namely that somebody in a position of power will contact them and threaten them into silence. Reading that, you're probably dismissing it as paranoia, fanciful self-important notions of 'Men in Black' turning up on their doorsteps, but it's not. In Todmorden, it's actually a pretty sensible fear, because everyone here has already seen it happen.

I think it's time to talk about the man who has really brought us all together in this pub. He has come up in conversation several times tonight, referenced in the way Pelé would be in a chat about football, with an air of legendary reverence, famous enough to not require a surname.

'We wouldn't be here if it wasn't for Alan,' says Colin.

Because if Todmorden was once known far and wide for its cotton mills, the town's reputation is now built on something else, or rather, someone else.

Alan Godfrey.

Alan is a local man who experienced something in November 1980, about 11 months after Peter saw that figure outside his house. It was an encounter that would change Alan's life and forever leave its stamp on this town, weaving itself into the DNA of Todmorden, becoming part of the local folklore – the origins story that all of these UFO witnesses at Tod UFO Meet can trace their lineage back to, when it became clear that something really strange was happening in this part of the world. What happened to Alan that night is now generally recognised as one of the most significant UFO events in British history, but it also acts as a cautionary tale for everyone here about what happens if you tell people you saw a UFO.

Whilst Alan's encounter happened in November, many people believe that, just as with Peter, the reasons for it lie in something that happened to him earlier, a few months before, on a rainy June night. To find out more, we need to do something that used to be the default advice in any time of trouble.

Ask a policeman.

CHAPTER 15

IT WAS RIGHT WEIRD

Rain falls on the windscreen as the car pulls up outside Todmorden railway station, the radio still crackling. Alan shoots a look at his colleague Malcolm; there's nothing for it, they're going to get soaked.

They open the police car doors and Malcolm leads the way, towards the coal yard at the bottom end of the station. The coal is arranged in a horse-shoe shape, with a large, taller pile in the middle, and that's where it is apparently, according to the report that was phoned in. Looks like they're going to get covered in coal then, as well as getting soaked.

Malcolm clambers up the heap first and Alan can tell from his reaction that this isn't going to be the quiet night they'd hoped for.

'I think you'd better come up.'

Malcolm climbs back down, his face grim, and Alan takes his place. At the top of the coal pile, laid out, almost neatly, is a body.

He swears under his breath, scanning the corpse with his eyes, taking in the crime scene, and instantly he has a feeling that this is just ... wrong. He's seen plenty of dead bodies before, but there's something about this particular one that feels deeply odd. The dead man looks like he's in his fifties. He's wearing a jacket, but it's fastened in the wrong place and underneath the jacket is just a white string vest, no shirt. The trousers aren't done up right either, sitting in a funny way, not quite properly on, and his shoes aren't tied.

'He was dressed after death,' says Malcolm.

Alan nods. The dead man has close-cropped hair. Alan leans in. On the crown of the corpse's head are a series of individual black burn marks in a ring, and at the nape of the neck is an open wound. A yellowy-green gel-like substance has been smeared across it.

No, this is not your average suspicious death, but the thing that really unsettles Alan is the look on the man's face. That won't be easy to forget. The eyes are open and the face is set into an expression that can only be described as terror.

Alan shivers. The strangest detail of all, though, is what is *not* there. Alan has run his eyes over the entirety of the body now, from head to foot, and there is not a single mark of coal on him. How in the hell do you get the body of a man on top of a coal heap, without getting any coal on it? With this rain, the coal dust is like glue.

'It's an odd one,' says Malcolm.

Alan nods again. It feels pretty clear the dead man did not get himself up here by his own steam and he can't have been dragged up either. It feels as if the body has just been placed there, which is impossible, of course. The bigger question though, is why somebody who had committed a murder – if that's what this really is – would want to place their victim at the top of a coal heap in the middle of the station yard. You'd go up on the bloody moors to hide the body, wouldn't you? Not dump it on public display like this.

Alan scratches his head. This feels like the sort of puzzle they'd get Sherlock Holmes or Hercule Poirot to solve, not a bobby on the beat in Tod. He doesn't have a good feeling about this at all.

It's the eyes. He can't stop looking at the eyes. It looks like the man was frightened to bloody death.

'So it was almost like he'd been dropped on top of this mound?' I ask.

'Well, yeah,' says Alan when I meet him, 'but no injuries to suggest he'd been dropped from a great height. He didn't have broken arms or owt, the only thing that were up with him was his heart had stopped and these burn marks on his head. Very strange. Very, very strange.'

Alan's still lives in Todmorden, and his Yorkshire accent is as strong as the gritstone rocks that litter the moors surrounding the town, where he grew up. His countenance could almost have been carved from rock too, solid and dependable if a little mournful. He's in his seventies now, with thick, bouffant white hair, but the photographs that you can hunt out of him online show it was once jet-black and that he had an impressive handlebar moustache, like a northern Magnum PI, appropriate for someone patrolling the mean streets of his hometown.

Certain things were learnt about the body on the coal heap in the wake of the discovery. A missing-person report emerged that matched the corpse. His name was Zigmund Adamski, known to his friends as Ziggy, a 56-year-old Polish man who'd gone missing from his home in the nearby village of Tingley five days previous. He'd been due to go to his god-daughter's wedding.

'But the day before,' Alan tells me, 'he went to Wakefield to do some shopping with one of his relatives. They came back and they had lunch at his home with his wife Hettie, and, after lunch, Hettie sent him out to go to the local shop for some groceries. As he left his house, he was wearing his coat and everything, fully dressed, and he had thick wavy hair.'

Note that detail.

'He spoke to one of his neighbours. It was a sunny day, and he said he was very excited about his god-daughter. He got to the local shop, he had a bit of a conversation with the shopkeeper, he left the shop and he never arrived home. He just disappeared off the face of the earth. And he turned up five days later, dead, on top of the pile of coal in Todmorden.'

'So he'd had wavy hair when he left the house, but the body you found had close-cropped hair?

'Baffling, in't it?'

It is. In another odd little twist, Adamski's job was as a coal miner, so was there any link between that and the fact that he'd been found on a heap of the very stuff he mined?

To this day, the case has never been solved. The autopsy concluded that Adamski had died of a heart attack, but given the fact that the evidence suggests there is no way he could have got himself to the top of that coal heap, that expression on his face that made Alan feel he'd been 'frightened to death' feels rather haunting. I can't help thinking of a little correlation with Peter's story too. It's probably nothing, but the way in which Adamski's body had no coal on it reminds me of the lack of snow on the ball by the gate, that sense that it had been just placed there without interacting with its environment.

Whether you're Team Believer or Team Sceptic, I think we can all get behind the fact that this is a bizarre and inexplicable death, which may well have been murder, and it would probably have stayed as just that, a weird unsolved crime, if it wasn't for what happened to Alan next.

It's six months later, in the early hours of the morning of 28 November 1980 and it's raining again – it does that a lot in Todmorden. The police station has received several calls from residents of a local housing estate saying that a herd of cows has been seen wandering around, so Alan goes up there in his car to investigate.

As he passes Centre Vale Park, there's something blocking the road up ahead. His first thought is that it's a bus, overturned, maybe one of the ones that take workers up to the mill. He drives the car towards it, but as he gets closer he can see that his theory was wide of the mark. The thing he's looking at is no bus. It's … well, it's nothing he has ever seen before.

It's a solid, metallic object, diamond in shape, big, roughly 20ft wide and 14ft high, and it looks like it's hovering about 5ft off the ground, spinning slowly, rotating anti-clockwise, a maelstrom of leaves spinning beneath it. Around the top of it, there are black panels or dark windows, he can't be sure which. Oddly, for something so big, it isn't making a single sound.

Following his training, he reaches for his radio to call it in. Quite how the heck he'll describe what he's looking at, he's unsure, but he figures somebody had better be told about a weird flying metal thing blocking a main road.

The radio's not working. All he can get is static. Damn it.

He decides if he can't phone it in, he'll draw a sketch of it, like he would for a road accident, to keep a record of the scene as evidence. He pulls out his police notebook and quickly outlines the shape of the flying thing. As he is glancing down though, he hears a tremendous whoosh, accompanied by a white burst of light. He blinks, his ears ringing.

The object is gone.

Well, that was bloody odd. Alan looks about, his eyes still adjusting, and something rather unsettling becomes clear. He is no longer in the same spot where he had pulled the car up. He is further down the road. Somehow, in the time it took that white flash to make him blink, his stationary car has travelled to a point beyond where he had seen the object! He looks in the mirror. The object isn't behind him either. It has just disappeared.

He starts the engine and turns the car around, his hands shaking a little, driving back to where the object had been hovering. All across the road is debris, leaves and bits of branches, but that particular patch of road is entirely dry, whereas the rest of the road is slick from the rain that has been falling all night.

Bloody heck. This is not what he signed up for. He wants to just head home, forget all about it, but the detective in him thinks he should probably investigate the surrounding area, to see if he can find any clues to what just happened. Next to him is the park, the moors looming darkly behind it. He opens the gate and goes in and there, right in front of him, is a sight he definitely hadn't expected ...

The herd of cows, gently mooing.

Now this really is strange, because the last time he checked, cows couldn't open metal gates and at this time of the morning there's no other bugger about. It feels almost like ...

They've just been dropped there from above.

His mind flits backs to Ziggy Adamski, his body positioned on that coal heap, and he sighs deeply, knowing he's going to have to write all this up in a report, and it's going to sound utterly bloody nuts.

'It was right weird,' says Alan, thinking about that night now. It's a line that seems to perfectly encapsulate not only his UFO experience but pretty much everything we have experienced on our journey so far. Peter's experience made us realise how unsettling it is to see a parent lost for answers, but is it even more troubling to see a police officer completely flummoxed? They are the people we have appointed as a society to protect us, but here was Alan confronted by something he had absolutely no idea how to deal with.

He was right to worry about filing his report, because somebody at the police station, whether through mischief or spite, leaked it to the local newspaper, the *Todmorden News & Advertiser*. From there, it was picked up by the *Yorkshire Post*, which has a far larger circulation, and somebody there put together the two strange crime reports Alan Godfrey was linked to – the unidentified flying object on Burnley Road and the mysterious death of Zigmund Adamski (whose surname, coincidentally – or not, if you are a conspiracy theorist – was the same as George Adamski, a Polish-American who became very famous in the 1950s for writing books claiming that he had travelled onboard alien spaceships). The ingredients were there for a great tabloid story speculating on whether the two could be linked, and the Todmorden UFO legend was born.

Of course, Alan's life became a nightmare, as he faced mockery and suspicion, with colleagues gossiping about what 'Gobby Godfrey' had really seen and whether he was just making it all up.

And then, a few weeks later, early in 1981, things got even more complicated when he received a letter with Russian stamps on it. It had been sent from Moscow by a university professor who asked if Alan would kindly write back to him with any information he had on his sighting and also any links it might have to 'the one in Suffolk'.

And this is where the plot really thickens, because 'the one in Suffolk' can only refer to the Rendlesham UFO incident, the other great UFO sighting in British history, where, at Christmas 1980, a group of American servicemen stationed at a US Air Force base there believed they saw a UFO land in Rendlesham Forest.*

Who was this Russian contact? Was Alan suddenly finding himself dragged into some sort of Cold War intrigue? And were there really links between these two incidents that happened just a month apart in different parts of the UK?

It's tantalising wondering what it was about 1980 that sparked so much UFO activity. Here we have what would be considered as two of the most significant British encounters occurring just a few weeks from each other. There were other reports in the vicinity of Todmorden in the build-up to Alan's encounter too that made it seem like it could be part of a pattern; and, of course, it all happens in the same year as Peter sees the alien-like figure in Middlesbrough.

One explanation that sceptics reach for is the release of the Steven Spielberg film *Close Encounters of the Third Kind* in 1977. If *The Exorcist* changed how people perceived Ouija boards, then Spielberg's movie certainly revolutionised interest in UFOs. Could it be that it primed a generation of people to imagine flying objects? It's a tempting explanation, but I'm just not that sure it would have made much impression on a down-to-earth Yorkshire bobby like Alan. Chatting to people in town who've known him since long before he had his sighting, I'm told he was somebody who resolutely did not

---

* I made an episode about the Rendlesham Incident for the second season of the *Uncanny* podcast; it's another fascinating rabbit hole to go down if you have time. Soldiers, like police officers, are the sort of people you expect to be immune to flights of fancy, so what did they see in that forest?

believe in UFOs. In fact, he used to laugh at the idea of them. One man I meet in town says he reported his own sighting to Alan in the late 1970s when he was on his police patrol and Alan told him to clear off and stop making things up!

But now, here Alan was on the wrong side of a close encounter, not only with a UFO but with the Russians. He handed the letter in to his superiors.

'About a week later, I was informed to write back to him, and he wrote back to me after that, and I had to hand the letters in.'

Alan had gone from beat policeman to spy, trying to ascertain what the Soviets knew about the Todmorden and Rendlesham incidents. Alan was deeply uncomfortable about it, but things were about to get worse as, one day, he was called into his chief inspector's office.

'Sat at one side was a guy in civvies with a file on his knee. And of course, me being me, I asked who he was, and he just said, all you need to know is I'm the Man from the Ministry. What he meant by that, whether it was Ministry of Defence or, I don't know, MI5, who knows, but I took an instant dislike to him. He was a bit arrogant, a bit cocky. The file he had was probably about as thick as your finger, a big, bulky thing. He opened it, and inside, I saw my drawing.'

The one that Alan had sketched of the object he saw hovering on Burnley Road. The Man from the Ministry had a clear message for Alan.

'I was ordered under the Official Secrets Act not to disclose anything about Adamski, or my own encounter.'

'So he actually raised the subject of the Adamski murder?'

'Oh yeah, definitely.'

'Do you think the Adamski case notes were in that file of his alongside your drawing?'

'I'm damned sure it was.'

I feel like even I am channelling my inner conspiracy theorist now. What were the powers-that-be, whoever they were, trying to conceal here? And could there be a link to Peter's sighting earlier that year? My head is abuzz. Alan had several other encounters with 'the Man from the Ministry' after this. He got the sense that he was being watched, or even followed.

'He came into my local pub one afternoon, when I were having a drink, and he got within an inch of a good smacking. I told him to – well, I told him to take a long walk off a short pier, but in a good Yorkshire version of it.'

It's another interesting analogy with the Rendlesham case. The US Service personnel who witnessed the UFO felt there had been an attempt by military intelligence to intimidate them into silence. Certainly Alan's police career never recovered. Over the next few years, he believed there was a systematic attempt to drive him out of the police force, something which pushed him to despair.

'I ended up drinking a bottle of whisky every single day. It wrecked me, completely changed me. My marriage broke up. I ended up in a friend's attic bedroom. I'll always remember that Christmas Day. I had no money, I couldn't even buy my kids presents. I were a shambles, an absolute shambles.'

Alan's chiselled, lined face settles into its most mournful expression yet, perhaps wondering how different his life might have been if he hadn't driven down Burnley Road that night in 1980.

I muse on the tragedy of Alan's story as I leave him. There's something about him and Peter, and all of the people I heard speak at Tod UFO Meet, that makes me think of the mortals who came into contact with the gods in Greek myths, granted secrets or gifts that became too much for them, overpowering their minds and eventually leading only to misery and madness. What do you do with your impossible knowledge? It's too strange to sit filed away neatly in your brain, instead throbbing like something radioactive, demanding an answer, and yet to try and find one, to discuss it openly, leads only to mockery or disgrace.

One question will always hover over Alan (no UFO pun intended) – the uncertainty of whether or not he is telling the truth about what he saw that night. I suppose it's a question that sits uncomfortably there with every encounter, ghost or UFO.

Could this person have been lying?

But Alan had so many chances to back out of his story, say he was mistaken or that it was a joke, save himself from ridicule, the loss of his career and the destruction of his marriage and health. Would he really do that to himself because he wanted some sort of fleeting tabloid fame? It seems a high price to pay, to live the rest of his life out, Prometheus-like, tormented until the end of his days.

CHAPTER 16

LIGHTS IN THE SKY

'I believe Alan saw what he tells people he saw,' says Colin Lyall.

It's the morning after Tod UFO Meet and I'm standing in the second-hand bookshop he's run for the last 22 years alongside his other pursuits, a cosy emporium packed with books of every genre, but with, of course, a big science-fiction section. It's not easy to keep an independent bookshop afloat these days, but Colin says the arty demographic of Todmorden helps.

'I get a lot of *Guardian* readers coming in. Everyone in Tod is just about to become an artist or just about to become a writer.'

Or just about to spot an Unidentified Flying Object.

'How many people in Todmorden have seen a UFO, do you think?' I ask.

Colin strokes his beard. 'I think it's a fairly high percentage, probably about half the population.'

'Wow.'

It seems incredible. Todmorden is to UFOs what Venice is to gondolas or Kendal is to mint cake, but could the answer to the boom in the town's sightings since Alan's experience actually be Alan's experience itself? If sceptics believe the *Close Encounters* movie could provoke a rash of sightings globally, isn't it possible that one well-known case could have the same effect locally? Once a place has developed a reputation for UFOs, there's a danger that people start to imagine them everywhere, like somebody staying in a bedroom they've been told is haunted is more likely to imagine a cold breath on their neck.

I ask Colin about the paranoia I saw sweep the Tod UFO Meet circle in the pub last night, the group's anxiety that somebody like 'the Man from the Ministry' would come to call on them. There is a lot of debate in town as to who that man really was – a government operative or just somebody from the upper echelons of the police who felt Alan was embarrassing the force and wanted to shut him up. Whoever he was is irrelevant now really, because the effect on Todmorden has been the same, to create a climate of fear at the idea of becoming the victim of a modern-day witch-hunt.

Colin feels that the whole subject of UFOs is bound up in a narrative of fear.

'Current governments want us to revisit the Cold War notion of aliens and spaceships,' he says, outlining the traditional view held since the 1970s that these unidentified flying objects are either foreign superpowers testing their most secret weapons or aliens up to no good, the view pushed in the enormous amount of science-fiction movies like *War of the Worlds* or *Independence Day*, that have humanity being threatened by extra-terrestrial invaders. More and more, Colin feels that it's a narrative that has been imposed on us by those who seek to divide and rule.

'I am frightened that governments will use UAPs* – their rebranding of UFOs – to create conflict and take control of space. There has to be a bogeyman, something that puts fear into the community you live in. Normally, that's nationalism, a threat to sovereignty, but I think in the future that's going to be UFOs.'

The more stories that Colin has heard through his meetings, the more he has started to think of UFO encounters in a very different way to this adversarial approach.

He tells me about a man who came to the group, a night fisherman who had a series of strange experiences, observing lights in the sky above him that moved at high speed and in a seemingly random manner. The more frequently he saw them, the more the man became convinced that the lights were there for a reason, that they wanted to be seen. One night, the man was feeling very sad, a close relative of his was extremely ill and dying, and he called out into the night, a primal roar of angst and pain poured into the universe.

Above him, the light blinked!

It was as if his message had been received. Colin has heard other stories like this – another man who felt, like Peter in Middlesbrough, that he was being followed by lights in the sky, then when his children's kittens died and he had buried them in the garden, the lights appeared and hovered over that very spot as if showing some sort of empathy for the loss.

It's stories like this that are pushing Colin into a radical new personal theory on UFOs. That what people are experiencing in

---

* Unidentified Aerial Phenomena, the acronym the Pentagon has chosen to refer to these sightings. It is also sometimes referred to as Unidentified Anomalous Phenomena – try saying that after a couple of glasses of wine.

these sightings is not a literal physical encounter with an object but some emotional connection with an energy force, and that the reason not all of us see them, is because some people, for whatever reason, are more able to tune in to that energy than others. It's almost exactly what Gordon from Newark Museum told Jenny Turner. Some of us are like radios.

I came here thinking that ghost experiences and UFO experiences had similarities but I'm suddenly hit by a realisation that it might go beyond that. Could they actually be just different aspects of this same energy force, different notes in the same tune?

'Do you think ghosts and UFOs could actually be one and the same?'

'I think they have the same source,' Colin says. 'Call it a ghost or an alien or whatever, and it has a consciousness because it responds.'

Colin is using a word that I feel I've heard a lot in the emails I get sent. That word that Vee used to describe the presence in her house.

'It'. The unknowable thing.

'Colin,' I say, 'what do you think "it" is?'

'It is the source of all consciousness. I think we come from it and we all go back to it.'

'And this would be what that some people call God?'

'Yes, some people label it that.'

'I started out on this journey, fascinated by belief. I actually said, "Some people might have chosen God, I chose ghosts ..."'

'But actually you're choosing the same thing,' says Colin. 'It all goes there. When you hear people describe near-death experiences, the language they use to describe them correlates almost exactly to how people describe a UFO abduction experience. I think that possibly, when you die, your consciousness leaves you and goes into some sort of greater consciousness which every so often we are able to make contact with, and that contact is some kind of emotional connection between you and it, because that is the one thing that everyone says when having these experiences, you have that sense that you are looking at it but it is looking at you.'

I think of Peter and that sense of personal connection he felt with the object he saw in the sky. The idea that metallic alien warships might be following a teenage boy in Middlesbrough seems ludicrous, but the idea that he might be having an emotional connection with some sort of higher state of consciousness feels poetic and beautiful, like some rite of passage. I love Colin's theory, but ...

You know me and my buts ...

How does the figure emerging from the ball fit into all of this? Lights in the sky, I can buy into them being ethereal drifting emotions, but how do we explain physical things like a figure walking down a garden path, or the craft that Alan saw in front of him? Those aren't emotions, are they?

I describe Peter's story to Colin in all its unsettling oddness, hoping desperately that he can make it fit into his theory, because I now want to believe it more than anything. It feels like a deliciously vast cup of sweet tea to counteract all the fear and shock that people feel about these experiences. Has he, I ask him, ever come across anything like what happened to Peter amongst all the many encounters he's been told of?

He nods and tells me about a woman who came to Tod UFO Meet whose daughter had seen a mysterious flying object out of the window of their house.

'Then the daughter became quite ill and the woman wondered if she should take her to see a doctor. But before she had made her decision, there was a knock on the back door. A man was standing there. He announced that he was a doctor and said that he had heard the woman's daughter was ill. He gave the woman a prescription for some medicine that would help her daughter get better. The woman went to the local pharmacy to get the medicine then came back and gave it to her daughter.

'After the daughter had taken the medicine, something very strange happened. A bright light came out of her daughter's ear. It was a fluorescent green object that the woman described as being about the size of a lozenge. It came out of the girl's ear, hovered up and around the room and then went out of the window.'

Colin pauses, looking me in the eye.

'Where do you go with that?'

We both reflect on this for a moment, staring out of the window. I can see the similarities with Peter's tale – the palpably, almost ludicrously bizarre event described by the sensible person that you trust.

'Who was the doctor, how did he know her daughter was ill? The prescription was real, it got real medicine, but how do we explain the thing that came out of her ear? I've heard a series of stories that have these curious elements in now, this "something extra".'

I look up sharply, stirred from my contemplation. Colin's use of those words, the same ones Ailsa used to describe the presence in her apartment, have caught me off guard.

'It's just a total random event in someone's life,' he says. 'It doesn't fit any of the patterns or norms, but it happened.'

I email Peter when I get back to London. I tell him about my experiences in Todmorden, and Colin's theory on the emotional connection between people and the lights in the sky. He tells me he can relate to this, and describes another experience he had when he was much older and married with children. One night he saw a set of five lights in the sky above Portobello, a seaside area of Edinburgh in Scotland where he was living at that time. He felt a strange connection to them and, a week later, he got his wife's parents to babysit and took her out for dinner near to where it happened. He had an ulterior motive; he wanted to see if the lights would appear again, and if, this time, she would see them too.

'I thought, I don't want to be one of these people who is always by himself when he sees things.'

Sure enough, as they left the restaurant on the seafront, there they were, five lights hovering in the sky above, and Peter had a crazy idea.

'I thought I might as well try and communicate with one of them. I didn't tell my wife I was doing this, I just said in my head, "If you can come down, I'll know you can hear me." And at that, one of them flew straight down and hovered about two metres away from us both, this ball of light. It wasn't a craft or anything. It was like a bubble, but lit from inside, a huge amount of lights flashing around inside it, almost like a jellyfish. It had that kind of luminosity. And it just hovered there in front of us. And I said, "Oh, well, thanks for that. We don't mean you any harm." That's the only thing I could think of saying in my mind to it, and then it just sort of bobbed in a very slow motion, out over the sea, and vanished. It was the weirdest thing ever.'

If Peter was fascinated by what he saw, his wife was frightened. 'She said, "I saw it, but I don't want to believe it's true."'

I'm intrigued by the similarities between the night fisherman's story that Colin told me and Peter's seeming ability to will the lights into being and then communicate with them. I ask him if he's ever had the urge to try it again.

'Yeah, once or twice, but I don't act on it.'

It's sad, I think, and I wonder how much of an effect his wife's reaction had on him, whether the excitement of making contact with something is outweighed by his inability to ever explain it to somebody else.

I'm still thinking about it that night, as I read my kids a *Star Wars* storybook at bedtime and then turn off the light. As I lie next to my youngest son in the dark, listening to his breathing change as he slips into sleep, I think about how very complicated we adults have made the whole concept of belief.

You and I have ruminated on the desire we have as humans to impose patterns and find narratives. When investigating ghosts, we set ourselves the challenge of making sense of what happened. We wonder if the banging on the wall could be the ghost of the former owner of the house, and when we learn that he died in the bedroom where the banging took place, it feels like a victory for logic. We have managed to impose order on chaos, like tidying a messy room, taking all the strange bits of someone's odd experience, and sorting it into a neat narrative that, however fantastical the events may be, makes sense. Sceptics do the same, taking the same set of events and weaving them into a different story, though often with the same reference points – 'You knew the former owner died in that room, so when you heard the sound of mice in the walls, you imagined it was him'.

Black and white polarised theories, as ordered and satisfyingly logical as the squares of a chessboard. And it is only by imposing this order that we judge whether or not we believe in the thing before us. But, perhaps, between this black and white, there is grey; a place where our experiences cannot be explained so easily and resist categorisation.

Because there is an alternative way of looking at the encounters people have described to me and to Colin, to not judge them by our ability to explain them but rather by our failure to. Perhaps we should embrace the randomness of these mysteries of the universe and see that not as a frustration but as the proof that these things are paranormal, in its most literal definition of being beyond or outside the normal.

Colin and I are both spending our lives trying to make sense of the experiences of the people we meet, but making sense of them doesn't have to mean coming up with an answer, it can be to accept that they are unexplainable and be able to live with that.

Colin's last words to me before I left were, 'I love the fact that the problem is never going to be solved. There is no answer, the important thing is the human perspective, being able to make sense of and understand ourselves.'

Once we stop seeing these things as problems to be solved, we can step back and see them for what else they are, moments of random magic, burps of chaos that we just happened to be near to, and instead of fear, we can perhaps feel lucky to have had an insight that very few others will ever have, insights like Harry Martindale's in that cellar in York, or Graham Morris's in Enfield, a sudden moment of awareness that there is more to life that we had previously thought.

It's a theory, right? And it'd be a really nice way to tie up a book. There's a big part of my brain saying, wrap it up now, Robins, walk away from the laptop, leave the reader on this philosophical, poetic note. But you know what? I haven't devoted my life to the pursuit of trying to understand the paranormal just to walk away from it that easily. Maybe some people, like Colin, can accept the joy of things remaining unexplainable, but I'm nowhere near that Zen.

I want answers.*

And I want one answer in particular, because of all the mysteries in this book, there's one that troubles me more than any other. An intriguing, frightening enigma that we have only heard the half of.

What the hell happened to Andrew in the Wilsons' apartment in Rome? I don't know about you, but I never ever walk away from a challenge, and there is no way I am leaving you without trying to make sense of that poltergeist.

So, as I leave the kids' bedroom, I go into my own to pack a suitcase. I have an early start tomorrow, taking a flight to Rome, because I have finally had an email from Andrew that made my heart leap. After weeks of trying, he has managed to change the Venerable English College's mind.

We can get into the apartment.

---

* Copyright Tom Cruise in *A Few Good Men*.

REASONS TO BELIEVE #3

NEWCASTLE, DECEMBER 1996

This is the way the world ends. Not with a bang, but with a feeling of intense disappointment and regret.

I am certainly dying.

It's the early hours of the morning and I am crouched on the bathroom floor having a heart attack. It's like my heart is actually attempting to leave my chest, so violently is it exploding in its uneven, arrhythmic last dance, a shitty out-of-time tango.

I'm in Newcastle, in my childhood home, which feels oddly, sadly fitting. Might as well nick another T.S. Eliot quote: 'In my beginning is my end', though I hadn't expected it to come quite this quickly.

I'm 20, back home for the Christmas holidays from university, back on the street I grew up on, where games of cops and robbers sprawled for hours, bikes were ridden until our parents called us in for tea, and footballs were lost over the walls of neighbours so grumpy you did not even dare ring their doorbell, the street we roamed as teenagers when no parent wanted us in their house and where first romances were contemplated under the hazy glow of streetlights. I'd half expected to tell you all of that is flashing in front of my eyes now, but it turns out that's a load of bollocks. You don't get a highlights reel of your achievements when you're dying – one final victory lap around your life – you don't have time, you just have a torturous moment of feeling everything slipping away and being really bloody sad and scared.

Maybe it's the English Literature student in me – I mean, that's what I would be going back to study next week if I wasn't dying – but I keep thinking of great lines about death. Hamlet, someone who thought about it more than most, described death as 'the undiscovered country', which makes it sound kind of romantic, the sort of place you'd have considered visiting on your gap year, provided you could get the right vaccinations, but right now, having actually bought a ticket for that trip, I'm thinking it's probably undiscovered because it is really shit, like one of those package hotels you instantly regret having been duped into booking by the misleadingly cropped photo on their website that omits the building site, swamp and active volcano.

But all these musings are really split-second distractions from the main event here. The pretty mutha-fizzling terrifying main event, which is –

I can see angels.

I can see actual angels.

I'm hallucinating, I get that, but they still feel pretty real and it DOES NOT feel at all comforting. It's disorienting, frightening, strange. When you hear people describe near-death experiences, they often speak of seeing a white light. Well, this feels like a strobe, pushed right up into my face. I don't feel some sense of blissful calm or acceptance, being lifted by gorgeous blonde figures clad in robes of most brilliant Daz Doorstep Challenge levels of whiteness. Or some sort of euphoric 'becoming an emotion', like in Colin's view of consciousness. These angels are trying to force me to a place I do not want to go, a state I would do anything to escape. All I want now, with every fibre of my soon-to-be-deceased being, is to pull a U-turn, to reverse away from the light and get the hell back to normality.

Because this is what is making me so sad. I really enjoy my life. I've been having such a good time at university, I have friends I really like, so many plans of things I want to do next term, plays I want to direct, comedy sketches I want to write, books I want to read. There is so much I want to DO, and I feel like an utter fool because, like a character in *The Ring*, or Ouija board-possessed Regan in *The Exorcist*, I can't help feeling this is all my own fault. I have transgressed.

The reason I am here, now lying on the mat on the bathroom floor, taking my final few desperate dying gasps, is that I have had TOO good a time. I've spent the last year and a bit since arriving at university partying hard, enjoying myself to the max. After a first 18 years of my life characterised by being a really good boy, thoughtful, diligent and with an almost pathological fear of getting into trouble, I have really let my hair down since leaving home and gone on a non-stop tear-up of parties, clubbing, endless late nights and very little sleep. I have pushed my body too far, too hard. Done too much, much too young, to quote some other great poets, The Specials.

And I regret it. I really regret it. Seeing how it's all turned out, having to exchange my friends for hallucinatory angels and the fun and buzz of student life for the enforced retirement of death, I just feel stupid. Like when you're a little kid and you're told not to touch an ornament because you'll break it and then you touch it and you do. A huge face-reddening surge of feeling really bloody dumb and wishing the ground would swallow you up.

Except actually that's the last thing I want this time around – I have no desire to go into that ground, to be an absence, a memory, a plot to be visited and cried over, marked only by a piece of stone carved with words that struggle to express even a fraction of all the many things you were and tried to be when you were alive.

To be honest, more than anything, I feel embarrassed.

But ultimately fear wins out over embarrassment and, as I look down at my heart visibly trying to break through the skin of my chest in its last few sledgehammer blows, I decide that there's really only one thing to do.

I'd better go and tell my mum.

My body is laid out on the bed, a sheet over me, a doctor standing by my side.

'What has just happened,' he says to my tearful mum, 'was a panic attack.'

I look up at him. As well as being a doctor, he is also my uncle, my mum's brother, who, in one of those moments of blessed synchronicity, was staying with us this Christmas, visiting from his home in Australia. It was he who was able to calm me down, who gave me one of his sleeping pills and who is now, in the reassuring light of morning, talking me through exactly what my body was up to in the (no pun intended) dead of night.*

I had been so completely convinced that I was dying – and let me tell you it's a horrific thing to have to wake your mum up and tell her that – but it was not a heart attack.

I was right in one way though, it was my body reacting to the last year and a half of relentless partying at university, telling me that I had pushed it too close to the edge and that I needed to back off.

As the sun glints off the white bedsheets, last night feels other-worldly, like I'm a character from *Nightmare on Elm Street*, fresh from doing battle with Freddy Krueger in my dreams. This should be a happy ending. I get to live to see another day, having learnt my lesson, without that lesson costing me my life. What felt like a medical emergency of the most serious kind was actually some-thing that many thousands of people experience at some point in their lifetime, scary and unsettling, but not deadly.

I should be able to move on, but … I can't. *In my end is my beginning.* This moment is the start of something.

I often talk about the life-changing nature of the experiences people describe to me. How once they believe they have seen a ghost, they find it impossible to go back to being the person they were. They are marked. This is how it is for me. That night engen-ders something that slowly but surely takes form inside me.

A deep and profound fear of death.

It gnaws away like a parasite, finding its way into every inch of my being, until all I can think about is death. Every little twinge in

---

* Actually there was a pun intended, I tricked you.

my body or head is a heart attack or brain tumour. I live in a perma-
nent state of being braced for my immediate demise, gripped by a
constant fear that the next breath will be my last. It is, as you can
perhaps imagine, utterly exhausting. It gets in the way of everything,
making it hard to concentrate on my university work. Why bother
writing essays if you are about to pop your clogs? It stops me from
sleeping and socialising. I can't concentrate on what anybody is
saying to me because I am a sweaty, terrified mess. I have to leave
parties or other events because I am overcome with an utterly
numbing dread that I am about to die that makes me want to cry.

It is the worst time of my life. All of the fun and carefree joy
I had in me before this point has vanished, to be replaced by a
morbid, nihilistic despair. And it lasts for a really long time. Most
of my second year at university is spent in this way, a private terror
that locks me into my own head, unable to explain it to people as I
know how mad it will sound.

Familiar, huh?

It is this, I realise now, many years later, that gives me an affinity
for and empathy with the people who send me their stories of ghostly
encounters. I am haunted by what I experienced in the bathroom of
my home in Newcastle. My own ghost that lives in my head. And I did
not know how to talk about it, how I could convey all the fear I felt
about it to people who had not experienced it themselves. It changed
my concept of reality, opened me to things I had never previously
contemplated, and made me question the very nature of my existence.

The thing that saved me was a form of scepticism. I had given
myself over by this point to a total, deep belief that I was really
about to die at some point in the very near future, that any day I got

through was simply a lucky escape, delaying the inevitable. There were enough people close to me who noticed what was going on and were worried, and I was encouraged and helped to see an NHS psychotherapist. They were able to explain to me that many of the sensations I was experiencing were physical rather than mental, my body going into defence mode in reaction to the amount of danger my brain was signalling to it. So when my heart beat incredibly fast it wasn't gearing up for a heart attack but was actually pumping blood around my body faster to get me into a state of readiness for whatever threat my mind was perceiving.

I had become a lizard.

When you have the evolutionary biology of the 'fight or flight' mechanism explained to you, it all makes a lot of sense. Your body preparing you to be able to outrun predators is incredibly useful if you are a caveman surrounded by them, but actually quite disturbing and inconvenient if you are a modern-day student sitting in a lecture hall and your brain has somehow got confused and pushed the panic button.

Eventually, during these few sessions, I came to understand why I was feeling how I was, and, somehow, knowing my enemy made things easier, no longer having to imagine the very worst form my personal bogeyman could take. I was still often gripped by panic and thoughts of death, but, over time, I was able to talk myself down from these precipices, to remind myself that *I* was in control here, I was the one sending those danger signals and if I concentrated really hard I might be able to make the signals stop. It took a long time, but eventually the panic morphed into anxiety and then the anxiety morphed into worry and then, sometime in my third year at uni, I found I felt happy again, that I could concentrate on the business of living rather than fixate on the sadness of dying.

But it never truly left me. For a long time after that, I had a very deep fear of death that still resides in me today. I think it is why I have become so frightened of heights, that proximity to death I felt walking down those steps on Skellig Michael, and I am convinced that it is, more than anything else, the motivator for my deepening interest in ghosts.

I have a theory that the reason we Brits and Americans are so scary-ghost-fixated is that we are particularly bad at dealing with the idea of death. There are cultures in other parts of the world that are more at peace with the fact of mortality, more in tune with the idea of ghosts as a celebration of the continuing relevance of our ancestors.

I wonder if, secretly, that desire to overcome death is what unconsciously spurs all of us into an interest in the supernatural. I've realised over the last few years that 'Do ghosts exist?' is the one question you could start a conversation with with anyone anywhere in the world. Because we all have skin in this game; trying to make sense of what happens to us after we die is the basis of every religion ever formed. I said earlier that my atheist upbringing made me fascinated by belief, but that I chose ghosts over God. I think what I've realised is that they are two prongs on the same path towards trying to find an answer to that biggest of all questions. It seems so senseless that we would spend a lifetime building up an incredible array of skills, memories and experiences – living, loving, laughing and endlessly communicating – for it all to just stop in a heartbeat or, rather, the absence of one. That was the most overwhelming feeling I felt lying on my bathroom floor, that it seemed utterly, tragically pointless if we simply cease to be.

So I am drawn in the most magnetic way to the idea that there is something beyond death and that our unique human ability to communicate goes on; that the loved ones we've lost might still be out there, or that one day we could return to those we leave behind. I am pretty certain I am not alone in that. Maybe deep inside you feel the same way?

In 1972, a group of people gathered around a table at a university research facility in Toronto, Canada. Their aim was a strange one. They had created a fictional 'ghost', a character they had constructed fictitious biographical information for, who they then planned to try and make contact with through a séance. If this sounds like another BBC Christmas ghost story like *The Stone Tape*, I assure you it is completely and utterly true. It became known as The Philip Experiment, after the name the researchers gave to their ghost. 'Philip Aylesford', as they called him, had a life story worthy of a classic ghost tale. They decided he'd been born in 1624, had been knighted aged 16 and fought in the English Civil War, becoming friends with the future King Charles II and working for him as a spy. Philip's marriage was unhappy though, and he fell in love with another woman who was accused of witchcraft and burnt at the stake. All this was too much for the poor man and Philip died by suicide in 1654, aged 30.

The group of people who met to attempt to make contact with this imagined person was led by mathematical geneticist Dr A.R. George Owen and overseen by a psychologist called Dr Joel Whitton. They met over weeks and months, conducting séances with absolutely no result.

You can't contact a fictional ghost, right?

But then, Owen changed the test conditions, dimming the stark lights of the lab room and changing the set-up so that it felt more akin to a genuine séance environment. With the stage set in this way, things began to happen. The group started to feel a sense of presence, the table vibrated, there were strange breezes, inexplicable echoes and rapping sounds that seemed to come in response to questions they asked about Philip's life, as if he really had taken shape and decided to reply to them. On one occasion, the table tilted onto one leg, and some other times it seemed to move across the room of its own accord. The sitters appeared to have got what they wanted. Somehow, through a collective act of will, they had made the fictional Philip real.

There's a concept within the paranormal called a 'tulpa'. The word is derived from Tibetan mythology and it describes the concept of a supernatural entity somehow brought to life by an act of collective will like this. It's the idea that belief can literally bring something into some form of existence, like the surge of electricity passing through Frankenstein's monster.

Is this what ghosts are, I sometimes wonder? The human race unconsciously engaged in a mass act of prayer, desperately willing to life the fictitious wraiths we have created as barriers between us and the bleak finality of death, until we have been wishing for so long that we do actually see them?

Belief in ghosts has been a constant in all human civilisations since prehistoric times. We have stubbornly refused to consign them to the scrapheap of redundant superstition along with elves and unicorns and other such things once held to be true, because they offer us a comfort blanket, a buffer zone between life and its opposite. And, standing here, after thousands of years of stubbornly believing in these things (or stubbornly not believing in them – Team Sceptic, I hear you), the million-dollar question is *why?*

Is it because they are real, actual proof that there's an afterlife? Or are they a fantasy to block out our buried knowledge that there is not? Basically, do we see ghosts because they exist, or because deep down we can't bear the idea they don't?

I know which one I want to be true, and this is why Andrew and I are now at Stansted Airport, boarding a flight to Rome to investigate a poltergeist in an apartment owned by priests. What will my mum, the lapsed Catholic turned devout atheist, make of this?

Andrew has never travelled budget before; he's more used to luxurious business-class transatlantic flights, so we are each introducing the other to fantastical new experiences here, though I suspect he may find Ryanair even more horrifying than poltergeists.

As the plane takes off Andrew insists on pulling out a speedometer app on his phone, measuring the plane's take-off speed with a boyish enthusiasm. He keeps waving it in my face, the numbers spinning and racking up in a blur, but I can't bear to look. I am a nervous flyer. It's not so much the flying I don't like, but what would happen if we crash. You know me by now, right?

'Two hundred and sixty kilometres an hour!' squeals Andrew as we lift into the blue blue sky over Stansted. 'Can you believe it?'

This whole journey has always been about belief, and there's something I want to believe in more than anything else, the thing that lies hidden under all the fear.

Hope.

Are we really about to find proof of life after death in an apartment in the eternal city?

CASE ONE PART TWO

THE
ENGLISH
COLLEGE

CHAPTER 17

A STRANGE MEETING IN THE CAMPO DE' FIORI

The taxi driver says he's never seen rain like this. It lashes down in suitably dramatic fashion on the Piazza Navona, one of Rome's most theatrical squares. Central to its baroque grandeur is the architectural equivalent of a rap battle. Gian Lorenzo Bernini designed the Fountain of the Four Rivers, the spectacular sculpture in the middle of the square, and his great nemesis Francesco Borromini designed the Church of Sant Agnese that stands proudly opposite. It's said that Bernini carved one of his statues holding up a hand to its eyes to block the view of the church, as a diss to his rival.

It's a great historical anecdote. It'd be even better if it was true, but the fountain was actually built before the church. A good lesson in human beings' enduring ability to discount the facts if they get in the way of a good story. I love these urban myths and half-truths about a city that get passed down by those who fall in love with it. In my case that is Andrew, who's clearly retained a deep affinity for Rome since his formative teen years here and has been impressing me with his Italian banter in the cab. It's how I know the driver's view that we are witnessing the worst weather

Rome has ever seen. Even in January, he wants us to know, this is not normal.

It feels fitting, I think, as we pile out of the taxi into the torrential downpour, to have come to one of the most beautiful cities in the world on the hunt for a poltergeist and find it transformed into something hellish by a near apocalyptic thunderstorm. I remember a term from my English A level – 'a pathetic fallacy'. It always sounded to me like something a man might have to apologise to his date for* ... but it's a technique used by writers whereby the weather in a scene mirrors the inner feelings of a character. If I was making this story up, I'd definitely have picked today's weather for the moment we potentially go head-to-head with the kitchen-based poltergeist. The view over the square reminds me of the 1970s horror movie *Don't Look Now* – a great film if you haven't seen it[†] – set in Venice in the winter, the pomp and splendour of an iconic city rendered mournful and sinister out of season.

We run, trying to dodge huge, deceptively deep puddles that have formed, like mini-lakes. The gusts of wind add an extra challenge, turning our umbrellas inside out in that way you normally only see in comedy films, forcing the rain horizontally into our

---

* I now know that is actually a 'pathetic phallus'.

† There's a recurring motif in the movie of a figure in a red raincoat, which was one of the inspirations for the red coat I wore for the photo on the front cover of this book, and has now become something of a signature look for me. I was lucky enough recently to meet one of the people who wrote the movie, Allan Scott, now in his eighties and something of a writing legend – he also co-created *The Queen's Gambit*. I told him that my *Uncanny* image was a loving homage to his film. He insisted I drank Chablis with lunch. It seemed like a fair exchange.

faces. By the time we make it to the other side of the piazza, we are soaked, water sloshing around our shoes, trousers plastered to legs. I'm following Andrew, partly because I might drown my phone if I pull it out for directions in this rain, but mostly because I can see he's already working off the inner compass he had as a 17-year-old, leading us down narrow streets towards our destination ...

Via Di Monserrato. Home to the Venerable English College and the apartment owned by them, where Andrew and Ailsa had their experiences in the early 1980s. It's fair to say that getting access has not been easy. Andrew's first emails to the English College were met with a flat no, but a career in film producing and a family background in diplomacy has taught him that the key to getting what you want is who you know, so he drew on a few well-placed ambassadorial contacts over here to pull a few strings. Brilliantly and surprisingly, a message came back saying we could visit, but ideally on just one particular day in less than a week's time, when the apartment would be vacant as the previous tenants moved out and another set prepared to move in. Cue a mad flurry of flight and hotel booking, and here we are, soaking wet, but very excited. The game, my friends, is definitely afoot.

But first, we have a stop to make, because I want you to hear the next, deeply bloody odd, instalment of Andrew's story in the place where it happened – remember, he told us it was about to get scary, and he really wasn't wrong – we just need to find the exact spot where the scares started to set in ...

'Aha!' Andrew barks, as, almost perfectly on cue, the rain subsides and we emerge from a narrow passage into Campo de' Fiori. The campo is in itself an impossibility – a rectangular square. It now houses a bustling street-market, but it has been many things over the years, including a place of public execution. On 17 February 1600, the philosopher and cosmologist Giordano Bruno was brought here to be burnt alive for crimes of heresy that included claiming that the stars were distant suns surrounded by their own planets and that the universe was infinite and could have no centre, something considered utterly unacceptable by a Catholic Church that believed itself to be that centre. Bruno has proved to have the last laugh though; his statue now stands in the square, defiantly facing the direction of the Vatican. High on his stone plinth, he cuts an impressive hooded, caped figure, like a Renaissance Luke Skywalker preparing to square off against Darth Vader.

We pass him and head for the furthest corner of the square. 'Yes, yes, yes!' whoops Andrew triumphantly, as we reach a bar called The Drunken Ship, positioned insalubriously opposite a kebab takeaway called Shawarma Express, the two clearly locked in an unhealthy reciprocal relationship, one feeding the sloshed customers of the other. Andrew looks in through the bar's windows, then nods happily. 'This is it! We were sitting … right about here …'

He spins and points to an outside table made out of a barrel. His eyes are alight, and I realise that this is an emotional experience for him, retracing his footsteps through a labyrinth of long-buried memories, in search of his own personal minotaur, an experience that's lurked in the darkest recesses of his psyche, never fully acknowledged, and certainly never explained. I realise how reassuring it must have been to hear Ailsa recount her own experiences of the apartment, confirming that this must have been real.

We take shelter under an awning; the rain is easing but the weather today is very different to the balmy summer evening when Andrew sat here back in 1983.

'I was on this side,' he says, tapping the table, 'and they ... they were there, opposite me, staring in utter shock.'

And so I ask him to tell me what happened here at this little touristy bar, because it turns out Ailsa was totally right when she thought the priests of the English College weren't being totally honest about what they knew regarding the happenings in the apartment.

There was a lot, lot more going on.

☦

It's tempting to wonder what Giordano Bruno's brilliant mind would have made of the mysteries of the Wilsons' kitchen, thinks Andrew. It's two days since that night and he has been able to think of little else, the strangeness of those few hours of babysitting throbbing disconcertingly in his brain like an arrhythmic pulse.

Right now, though, he's sitting in the shade of this far corner of the Campo de' Fiori, feeling deliciously, intoxicatingly grown-up. He's wearing the new Fila coat he persuaded his mum to buy him, the height of current fashion – a young man enjoying observing the early evening social life of a Roman summer's night, sipping a cappuccino, only slightly jealous of the pints of Guinness his two companions wield.

Who would have known that priests drank Guinness?

But it's easy to forget these two young men with him are priests; they're only about three years older than Andrew, affable, handsome, athletic, chatting easily about cricket and rugby, the common language between Australians and Brits. They're students from the English College that Andrew has befriended through the social circles linking the college and the Australian Embassy. It's a mystery, he thinks, why two charismatic young men would want to give up the world for a life of celibacy and devotion, but they seem happy and contented in their choice, and it's done him good to spend the last hour laughing and chatting with them.

Only now, as the two lads return from the bar clutching a second pint each – who would have known that priests drank more than one pint of Guinness? – do the strange events of two nights ago force their way back into Andrew's mind. A street-hawker wanders past their table selling red roses, takes one look and realises the boys are not his crowd. The priests sip the white head from their jet-black pints, ready to slide back into chatting sport.

What the hell, thinks Andrew, I'll tell them about it.

The worst that can happen is they'll laugh, right? Say that his imagination got the better of him. And perhaps that's what he secretly wants to hear? To have his experiences explained, and dispelled, the minotaur slain. Or maybe they'll be mildly intrigued, congratulate him on a fascinating anecdote and he can move on from feeling so unsettled, relocate the story in his head from the 'troublingly weird' drawer of his mental filing cabinet to the 'good to bring out at parties' one.

Instead, something very odd happens.

As Andrew says, 'You'll never guess what happened to me', and launches into his account of that evening, detailing teleporting postcards, stacks of plates, and taps with a mind of their own, he watches their whole demeanour change. With each instalment, each new kitchen item weirdly out of place, they go quieter and quieter, until, by the time he's reached the return of the Wilsons and the final dramatic act of the kitchen misbehaving, the two priests are silent, the colour drained entirely from their handsome celibate faces.

Andrew is worried. Has he accidentally offended them? Is it a faux pas to raise the possibility of paranormal activity to representatives of the Catholic Church, he wonders, with a nervous backwards glance to the statue of Giordano Bruno.

The boy priests look to each other, and then back to him.

'You need to come with us,' one says.

All trace of the jocularity of earlier in the evening is gone. They both feel older, their faces set in an expression Andrew can't quite interpret.

'Where?' he asks.

'To the English College.'

And then, from the other priest: 'We need you to tell this story to the Monsignor.'

Oh dear. This does not sound promising. The Monsignor is the most senior figure at the English College, the boss of these student priests, most venerable priest at a venerable institution, and Andrew doesn't suppose it's a particularly good thing to be dragged in front of him, though at this moment he also can't think of any good reason to refuse.

The priests are already on their feet, their nearly full pints forgotten, an urgency to their movements.

'Now?' says Andrew, flustered.

'Right now.'

Andrew rises, zipping his fashionable Fila coat up to fight off a strange shiver now coursing down his spine. Because he has recognised that expression on the young men's faces.

It's fear.

CHAPTER 18

THE APARTMENT

The door to the English college is huge, wooden, medieval. It feels oddly surreal to be here, I think, as I push against the ancient wood and enter. Inside, the building is even more impressive, ornate yet sparse corridors lined with rows of portraits of English cardinals, their robes and caps a vivid blood-red. Andrew is next to me, emitting little noises of recognition, seeing the place again for the first time in 40 years, with the eyes of a man rather than a daunted teenager, though what he is seeing is largely unchanged. I suspect the English College hasn't really altered much for centuries. The two priests led him to this very entrance hall on that evening in 1983, rushing him through the corridors, past the painted cardinals, on a hunt for the Monsignor, Andrew at a loss as to why things had become so urgent and dramatic.

'Danny! Andrew!'

The friendly Italian voice comes from Emanuela, the college's finance manager and holder of the keys to the apartment, who we've been corresponding with by email. If she's perplexed or unsettled by our ghost-hunting mission, she doesn't show it, chatting away politely, asking about our journey, apologising for the weather, as she leads us back out of the college on to the street, towards the beige-coloured residential building next door.

Last night, after we'd landed at Ciampino Airport and driven into central Rome, I made Andrew come with me to Via Di Monserrato. I wanted to case the joint, see if there were any clues I could pick up about the apartment from the outside. Was there some obvious way a wily kitchen-rearranging intruder might climb in through a window unseen? Or perhaps a nest full of jackdaws on the roof who'd got tired of building fires in Wales and gone on holiday to Rome to mess with Ailsa's kitchen.

We walked up and down the street several times. The weather was fine then, the calm before the storm. Caffe Peru, the little coffee shop and bar directly below the apartment, was in full swing, conversation wafting through the night air. I stood and gazed up at the apartment's windows with its dark brown shutters, the smooth, light surfaces of its walls. I could spot no obvious anomalies that would yield such weirdness. The experience was interesting but frustrating – like that first hour of the Boxing Day sales when you're only allowed to browse. I wanted to be inside, investigating and now …

Clang!

We nearly are. The metal gate closes firmly behind us as we mount the stairs, each flight leading me closer to what has now taken on the mystique of a crime scene in my head. I look to Andrew, his face shifting into a serious, apprehensive expression.

'We are here.'

It's Emanuela, but I can see Andrew mouthing the same words, looking at the familiar door.

Click clunk.

Emanuela turns the key in the lock and ...

We are in.

Andrew and I enter the hallway. Emanuela doesn't follow, telling us she'll meet us downstairs when we are finished. The door closes softly and we are alone, standing in what seems to be an almost entirely empty apartment, devoid of any furniture or personalised touches.

Well, not quite. As we begin to explore, we see that there are little piles of discarded or forgotten objects in some corners, the detritus of the previous tenants. In one room I enter, there's just a solitary chair sitting eerily in the middle. My horror-movie brain kicks in and I imagine either Andrew or myself tied to it later on, a flickering lightbulb illuminating words written in blood (probably ours) on the walls –

'Why did you come back?'

'Want to see just how badly this kitchen can behave?'

'Now this,' comes Andrew's voice right behind me, 'was the music room. There was a piano in here.'

'This place is bloody massive,' I say.

Which is an understatement. The apartment is absolutely enormous. As we walk through room after room, it's hard to imagine how any family could ever find a use for them all, in fact you could comfortably accommodate several families here, and they'd never need to meet. I have to be honest, though, I'm finding it hard to reconcile the rooms I'm seeing with the splendour Ailsa described, the bustle and excitement of diplomatic soirées attended by the great and the good. The cardinal's golden jelly moulds are still resplendently glued to the dark wood ceiling, but there's something forlorn about everything else that sits underneath them. The degree to which the apartment feels abandoned is almost shocking, every fixture and fitting ripped out, leaving it feeling like an empty shell, sad and lonely, and nowhere is this more true than …

'The kitchen!'

'Oh my flipping God,' I say, realising that casual blasphemy in somewhere owned by priests is probably taking a liberty, but I have the heady sensation of being a paranormal version of Neil Armstrong finally stepping onto the moon after years of planning. I'm in a room that had begun to feel almost mythic to me, as I combed through Andrew's testimony during late nights in my shed in Walthamstow, trying to make sense of it, to visualise the cupboards, the sinks, the fridge.

As it turns out, that doesn't get much easier actually being here. Literally every single item, apart from the boiler, has been torn out of the room in preparation for a full refurbishment, holes and

loose wires in the walls the only evidence of their former positions. Not even the sinks remain. But I can get a sense of the space, and Andrew's memories are kicking into gear to paint the scene.

'So the fridge was here, and where I found the postcards was ...'

He takes several large paces across the green tiles.

'Here.'

He points to a patch on the floor. It's clear to me that not even the most extreme freak gust of wind would have transported them that far. Likewise, the idea of plates travelling down from the height of where the top cupboards would have been to this hard tiled floor without breaking seems equally impossible.

I breathe out, closing my eyes a moment, trying to imagine myself in Andrew's shoes that night, envisaging the scene before him. I've been in 'haunted' locations before. I spent a night once at 30 East Drive, a house in Yorkshire that is the scene of the notorious 'Black Monk of Pontefract' case, a vividly violent alleged poltergeist haunting. The house is now owned by a film producer who made a movie about the case, and has become something of a go-to destination for ghost hunters, a paranormal Airbnb.* The official website recounts all the things that visitors have witnessed there, from seeing objects move, to finding strange scratches and bruises on their bodies. I went there with the hope that I too might be in some way affected, and I find myself doing the same now, desperately willing 'something' to happen, yearning for 'a sign'. As I open my eyes, I'd like nothing more than for something to fly right past them across the room, a reprise of what Andrew witnessed here to welcome him back.

---

* Or should that be Scarebnb?

Nothing happened to me at East Drive, the only feeling I experienced was one of anticlimax, and I seem to be equally out of luck with my poltergeist-baiting here. Perhaps the problem is there *aren't* any objects to hurl around, just a 2022 calendar hanging limply on the wall, full of twee pictures of animals – the solitary thing to survive the ruthless clear-out. I look at it for a moment, mentally urging it into action.

'Go on, my son, jump off the wall and fly towards my head.'

I turn away, in case it has performance anxiety and would prefer to move behind my back.

'Come on, do it for me!'

I wait a moment, hoping to hear, at the very least, the sound of it sliding down to the floor, but as I turn back around, it is still in place, the eyes of the cow in the January picture meeting mine, stubbornly refusing to leap across the kitchen despite my clear disappointment.

I look out of the kitchen's only window down to a quiet scene, the back of the English College, priests' garments hanging on a washing line to dry.

The window is actually French doors, opening onto a little balcony. Andrew swears it was shut on the night in question, but what if he was wrong? It is just about theoretically possible, I think, that somebody could have climbed up and entered this way. They would have to have had a serious head for heights, though. Looking down, it's quite a drop, a big risk just to play a prank on a teenage babysitter. Since chatting to Andrew, I've read up about a practice the Mafia used on people they hoped to intimidate – for instance, witnesses in trials they wanted to scare off. They'd enter the person's house and cause a small disturbance to show they had been there. A subtle demonstration of their power, to say, 'We can get in whenever we want and next time it might not be just your possessions we are messing with.' But again, would the Mafia really waste their time abseiling up an apartment block and then rearranging the contents of Ailsa Wilson's kitchen?

No, if the answer to this mystery is not a ghost, then I feel it has to have come from inside, not outside the apartment.

'This was the girls' room,' comes Andrew's voice from elsewhere in the apartment. I follow him out, and find him standing by the doorway to another unlit room, this one slightly smaller than the others. I picture teenage Andrew sitting in here with two laughing children, playing Monopuedo, then convincing them it was time to get to sleep.

'Were you a good babysitter, Andrew?' I ask.

'Yeah, I think I was actually,' he says with a smile.

I remember the teenage babysitters of my own childhood, how exciting and glamorous they felt, their presence an intoxicating advert for what I might one day become, 'when I was grown up', and yet, they still had a sliver of a connection to childhood, still at school, not yet fully crossed over into the unimaginative land of adulthood; like Wendy on the last night in the nursery, still able to tell her tales of Peter Pan. Standing here, I am hit fully for the first time by a realisation, previously obscured by the fact that middle-aged Andrew has been telling me this story. On that summer's night in 1983, there were *three* children in this apartment. The two Wilson girls and a teenage Andrew.

So, maybe there is an elephant in this room.

Not an actual elephant – though to be honest in some of the rooms in this apartment you could probably fit one – but there is something knocking on the door of my brain right now that anyone who has made even a casual study of poltergeist cases would consider. One of the golden rules for any paranormal investigator confronting this sort of activity.

Look for the teenager.

Time and time again, if you study poltergeist hauntings, you will find that the person who is perceived to be the 'focus', the one around whom most of the activity seems to occur, is an adolescent. The case that I based my series *The Battersea Poltergeist* on revolved around Shirley Hitchings, a 15-year-old girl living in South London in 1956. She seemed to develop a relationship with the poltergeist, who the family nicknamed 'Donald', whereby they appeared to communicate with each other through a code of knocks on the wall. It seemed almost as if Donald responded to Shirley's commands. The tabloid press had a field day with this, suggesting, rather creepily, that Donald was Shirley's 'ghost boyfriend'. Ten years later, in 1966, came the Black Monk of Pontefract haunting I mentioned earlier, so called because the theory was that it was a monk who had been hanged on the very spot that 30 East Drive was built on who was doing the haunting (a theory that sadly was based on zero historical evidence). Again, the affected family gave a nickname to their poltergeist, 'Fred' this time. Fred was even less pleasant than Donald, and is sometimes dubbed 'Europe's most violent poltergeist'. There were two teenagers at the heart of this case, a brother and sister named Phillip and Diane, and, in the most extreme moment of the haunting, Diane was alleg- edly dragged up the stairs by her neck, screaming, angry red finger marks left behind on her skin afterwards. Many things happened to Phillip too, suggesting that the focus was split between them. Ten years on again – funny how each decade seems to yield one major poltergeist case – in 1977, we have Enfield, with 13-year-old Margaret and 11-year-old Janet being the centre point of the activity, Janet seemingly channelling the voice of the poltergeist, 'Bill'.

I could list you dozens and dozens of other cases, reaching back centuries – including the famous poltergeist of Cock Lane* in London in 1762, which gripped the nation, and the 'Drummer of Tedworth' in 1661, often argued to be the first recorded British poltergeist haunting, where a family were haunted by a banging said to be the restless spirit of a vagrant drummer – all of which feature children near to or going through puberty.

If this is a coincidence, it's a pretty big one.

Could there be something that happens during adolescence that makes you statistically more likely to experience a poltergeist, in the same way men of a certain age are more likely to experience hair loss, heart trouble or the need to patronise young women on social media?

Essentially, what is going on here? And why has it been going on for so long? You can't say that a teenager back in 1661 was influenced by watching *The Exorcist*.†

Well, there's a theory that's popular amongst some parapsychologists, revolving around the term 'RSPK'. It might look like the Royal Society for the Protection of something (Kangaroos,

---

* Yes, that is the real name of the street, and the poltergeist was nicknamed 'Scratching Fanny'. Do your own jokes.

† It's well known that the earliest director's cut of that movie dates from the realm of George III. It sent him mad.

perhaps, or Kit Kats), but RSPK stands for Recurrent Spontaneous Psychokinesis.*

Psychokinesis is the ability to move or affect objects through simply concentrating on them, literally 'mind over matter'. One of the most famous alleged proponents is Uri Geller, an Israeli former paratrooper, model and magician who became a celebrity (and friend of Michael Jackson) from bending spoons on TV by staring at them. He was absolutely massive when I was a kid, cropping up on every TV chat show to demonstrate how he could bend solid metal simply by looking at it. There was also Nina Kulagina, a Russian woman who, in the 1960s, found controversial global fame through supposedly moving objects without touching them. But both Uri and Nina were plagued by accusations of fraud, and no one has ever been able to prove in any definitive way that has convinced scientists that psychokinesis is possible.

Yet.

But there are those who think that a form of involuntary psychokinesis could explain poltergeist activity, that the noises and moving objects are not being caused by the spirit of a dead person, but by something that comes from inside a living one without them even realising – hence the 'spontaneous' bit of RSPK, and that it happens repeatedly, hence the 'recurring'. In a nutshell, it's the notion that some sort of psychic energy is produced within the person who is 'the focus' of the haunting and that this energy manifests outwardly to cause the disturbances in the house.

---

* Yes, they're cheating slightly getting the P and the K out of psychokinesis, but they are dealing with vengeful poltergeists on a daily basis, so let's cut them some slack.

RSPK was coined as a term by a parapsychologist called William G. Roll. Roll was born in Germany in 1926. Funnily enough, his father was a diplomat, just like Andrew's. He was stationed there as vice-consul, and would later be instrumental in the early organisation of NATO. When his parents divorced, William went to Denmark with his Danish mother and it was there that he claimed he started having 'out-of-body' paranormal experiences. After his mother's death when he was 16 – presumably another hugely formative moment for his study of the subject of ghosts – he relocated to America with his father, studying at Berkeley. He then moved to Oxford University where he studied parapsychology for eight years. Increasingly, Roll specialised his interest in poltergeist cases. He came up with the idea of RSPK whilst investigating a haunting in Seaford, New York. He became convinced that the activity there was the product of the family's 12-year-old son.

And here we get to the nub, potentially, of why so many of these cases feature a teenager, because if we are talking about poltergeists being the product of inner turmoil, is there any more tumultuous, uncertain, emotionally unbalanced period of our lives than adolescence? There's an aspect of this theory, though, that I always find slightly prurient and unsettling – middle-aged paranormal investigators deciding that all the bad stuff that is happening to a family is the fault of the teenage daughter going through puberty. It comes with all sorts of horrible old-fashioned connotations, like calling menstruation 'the curse'. I'm thinking again of Janet in the Enfield case, all that she had to contend with, becoming a tabloid figure at the age of 11 and then to be told that it's all 'her fault' because she started having periods?

Of course, there are other, more sceptically minded, people who agree completely that teenagers are the focus in these cases, but not because of RSPK. In each of the cases I've mentioned, it has been suggested that the 'poltergeist' activity was faked by a teenager in the house, and that the more they became the 'focus', not of a ghost but of those middle-aged paranormal investigators, the more they played up to it.

Either way, it feels a huge pressure as a kid – to know your mind is making weird stuff happen, or to be keeping a secret that you are maliciously faking things that are causing disruption and chaos to your family's life.

Personally, I find the idea of RSPK unsettling. It feels a little too much like victim-blaming, telling the frightened person at the heart of a poltergeist case that they are the one causing it. But there is another more positive way of looking at it, viewing the activity as almost like a superpower. Graham Morris told me he tried to describe it to Janet in these terms. He related helping the kids with their science homework one night at the house in Enfield, showing them that old trick with some iron filings on a piece of paper and a magnet underneath, moving the filings about. It was an experiment that helped them with their homework but was also designed to show something else.

'It was saying that, Janet, you're like the magnet, and all these things, whether they're Lego bricks or ashtrays or cupboards or books or tins or whatever that fly around, they're the iron filings.'

If there's even a small possibility this is possible, it's revolutionary. Because if it is the person and not the place causing poltergeist activity, that means that other people could indeed live in a house or apartment and never experience any element of paranormal activity, and it also means that the affected person could move to another place and take the activity with them, which chimes with what Graham noticed about Janet.

'She'd be at school and things would happen there. Things would fly around the classroom. She'd go in the local shop and things would fly off the shelf. That's what convinced me that it wasn't the house. *This House Is Haunted* was the name of the book about what happened,* but no, I don't think it was. I think it was something that Janet had – this sort of force that attached to her, and it just happened wherever she went.'

The very same thing occurred in the *Battersea Poltergeist* case, the knocks and taps that the family believed were signs of 'Donald' communicating followed Shirley to work, to the doctor, even on the bus. When she was working in the alterations room of the Selfridges department store on London's Oxford Street, a pair of scissors flew across the room, witnessed by another woman working there.

Could that possibly be what happened here at Via di Monserrato?

We've done a full circuit of the apartment now. I look at my watch and realise, incredibly, that we've spent three hours wandering around, talking. During that time, I've felt a strong sense of melancholy about the place, but I haven't been struck by any sensation of 'presence'. Has whatever was responsible for the activity left? Or does it sit dormant, waiting for the next tenants to arrive, or ...

Am I standing next to it?

Could Andrew have been the focus?

---

* By Guy Lyon Playfair, one of the lead investigators. Published in 1980, it's a good read if you want to find out more about the case.

Could he have been the trigger that brought the poltergeist activity into the apartment somehow? He told me he had babysat a few times here before that night; could any of those have been around the time that Ailsa witnessed strange things? Could, for instance, her special bowl or Emma's jumper have reappeared after a visit from Andrew?

Oh my God. What a thought. Have I been looking for an answer and been standing here talking to it all along?

But, for this to be the case, we'd ideally want to find evidence of poltergeist activity connected to Andrew, but in a location other than the apartment, to try and prove that theory that it could have travelled with him.

Well, what if I told you there was?

'I think we'd better go downstairs,' I say. 'I want you to tell me all about the Swedish nuns.'

CHAPTER 19

THE CONVENT OF
THE SWEDISH NUNS

A thunderous banging fills the air.

'They're giving it a facelift,' says Andrew, gesturing to an enormous building to our left, its architectural charms hidden behind an equally enormous tarpaulin.

'We're currently standing in front of the Michelangelo façade on the front of the Palazzo Farnese, which is now the French Embassy to Italy.'

'You sound like a tour guide,' I say. 'Rome does that to you, right? There are so many incredible things here, something on every street corner that blows your mind, and it's so amazing you want to share it. It's like it becomes part of you and you become part of it.'

'Absolutely,' says Andrew. 'I lived here for four years and we did everything. Every museum, every secret museum, every nook and cranny. And it stays with you.'

And indeed, draws you back. Because this is not Andrew's first time returning here since those teenage days. A little warning, this story is about to get a whole lot scarier and it all starts in that building over there ... Not the French embassy with the banging

builders, but the one sat at a right angle to it on the other side of
Piazza Farnese, a white-fronted church with a more modest and
demure façade. The Latin inscription above the door tells us it
was built in honour of Saint Bridget, the patron saint of Sweden,
attached to a convent for the nuns of her order. It still performs that
purpose, but, if you're in the know, it's also a great place to stay inex-
pensively in central Rome, as the nuns rent out rooms to travellers.
It may not be luxurious, but you're in the beating heart of the city,
a stone's throw from loads of the major sights,* with a great view
of this charming little square to wake up to in the morning. More
importantly, it's the venue for the next instalment in this case that
keeps on giving.

---

* Be warned, though, the nuns take a very dim view of throwing stones.

'This is in 2012,' says Andrew. 'I'd come to Rome for some business and my then girlfriend wanted to come along as well. So I thought it'd be fun, to stay in a 500-year-old Swedish convent for nuns.'

It's an interesting approach in the romance stakes, I'll give him that. The convent is literally around the corner from the English College, positioned right by where Via Di Monserrato meets Piazza Farnese, so he couldn't have been much closer to the old apartment. How much was that playing on his mind, I wonder?

'We arrive, we are handed the keys to our room by a nun, head upstairs, and this is where it does get a bit strange.'

I think we all know by now that when Andrew says 'a bit strange' what he really means is 'terrifyingly weird'.

☦

Andrew pushes the single beds together. He's not sure the nuns would be happy, but it feels odd to be sleeping on opposite sides of the room. The trouble is, they're heavy, metal monstrosities – the beds, not the nuns – wrought-iron, each feeling like they weigh a ton and screeching painfully across the floor. Sarah helps him, but even so, by the time they have shifted them just about close enough together, he's sweating like he's in a sauna and has put his bloody back out.

That night, they lie on the puritanical beds, their iron springs creaking disapprovingly with every movement. It's not like they're actually doing anything the nuns would disapprove of, they wouldn't dare. Andrew can hear the sounds of people passing through the piazza. It reminds him of being a teenager again, in charge of the

Wilsons' apartment. His memory drifts back around the corner for the first time in many years, to those stacks of plates and scattered postcards, before he drifts into sleep, wondering what strange dreams, or nightmares, may choose to come.

And then, in that moment of magic that happens to all of us every night, with what feels like a mere blink of the eye later it is morning. The sounds of Rome starting its day drift in from outside. Andrew breathes a sigh of relief, he has actually slept well, he feels surprisingly rested, but he's not quite ready to open his eyes yet. The sound of Sarah's breathing, soft and rhythmic nearby, is comforting. He wonders if he might catch another hour or so of sleep before facing the world.

But even now he can feel her stirring, her back pushing into his.

And then, she lets out a startled gasp!

'Oh my God!'

He jolts awake.

THUMP!

'Ow!'

He cannot move.

His face is pressed against a wall. He twists round awkwardly and watches Sarah having the same struggle; they are both on one of the single beds, somehow trapped tightly between two walls.

What the hell has happened? Did the room close in on them in the night like that trash compactor in *Star Wars*? Is this what happens if you mess with the Swedish nuns?

Andrew studies his surroundings, turning his head to take in the scene.

What in the name of...?

The walls haven't moved.

He and Sarah have.

The single bed they are both now in is positioned under an archway that passes from the bedroom into a small living area. No, sod that, 'positioned' sounds too gentle. They are *wedged* into this tiny passage about 15 feet* from where they were last night. This bed, the heavy wrought-iron monster he nearly slipped a disc manhandling just a few stubborn inches last night, has somehow moved itself the length of the entire room. Without waking them up.

Sarah screams. And, frankly, Andrew is considering doing the same thing.

⳨

'Andrew, there must be a reason for this?' I say, raising my voice over the cacophony of building works.

'Yes, there must be a reason. And I have no idea what it is. Did I wake up in the middle of the night? Was I sleepwalking, and somehow pushed this almighty bed with Sarah in it halfway across the room? Maybe. But I've never done anything like that before or since.'

Or, I think, *does lightning strike twice?* Could Andrew have been the unwitting source for the disturbances back in 1983 and then again in 2012, unconsciously generating energy that manifested in items moving through psychokinesis? It sounds mad, but if this

---

* That's 4.5 metres for anyone not down with the crazy British imperial measurements system. Or, in other words, about the length of two and a bit basketball players. NB, please do not chop any basketball players into bits to try and prove this.

were a police investigation, he's the only 'suspect' we could place at both scenes.

These thoughts are going through my head as we huddle under our umbrellas, the Roman rain pounding again like an incessant drumbeat, mingling with the clash of hammers and the whirr of drills coming from the French Embassy. It's hard to think straight, but there is something that just doesn't quite make sense.

The sheer mundanity of what happened in that kitchen.

It's the very same thing that made me so sure that Ailsa was telling me the truth. The concept of RSPK seems to neatly fit the violent and dramatic poltergeist cases where objects fly across rooms and bangs reverberate from walls like explosions of an inner turmoil. You can interpret those cases as William G. Roll did with his idea that disturbed teenagers can project psychic energy, or like his many sceptic detractors, who said, yes, the teenager is responsible but from a very tangible fraudulent point of view, hoaxing credulous adults, but, either way, the answer comes out the same. The poltergeist, real or imagined, is an expression of teenage rage, confusion, anxiety. An inner scream turned 3-D.

But how many teenagers neatly stack plates or helpfully dig out hard-to-find strawberry bowls?

And, can we really see Andrew being responsible for it all? The more I unpick it in my mind now, the more I think of all the moments when things happened to Ailsa that Andrew could not possibly have been anywhere near: the feeling of dread when she woke in the night, the miraculous returning coffee cup which appeared when they got back from holiday – a chunk of time when Andrew wouldn't have been able to get anywhere near the house.

So is there another possibility then, that RSPK has been a red herring – an interesting detour, but one that leads us away from our real chief suspect?

Because in so many of the poltergeist cases where people rushed to point their fingers at the teenager being the cause, the family resolutely refused to believe that, because they were certain there was something in their house, something they called Donald, or Fred, or Bill in a bid to understand it, to personalise the presence that had taken over their home, their lives, their children.

Ailsa's 'something extra'.

If this is nothing to do with Andrew, then we really do need to consider the possibility that there was something else linking the strange events in the kitchen of the apartment and the bedroom of the Swedish nuns, and that that something might be …

A ghost.

And whilst so much of what it did was innocuous, rearranging a few kitchen items or finding a missing jumper, it was also capable of doing things that felt really bloody scary – remember the lamp-shade that nearly fell on Ailsa's mum, and there's something about this metal bed, forcibly dragged across a room with two people in it, that feels just a little bit threatening. Like … a message, to Andrew.

'It's as if this thing is following *you*, from the apartment to the convent,' I suggest. 'This is thirty years later, and you are just around the corner, with strange things happening to you again.'

'Yes,' says Andrew.

'That's pretty scary,' I say, a little shiver running down my spine. 'Something that has that kind of power.'

'It is,' he agrees.

'Do we feel like this … ghost … if we feel comfortable using that word, could be haunting this whole area? From the English College up here to the convent?'

We both ponder this for a long time as the rain thuds onto the umbrellas, big reproachful drops. Rome is doing everything it can to tell us we shouldn't have come here, poking our noses into this strange mystery.

Some stories do not want to be told, and some puzzles do not want to be solved.

BEEP BEEP BEEP BEEP BEEP!

The shrill noise makes us both jump. For once, it's not the builders. It's a reminder on my phone, telling me it's time to meet the people who may possibly hold the key to this riddle, because I can't help feeling the answer to the mystery may lie inside the walls of the Venerable English College, and we have been invited to lunch there.

'Let's go and meet some priests,' I say, walking back round the corner on to the Via Di Monserrato, and up to the college's giant, ancient wooden door. Like Andrew, lead there by those two student priests 40 years ago, I brace myself for whatever strange knowledge may lie inside.

CHAPTER 20

THE SECRET OF
THE LIBRARY

It's hard to tell if we've dressed appropriately. When everyone else is a priest, what is the dress code? Certainly, we are an incongruous splash of colour amongst the black-clad men now staring at us curiously.

'You look as if you've earned some wine,' says Stephen, the current rector of the Venerable English College, pouring it into my glass without waiting for an answer. We'd been expecting a Monsignor, like the one Andrew was marched to, but Stephen tells us they dropped that title a few years back. He is still the boss of all the students though, and we are his guests of honour.

We're in a really rather spectacular dining hall, wood-panelled, with a luscious trompe l'oeil ceiling and a massive painting of Mary Magdalene washing Christ's feet hanging on the wall opposite that looks very old and very valuable. You hear about the vast wealth of the Catholic Church, but it stills feels surprising to be sitting amongst it.

Of course, this is just the everyday dining hall to the student priests who fill the circular tables surrounding us. Like Andrew did with his friends back in the eighties, I find myself scrutinising their faces, trying to imagine what made each one decide to commit themselves to a life of celibacy and religious duty. It really does seem a huge sacrifice. I could almost understand it, I think, if you got to live here in the opulent English College forever, but each one will be posted to some local diocese back in the UK. One of the first students we get talking to is bound for Portsmouth. No disrespect to Portsmouth, but it will be a bit of a comedown after this.

Once he's poured us some wine – white, not bad quality, in case you were wondering – Stephen introduces us to his students. After our initial email exchange, I'd presumed that we'd be greeted here under some duress, tolerated but not welcomed, our paranormal purpose undisclosed for fear of bring the college into disrepute, I was definitely not expecting him to say:

'Hello, everyone, Andrew and Danny have come here to look for ghosts.'

Suddenly all eyes are on us, and, as the pasta is handed round, and we serve ourselves, it's clear that the priests on our table *really* want to hear Andrew's story. So I make him tell it to them and they listen, rapt. They're an interesting bunch in themselves. One is Finnish, in his thirties, another's from Malta in his late fifties and the third is British, only 19, here training to be a priest just one year after finishing school. I'm hoping for a repeat of the reaction Andrew got in the Campo de' Fiori, the colour draining from their faces, but as Andrew reaches his crescendo of poltergism,* no one bats an eyelid. I realise they aren't actually surprised by the idea of a poltergeist at all.

---

* Is that a word? I may have made it up.

'I heard of a case very like this,' says the Maltese student priest. 'It happened to a teenager, just like you were then.'

Andrew and I lean in, interested.

'They came to the conclusion he was possessed.'

'I wasn't possessed,' says Andrew, sounding slightly offended. I can understand why he's upset; to be recurrently spontaneously psychokinesing* is one thing, but to be actually consumed by demons is quite another ...

I take a sip of wine. I have been biding my time, because I have in my head what Ailsa told me about how she discovered it was an open secret amongst 'the boys', as she called the young priests, that strange things happened in both the apartment and the college, and I'm wondering if those stories still persist.

The apartment is certainly well known to the priests, and they tell me another name to add to the colourful array of former visitors there. In the guest book there is apparently a signature for 'William of Stratford', said to be Shakespeare himself. I probe them a bit further. They haven't heard of anything strange happening there, they say, but they have heard of two spirits that are said to walk in the college. The ghost of a nun, and the ghost of a martyr.

Just go for it, I tell myself.

'Have you experienced anything strange here yourselves?' I ask.

They look at each other. It is the 19-year-old who speaks first.

'When I first moved here,' he says, 'one of the very first nights, I was woken up in the middle of the night by a very loud scream.'

---

* I might have made this word up too.

A chill runs through me. That was one of the things that the boys told Ailsa had happened, that they would be woken at night by screaming.

I ask him if it scares him, the idea that something might be lurking here, some entity, and what if it is malevolent? 'No,' he smiles, 'because as Christians, we know who wins.'

His gaze is unwavering.

After lunch, Stephen offers us a tour of the college. This is what Andrew and I have been waiting for, because we have an ulterior motive for wanting to get inside the college, a particular part of it that Andrew desperately wants to see again, because … well, I figure you know Andrew well enough by now to know it's not going to be anything nice and cheery and reassuring. If you've got any of that whisky left, I'd line a large glass up.

Stephen leads us into the college's chapel and, if the dining hall seemed resplendent, then this is something else entirely, drenched in gold, a spectacular heavenly fresco painted on the ceiling. Andrew and I make impressed 'oohs' and 'aahs' of awe. Stephen kneels to open a cupboard that contains the college's collection of 'monstrances', ornate vessels normally used to carry the Eucharist host, though these ones contain relics of martyrs – to be specific, little bits of bone from priests who studied here and were then killed for their faith.

I am struck by the fact that 'martyr' is not an abstract word for the priests who study here. Young men like the fresh-faced 19-year-old we ate lunch with lived in this building hundreds of years ago, sleeping in the same dormitories, knowing that one day they would have to head back to England to spread the 'one true faith', something they would need to do entirely in secret due to its illegality, often forced to hide in priest holes for days at a time, sometimes with only room to stand, unable to eat or even properly go to the toilet, barely daring to breathe, because they knew that if they were caught they would be tortured and killed, their bodies hacked apart publicly in front of a baying mob for daring to speak their 'heresy' in Protestant Tudor or Stuart England.

That would be enough to make me wake in the night screaming.

We follow Stephen upstairs as he leads us past large paintings depicting some of these grisly martyrdoms. 'The story is that this is part of Christian life,' he says, 'so don't be afraid.' As we wend our way through the history-soaked building, I look across at Andrew. Inevitably, we are both thinking of the night he traipsed around these same corridors with his student priest friends until eventually, they found Stephen's predecessor ... the Monsignor.

☦

'Tell him what you told us,' says one of the student priests.

Andrew looks directly at the Monsignor. He is in his sixties, English of course, sent from the homeland to oversee the next generation of his country's priests. His face is friendly and kind, but as Andrew recounts his story for the second time that day, it darkens. Andrew desperately wishes he could somehow back-pedal out of this, because he is getting the very same response he received from the boys a little while ago. The Monsignor has gone deathly pale.

The powerful priest remains still for a long moment and then in a quiet voice he says, 'Follow me.'

Gulp. This evening does not feel like it is going well, the grown-up sophisticated Andrew of the Campo de' Fiori is giving way to an earlier draft of himself who wishes he could just run home and hide under the covers of his bed. But he has no choice. He follows the Monsignor, who leads him through long, dark medieval corridors, past pictures of martyrs, priests, apostles and cardinals, towards the college's libraries, the storehouses of all their theological texts for the last 600 years, a bastion of Catholic knowledge.

There are three libraries. The old priest passes through the first and the second and then stops in the third. To Andrew, it feels like something out of *The Name of the Rose*; dimly lit and dusty, you can almost inhale the history. A few trainee priests sit in front of yellowed books in attitudes of reflection, learning or silent contemplation. Maybe one or two are actually asleep. Andrew feels deeply out of place in his Fila jacket, a fashionable young atheist amongst these men who have devoted their lives to God, bearers of a tradition that you should be prepared to die for your faith if called upon.

Why is he here?

He's mostly regretting sharing his experiences in the Wilsons' apartment, but there is a part of him that's fascinated by what it is about his story that has so affected the priests, why they are all taking it so extremely seriously.

'I want to show you something,' says the Monsignor.

He leads Andrew into what feels like the furthest away, darkest corner of the library, a place where the dust circulates in the air like something living, until finally he stops in front of a set of shelves.

'This,' he tells Andrew, his tone grave and sonorous, 'is the section of the library specialising in books on the Antichrist. Beelzebub. Satan.'

Beelzebub. This is the first time Andrew has heard that strange-sounding name. It has an almost comic ring to it, he thinks, and this really is a turn-up for the books, no pun intended. He hadn't expected a college of priests to own volumes on the Devil, but as the Monsignor explains, 'To have Christ, you must have Antichrist.' It is important to know your enemy.

His eyes seem to bore almost right through Andrew, who shifts from foot to foot uncomfortably. Perhaps he doesn't want to know why he is here after all.

'Where there is light, there is also dark.'

In this moment, properly meeting the elderly priest's eyes for the first time, he could swear the old man had the power to see into his soul, and then the Monsignor surprises him, letting out a deep, profound sigh that seems to carry all of the cares of the world, every single trouble released from that box by Pandora in the myth created centuries before the Monsignor's faith was even born.

'Do you believe in ghosts, Andrew?' he asks.

Andrew considers this. He supposes he does, though in all of this business connected to the Wilsons' apartment, he has never actually once used the g-word.

'I do,' says the Monsignor. 'Of course I do. The Catholic Church, we invented them.'

He allows himself a small smile that doesn't extend to his eyes. He leans in, through the little cloud of flecks of dust, hovering like insects in the stale air, until his head is close to Andrew's.

'What I am about to tell you is fantastical, Andrew, but completely true.'

☩

We are standing in that library now. Updated and modernised, but still with that musty smell and a cloud of dust.

'This is it,' Andrew whispers urgently to me. 'He led me here.'

I can see Stephen is keen for us to move on, he's looking at his watch, politely hovering by the door, mentioning that he has a meeting to get to soon. I wonder if he has some inkling of our interest in this room. After his initial interest in our quest at lunch, he has been more businesslike on the tour. Perhaps there is a sense that the old ghost stories are best kept as that, not examined in too much detail, in case, like the cosmology of Giordano Bruno, they prove to be more complicated than the Church would like.

I remember the words of the 19-year-old priest at lunch when we'd discussed the idea that the ghosts stalking the college might not have good intentions.

'We know who wins.'

But what if the doors that this story opens up do not lead to neat answers that can be tied up with theology, but to a darkness that contains the greatest enemy of faith …

Doubt.

☩

'This library is locked at night,' the Monsignor tells Andrew. 'Nobody can get in. Or out.'

Is this a threat? wonders Andrew, looking around nervously. He wouldn't fancy being trapped here overnight.

'But, every two days for the last month,' the old priest continues, 'we have come in, in the morning, to find the books on these particular shelves, the books that deal with the Antichrist, strewn all over the library.'

He throws out his hands dramatically.

'Some have been found as far as fifteen metres away. As if they have been thrown.'

He paces the length of the shelf, agitated.

'We have been unable to explain it. If I am honest, it has terrified me.'

Andrew can see that he is not the sort of man who enjoys expressing weakness. Now he feels like he can see into the priest's soul, and it is troubled.

'But then,' says the Monsignor, 'you told us your story tonight, and, you see, I became even more frightened.'

Andrew is rigid by now as he gazes into the fixed stare of the other man's eyes, his watery pupils dark tunnels of fear.

'Because,' says the Monsignor, 'on the other side of the wall where these selves are ...'

He taps the shelves to emphasise his point.

'... is the kitchen in the apartment of Mr and Mrs Wilson.'

☦

'Wow, that freaked me out,' says Andrew. We are outside the college now, having said our goodbyes. The rain is worse than ever.

'What did you do?' I ask.

'I told the Wilsons, and then they liaised with the Monsignor directly. The two student priests told me a week or so later that the English College was flying out a qualified exorcist from England to deal with it. They didn't want me to tell anyone about my experiences in the kitchen, or what had been happening in the college library.'

Shades of Giordano Bruno after all, I muse. The Church's desire to control the narrative in a finite universe free of doubt.

It took me a while to leave that library, despite Stephen being desperate to show us out. I wanted to savour the moment, knowing that what Andrew was told by the Monsignor in that dark corner is truly fantastical.

I held on to a shelf for a moment, needing to remind myself of the reality of where we were, as my mind was racing now with the geography of how the college and the apartment block connect, because I'd realised from our tour that they connect in more than one place, and I found myself remembering something else from Ailsa's story, a small detail she'd told me that I didn't think much of at the time.

The one moment when she herself was truly unsettled by the presence there. The night she woke coughing and took herself into the living room, the strange sense of dread that suddenly overcame her. It happened as she lay on the couch, a couch which she said ... *backed on to the chapel of the college.*

The chapel that contained the relics of the martyrs who studied here and were returned to their alma mater as broken fragments. Standing in that library, wondering what it is about the strange connection between these two buildings, and whatever it is that may still reside within them, for a long moment, I felt closer than I ever have before to saying:

I believe.

A thought occurs to me as we pass the apartment block entrance. I glance up at the windows that we were looking down from just a couple of hours before. I had been so desperate to experience something inside the apartment myself. Even if it was just a feeling. But maybe, if Gordon from Newark Museum was right and we are like radios, then I was tuned to the wrong frequency. I am intrigued though; we know so much about Ailsa's family's experiences in the apartment, and Andrew's, and that, according to the priests Ailsa spoke to, people living there before them had had experiences too.

But what about the people who lived there afterwards? Did the phenomena continue after the Wilsons left?

To answer that one, we need to head back to that day in 2012, after the beds moved for Andrew and his girlfriend Sarah. Still shaken, they are sitting having breakfast exactly where we are standing now, at Caffe Peru, the little coffee shop directly beneath the apartment.

☦

Sarah raises her coffee cup to her lips, her hands still trembling. She is upset, or freaked out might be more accurate. She couldn't get out of the convent fast enough, and so now here they are, having a breakfast of coffee and a sugary croissant to calm her nerves.

Andrew is wondering how he should feel about all this. It's like being one of those men who have another child with a second wife later in life and are never quite able to fully take part in the exhilaration and anxiety of new parenthood – *This is her first poltergeist activity ... but I've actually had a few over the last thirty years.*

311

From where they are sat outside the café, he can see the apartment if he looks up. He figures it's about time he told Sarah the story of what happened to him there. Perhaps it will make her feel better, if she realises that these things are … well, things that can happen. He tells her about the night he babysat. She listens open-mouthed, and at the end, maybe he was right, her expression has changed. Perhaps what happened to them today doesn't feel quite so bad now. As she brushes the croissant crumbs from her lips, her face is a picture of intrigued curiosity.

'Wow,' she says. 'Wouldn't it be amazing to get in there, to see if anything happened again?'

It would, Andrew supposes. Here now, in such close proximity, directly below the misbehaving kitchen, he is feeling an intense curiosity to know if anyone else over the last three decades has ever experienced anything like he did.

Would it be reassuring? Knowing he and the Wilsons were not alone in this? Or does it make it even more frightening if this mystery deepens further? What would that mean, if a bricks-and-mortar building contains some energy force able to enact chaotic madness?

And then, he hears a sound that is instantly familiar and yet incongruous on this quiet street in Rome. Australian accents, coming out of the metal gate to the apartment block. A mother and daughter holding bags, off to go shopping.

He and Sarah look at each other. Could it be? It must. The apartment has always been rented by people working for the Australian Embassy. But should he? Sarah nudges him sharply, spurring him on. You cannot pass up an opportunity like this. Andrew rises.

'Excuse me …'

The woman and her daughter stop mid-conversation and look at him. Stumblingly at first, but forcing himself to channel the charm that he deploys on potential investors for his movies, Andrew tries to explain, in a way that won't make him sound completely mad or scary, why he would like them to invite him into their home. Knowing that, to live in the apartment, they must be involved in diplomatic circles, he drops a few names of people they will know at the embassy. Sarah chips in too, smiling warmly and assuring them that she would not be having coffee with a dangerous lunatic.

A few moments later, the two of them are following their new friends up to the apartment.

☩

'We went into the kitchen,' Andrew tells me, as the rain bounces off our umbrellas again. We're back in the Piazza Farnese, with the now familiar backdrop of building works.

'How did it feel?' I ask.

'It was all shipshape and it was quite different to how I remembered it. It would have been updated quite a bit, and so we just had a little look around. Sarah was interested to see it … but nothing happened.'

Just like Andrew's and my visit today, there was no amazing, magical, timely reoccurrence of bizarre activity. He and Sarah politely thanked the woman and her daughter and headed for the door.

'I gave them my card, and we left, and that was that.'

313

Well, almost. If there's one thing that we can take home from this story it's that that is never quite that.

'About a week later, I got an email from them. They said that a couple of days after I visited, they got back to the apartment, walked into their kitchen, which had been pristine when they left because their cleaner had been the day before, and … the place was a complete mess.'

My stomach lurches, my inner horror-movie score composer hitting a peak moment.

'Oh my God. Really?'

'Yeah. Things all over the place. All the cupboard doors were open. Things out of the fridge. A lot of the liquids were on their side, and a rubbish bin that was full of rubbish had been pushed over, the rubbish was strewn all over the floor. They said it was like a tornado had gone through it, but again, *nothing was broken*.'

I am aghast. The banging of the builders merges with the constant thud of rain on the umbrellas and my own quickening heart, a cacophony of drumbeats, pounding in my mind, a roar of excitement mixed with terror as I realise the implications of what he's just told me.

'How did you feel?'

Andrew ponders this.

'A bit guilty. I remember thinking, "Oh my God, what the hell is going on?"'

Again, that uncertainty of who was responsible. Had Andrew somehow reactivated the apartment by entering it?

'How do you explain it?'

'I can't. It felt quite unbelievable. The bed at the convent had moved in the night and then now this ... I could only wonder if perhaps it was whatever was there in that apartment, saying hello to me.'

We stand there in bemused silence. I came to Rome for answers and I have found even more questions. Now, how does my journey continue? There are two possible routes, one back to the nice, safe warmth of being able to dismiss all of this under the bright, rational lights of sceptic reason, but the other route leads to the edge of a precipice, beneath which lies the utter darkness of the unknown, a pitch-black void of uncertainty that just might contain ...

Something extra, the g-word, whatever you want to call it, but proof, that ...

We are not alone.

EPILOGUE

CHAPTER 21

BLOODY HELL KEN!

In my beginning is my end.

T.S. ELIOT, 'EAST COKER'

I'm sitting on stage with a man wearing an eccentric black wig, sunglasses and tweed waistcoat. If I encountered him on the street, I'd probably steer clear, but today, well, let's just say we are all here because of him.

Stretched out in front of us are hundreds of excited people wearing T-shirts printed with the words 'Bloody Hell Ken!' Camera-phones flash and smiles beam, and Ken looks on, slightly bemused from under his wig.

In real life, Ken is an extremely eminent scientist, a geneticist engaged in the study of the human genome, a man who has dedicated most of his life towards the good of humanity, trying to make breakthroughs in the study of hereditary diseases, someone so revered and well known in his field that he has chosen, in these other circumstances, to keep his identity a mystery, like a paranormal Superman.

Because scientists aren't supposed to see ghosts.

319

You see, Ken's many scientific achievements are not why hundreds of people have gathered in this London theatre, with hundreds more watching from home online. We are here because, over 40 years ago, Ken thinks he may have seen a ghost. A ghost that he decided to email me about for no other reason than a realisation that, if he didn't, then, when Ken eventually – hopefully many years from now – dies, the story would die with him, and he felt that it was such a strange and inexplicable experience that there should really be a record of it. He also wondered if anybody else had experienced anything similar. His scientific brain craved data that he could process to try to make sense of something he has never been able to explain or forget.

Ken's story became the first ever episode of my *Uncanny* podcast for the BBC.

Back in the autumn of 2021, it just seemed like a really good, creepy tale told by a reliable credible witness. We released it around Halloween and Ken ticked all the right boxes – a sceptic who didn't believe in ghosts and yet was convinced he'd seen one. His story was properly creepy, featuring experiences that had happened to him as a young man in Belfast in the early 1980s; it featured apparitions and poltergeist activity that he had witnessed in Room 611 of a student hall of residence, a 1960s tower block called Alanbrooke Hall, and had the added twist that he had learnt that the students who lived in that room the year before him and the year after had experienced almost identical activity. Incredibly, after we aired the episode, more and more witnesses came forward to say that they too had experienced what they believed was paranormal activity in that particular student bedroom, or in Alanbrooke Hall in general.

It was stunningly weird; the story was picked up on by the media and ended up going viral. Those 'Bloody Hell Ken!' T-shirts in the crowd were inspired by words I let slip after one of the scariest moments Ken described. It became a meme on social media, then a catchphrase for the podcast, and now I like to think it nicely sums up how people feel about listening to the stories people tell me – a mix of wonder, fear and empathy. It's a way of saying to Ken and all the other witnesses, 'We're with you,' but simultaneously, 'Holy fuck, this is scary.'

Today, sitting on stage at this live event, watching the wave of emotion and excitement that visibly swept across this crowd as Ken walked out in his (let's be honest, slightly rubbish) disguise, I realise his story has grown into something bigger than both of us. If we're going to get scientific about it, it has become a very public experiment testing the hypothesis that ghosts really do exist, and, by extension, that's what all of my work has become. Whether it's the podcast, on TV, in my live shows or in this book that I really hope you've enjoyed reading,* I'm not just telling you these stories for entertainment purposes. If that was the aim, I'd be better off making them up, because then I could shape them how I want, deliver neat little endings that tie everything up. No, I'm telling you them because I have a burning desire – actually, make that total, all-consuming obsession – to answer that question, and each of the people I have met, from Ken onwards, including all the people who

---

* If you haven't, I'm presuming you wouldn't have got this far, unless you are a complete masochist, or a book critic. NB, if you are a book critic, I still have some of that whiskey left and am prepared to share if you give me a nice review ;-)

feature in this book, feel like they might hold pieces of a complex jigsaw puzzle.

But experiments need outcomes. Data, once processed, needs conclusions, and that's why we're all really here, right? You bought this book, yes, because you enjoy that little pleasurable thrill that comes from a good spine-tingling story, but really, deep down, you want me to prove that ghosts exist. Or prove they don't. You want some kind of closure.

I often feel people I meet look at me with a mixture of hope and anxiety, as if, through all of the witnesses I have interviewed, I must have somehow finally cracked this eternal mystery, found the paranormal Holy Grail. At the earliest moment politely possible, they ask me, in an intense, expectant tone, 'What do you believe?'

So, for the record, here it is.

WHAT I BELIEVE

I believe that for years we have wrongly dismissed people who have stories of having seen ghosts and UFOs, to the point where it feels almost taboo to say what has happened to you, so that a scientist like Ken feels he can only tell his story by wearing a disguise. I believe that in listening to these stories, we learn more about ourselves as human beings and are enriched by a realisation of not only what we do know about our universe, but also what we don't.

I believe that every day, someone like you is sitting feeling entirely normal in their very normal house or walking down an extremely ordinary street and they are about to witness something that will change their lives forever.

I believe these cases pose questions I cannot currently answer, and mysteries that deepen the more we try to solve them, and, to use that phrase that I heard so many times at Tod UFO Meet, 'Where do you go with that?'

Well, let me tell you where I think we should go.

We live in a divided, and divisive, world right now, particularly on social media, where we are constantly encouraged to take sides in a combative way, defining ourselves by what we hate as much as what we love. Trenches are dug, shouting matches are had, and everything is black and white.

But actually, sometimes it's okay to be grey. To say you don't know what you think, to change your mind, and to keep an open one.

I asked you at the beginning if you were Team Sceptic or Team Believer, but I'd like to think that maybe you have been both at various points during this book and that maybe now you're still mentally flitting between the two, so, I'm going to introduce a new category:

Team Not Sure.

Because that's what I am right now, and I think that's an okay place to be. I want to believe with all my heart that the paranormal is real, I feel close, damn close, but I'm still waiting for that moment that tips me over the edge of the precipice, the moment that I experience something myself.

But until then, I'll hold on to the thing that has lured me away from that neat, brightly lit path to explaining it all away, and down the other trickier, darker route to stand at the edge of reason, looking down into doubt. It's the fact that when I meet the eyes of

Andrew, Ailsa,* Graham, Vee, Maureen, Jenny, Judy, David, Peter, Alan, Colin, Ken or any of the people I have spoken to over the last few years, I believe 100 per cent that they are telling me the truth, and that, well, it scares the hell out of me.

---

* Well, I would have looked into her eyes if she'd been able to work out how to use Zoom!

I would love to hear from you. You can write to me at danny@dannyrobins.com. All queries, questions, compliments and cake will be gratefully received.

And maybe you have a story to tell me yourself? To send me an account of your uncanny experience, you can write to experiences@dannyrobins.com. It could be anything you think may have been paranormal, from ghosts and UFOs, to strange beasts, premonitions, or other odd phenomena. I'd feel privileged to hear it, and I'll try and help you find answers for what happened. Who knows, you might even end up in my next book.

To find out more about my projects, including Uncanny Live tour dates, and upcoming podcasts, TV series and merch, go to www.dannyrobins.com.

ACKNOWLEDGEMENTS

Lots of people have helped me along the way on this intriguing journey investigating the paranormal. First and foremost, I would like to thank my beloved wife, Eva, who has had to put up with me working very long hours in the shed and being away a lot. I couldn't have done any of this without her incredible, thoughtful support and generosity of spirit. We are very definitely Team Robins. I also want to thank my sons Leo and Max, who aren't that fond of the fact their dad is so obsessed with scary stuff and would much rather I made podcasts about *Star Wars* Lego. Thanks too to my mum, Rose O'Sullivan, who nurtured my interest in reading, writing and performing as a kid and made me the person I am today, and to my parents-in-law Östen and Ulla Johnsson, who have been incredibly supportive over many years. I love all of you very much.

Thank you to all of the experts who have appeared on *Uncanny* and given me the benefit of their wisdom, in particular my close collaborators and friends Ciaran O'Keeffe and Evelyn Hollow, and to all of the witnesses who have told me their stories – it takes courage to say those words 'I have seen a ghost' and I feel humbled that you have trusted me to share your stories. A special thank you to Ken, whose story was a huge part of making *Uncanny* what it has become, and to the inimitable Andrew, Ailsa, Vee, Maureen, David and Peter for their bravery in allowing me to feature their experiences in this book.

Big thanks to my editors at BBC Books, Albert DePetrillo and Nell Warner, for their belief, enthusiasm and good advice – and for waiting for me to finish this long after I missed my first deadline! Thank you to Jessica Anderson, Ian Allen and Paul Simpson for their input during the editorial process, to Claire Scott, Patsy O'Neill and Shelise Robertson for all of their great work spreading the news about the book to the wider world, and to all of the booksellers out there who are supporting and stocking it. I have spent a lifetime loving browsing bookshops, dreaming of seeing my own book on the shelf, so this is a huge thrill.

Thanks to the inspirational Nancy Bottomley for all her help with research and organising my chaotic life, and for packing and posting all of those 'Bloody Hell Ken!' T-shirts. Thanks to my agents Hugo Young, Jessica Stone, Paul Stevens and Francesca Devas, who have been brilliant and supportive, through lean times and busy ones, and thank you to my friends Jenny Shaw-Sweet, Michael Shaw and Rob Streeten for early, very helpful conversations.

I'm grateful also to my dear collaborators Isobel David and Matthew Dunster for all the chats we have had about ghosts for *2:22 – A Ghost Story* and to the truly excellent Joe Myerscough for similar chats on the *Uncanny* TV series, alongside Francesca Maudslay, Ben Leigh and Sarah Patten, and to Jack Bootle, Alan Holland, Cate Hall and Naomi Benson for believing in the show and wanting to put it on television. A massive thanks also to Charlie Brandon-King and Evelyn Sykes, who have created the sound design and music, respectively, that has been such a huge part of *Uncanny* both in audio form and on TV, and to Lanterns on the Lake, who wrote our spine-tingling, atmospheric theme tune, with its iconic line, *'I know what I saw,*' which they astutely noticed was something that a lot of witnesses said to me.

Thanks to Sam Hodges and Pam Kehoe for all of their great work on the Uncanny Live Tour, which is happening very soon as I write this. All of these different aspects of *Uncanny* inspire me in different ways. It's a thrill to tell the stories across various formats.

Finally, though, my most enormous and heartfelt thanks to my colleagues at the BBC: the brilliant Rhian Roberts, my commissioner at BBC Radio 4, for seeing the potential in *The Battersea Poltergeist*, the show which really did change my life, and for all of her support since on all of my projects. It means a huge amount. Thanks to her wise and thoughtful colleague Paula McDonnell and to the Radio 4 controller Mohit Bakaya for all of his much-valued support. The BBC is sometimes criticised these days, but it remains a uniquely inspirational organisation that is a joy to work for. Community-building is at the heart of its ethos and it has been the perfect place to build the #UncannyCommuntity.

Last of all, I want to say a very special thank you to Simon Barnard, my long-time co-producer on all of the podcasts. He is a very self-deprecating man, so won't like being singled out, but he, more than anyone else I've worked with, has been instrumental in giving me the confidence to tell these stories in this way. It was him who encouraged me to take my idea for *The Battersea Poltergeist* to the BBC at a time when I was feeling stuck in a creative rut and wondering if I should pack it all in, and it is he who, along every step of the way since, has been the best of collaborators and friends, a yin to my yang.

If you've got through all of those acknowledgments, then thank you to you too. The #UncannyCommunity that has grown up around the shows I make is the thing I am probably most proud of. It feels quite unique in these times to see such kind and thoughtful debate going on on social media between people with utterly polarised opinions who are happy to agree to disagree. Long may it continue.

Until the next time we meet, sleep well and don't have nightmares.

INDEX

Page references in *italics* indicate images.
DR indicates Danny Robins.